"*More than a Game* captures the essence of all that is good about youth football. It captures the delicate balance between teaching and learning the values and lessons of teamwork, and the passion and joy that is the ultimate goal of youth athletics. Jim Brown captures the essence of all of these and focuses on the trials, tribulations, and above all else, the successes of the nationally recognized St. Raphael Football program through his compelling work. His literary efforts speak volumes about the everlasting value of a properly organized and managed youth sports leagues."

—New Orleans Saints Head Coach Sean Payton

"We hear so often about the problems in youth sports, but children and adults need to be reminded that there are many positive life lessons to be learned from the playing fields of our youth. To read *More than a Game* is to vividly recall those lessons. Jim Brown captures both the good times and the bad in these pages, while teaching us about the great value of sports along the way."

—Christine Brennan, *USA Today* sports columnist, ABC News/NPR commentator, author of *Best Seat in the House*

"*More than a Game* invites you into the simple truths of most any season of life. Practice makes perfect . . . as you discover the play-by-play teachable moments of this team of eighth-grade role models. Whether you coach a youth sports team, a business organization, or a family unit . . . you will learn meaningful insights into values, leadership, and relationships."

—Mac Anderson, founder, Successories and Simple Truths

"Jim Brown was a leader in the business world and now has applied his formidable leadership gifts to using sports to develop great people. St. Raphael's youth football is the kind of program that all youth athletes should have to help them become the best they can be. Jim has now brought the story of St. Raphael's to life with *More than a Game*, a book that will grab you and keep you involved from the preseason workouts to the banquet at the end of the year. This book is a positive contribution by an incredibly positive man."

—Jim Thompson, founder and executive director, Positive Coaching Alliance

"*More than a Game* will leave you defenseless as it tackles your mind, heart, and soul. Beyond the x's and o's, this playbook teaches you lessons applicable to every season of your life. Whether you've been a football coach for years or you don't know a thing about the game, this special season will keep you thinking long after the fourth quarter of the final game."

—John G. Blumberg, professional speaker and author of *Silent Alarm* and *Good to the Core*

"*More than a Game* is a must-read for everyone who has ever been associated with the game of football. Jim Brown's forty-plus years of involvement with football has allowed him to write an insightful and inspiring book about the game of football that goes way beyond the techniques, skills, and x's and o's of the game. Anyone who has ever played the game of football knows it is much more than just a game. Every person reading this book will come away with an appreciation of the game of football beyond the wins and losses. Jim's book should be required reading for any person wanting to start out in the coaching ranks."

—Gary Goforth, head football coach and athletic director, Benet Academy, Lisle, Illinois

"*More than a Game* brings youth football to life more than any newspaper, magazine, or broadcast possibly could. Through swift pacing and simple wording, on-field action smoothly leads to life lessons off the field. The powerfully told stories will touch your heart. If you don't walk away wanting to coach football, you'll surely leave wanting to lead your family, organization, or business in a better way—Jim Brown's way."
　　　　—Brad Engel, *Naperville Sun Sports* editor

"*More than a Game* is a very clear and powerful perspective of the reality of youth sports and the impact it has on our lives. As a former professional football player and currently a youth coach, *More than a Game* unveils so many teachable moments; it's simply a must-read for anyone with the responsibility of coaching kids in sports. Jim Brown is able to transcend sports and life by providing characters that we all can relate to. It is an awesome toolbox of applicable solutions that provides a lifelong playbook of teaching the balance between competition and character in our sports society today. Thank you, Jim, for having the courage to share forty years of your amazing experience with St. Raphael Football Program."
　　　　—Shafer Suggs, president of the NFLPA Retired Football Players of Chicago, New York Jets starting strong safety 1976–1980

"*More than a Game* is a must-read for people who 'coach' on the field or in the workforce and struggle with connecting and motivating a group to successfully function as a team. Jim Brown's decades of professional coaching and youth coaching success is the result of a sustainable foundation of guiding principles designed to build team unity. You will truly be amazed at the maturity of the youth characters in this book and their ability to learn and make defining choices that will shape the team and their lives for the future. Jim Brown captures the true essence of coaching as it truly is *More than a Game*."
　　　　—Dale Grosso, logistics executive and assistant coach, St. Raphael varsity football

"Jim Brown's *More than a Game* is must reading for any parent whose child is or has played youth football. Jim's love of the game and four decades of coaching and developing young athletes for the game of life as well as football are testimony to the way the game is meant to be played—for love, fun, and with dedication. As the author of the biographies *Papa Bear: The Life and Legacy of George Halas* and *Rozelle, Czar of the NFL*, I have seen firsthand how dedication to the game and the fundamentals build champions. Jim Brown has a winner in *More than a Game*."
　　　　—Jeff Davis, author *Papa Bear* and *Rozelle*

"Jim Brown presents a winning lineup in *More than a Game*. He carefully selects players, the characters in his book, who he's personally worked with—both on and off the field—in his forty years of coaching youth football at St. Raphael. He takes the reader through many of the hardships and triumphs he's faced firsthand, as a coach and mentor of the players in the program. Ultimately, the players come together and become a dream team."
　　　　—Margi Schiemann, team mom and mother of a Youth Football player

"*More than a Game* is motivating, intense, gut-wrenching, and exciting all at once. I could relate to the players in Coach Brown's book, and I think I may even know a couple of the players who he writes about in his starting lineup."
　　　　—Brian Schiemann, Youth Football player

"In this day and age of hypercompetitive youth sports, Coach Brown has put together a must-read manifesto for anyone who is charged with the responsibility for coaching youth sports. *More than a Game* and its lessons provide a moral and ethical roadmap that all youth coaches can and should follow. As a youth football coach myself, this book serves as a blunt reminder that we have an awesome responsibility to those we coach, and we have an enormous impact on how they grow and mature into the world around them. This book should be required reading for anyone given the privilege and honor of coaching young men and women."

 —**Frank Ribaudo, head football coach, All Saints Academy**

"When you're talking sports, you always hear that a coach or team member is "full of heart." That description fits *More than a Game* in a nutshell; it's a story about teamwork that's full of heart, and sets a great example for the next generation of team sports players."

 —**Carole Bellacera, award-winning author of** *Spotlight, Border*
  Crossing, Tango's Edge, Understudy, Shepherd Moon, **and** *East of the Sun*

"*More than a Game* is about love. It tells the story of one man's experience of teaching young people, through football, how to be kind, compassionate, and effective human beings. For forty years Jim Brown practiced his art, and the masterpiece he created is inspiring. Anyone who wants to learn how to give something back creatively and courageously should read this book."

 —**Lari Washburn, artist, Etsy.com**

MORE
THAN
a GAME

Published by Legacy Book Company, a Division of Greenleaf Book Group, LLC

Submit all requests for reprinting to:
Greenleaf Book Group LLC
PO Box 91869, Austin, TX 78709

Publisher's Cataloging-In-Publication Data
(Prepared by The Donohue Group, Inc.)

Brown, Jim (James L.), 1939–
   More than a game : a vehicle for child development / Jim Brown. -- 1st ed.

   p. ; cm.

   ISBN: 978-0-9841892-0-5

1. Teenage athletes--Psychology. 2. Coach-athlete relationships. 3. Parent and
child. 4. Sports--Psychological aspects. 5. Football--Coaching--Anecdotes. 6.
Football players--Naperville--Illinois--Anecdotes. I. Title.

GV959.55.C45 B76 2010
796.332/0835   2009935167

First Edition
Printed in the United States of America

09 08 07   10 9 8 7 6 5 4 3 2 1

Dedication:

To my mother and father for their instillation of values; to my family, Marcia, Susan, Mike, and Dan for their support; to John Blumberg and Lari Washburn for their advice; and the children of St. Raphael for their inspiration.

Thank you to my readers for their candid suggestions:
    Frank Ribaudo
    Dale Grosso
    Margi Schiemann
    Lari Washburn
    John Blumberg

Thank you to my LongRidge writing coaches:
    Carole Bellacera
    Roberta Roesch

Joe

I hope you enjoy the book as much as I enjoyed writing it. It may help one last able be a better person

MORE THAN a GAME

A Vehicle for Child Development

J.H. Brown

JIM BROWN

LEGACY BOOK COMPANY
A DIVISION OF GREENLEAF BOOK GROUP LLC

Contents

Prologue

IN 1992, I WAS RESPONSIBLE for changing the cultural and operational approach within Lucent Technologies to high-performing teams and a coaching style of leadership. That same year, I began my 28th year of coaching the seventh- and eighth-grade football team at St. Raphael parish.

During the Lucent implementation, I became aware of an amazing similarity between coaching Lucent executives and my football players at St. Raphael to high-performing teams. So I decided to write a book describing my experiences at St. Raphael and Lucent, which defined the similarities of concepts required to build high-performing teams whether in youth sports, families, or businesses.

However, as the book evolved, I found myself writing mostly about the children of St. Raphael and what they had taught me about values, team concepts, and leadership. They became my heroes as their identities and messages evolved with each story.

I enjoyed writing the book as I relived each experience. As I wrote, I became more aware of the value of the experiences as they provided insights beyond the obvious and my original interpretations. Writing the book helped me become more aware of what I thought, what I learned, what I knew, what I felt, and what we taught the children of St. Raphael.

I also learned that writing about the past constitutes a reapplication and relearning of principles and values long forgotten. Writing this book helped me rediscover who I am, what I believe, what I've learned, and what I've been able to teach others as a coach at St. Raphael. It also helped me discover that much of what I taught, I learned from my relationship with the children. They became some of the best teachers of my life.

For that reason, I want this book to represent the voice of those children who are shouting, "Hey, look and listen to me. I have some pretty neat things to say and I'm doing some great things too. I know more than you think and I can teach you something if you'll listen. I'm talking to you because I love you, and I need you to love me. Hey, I want to be your friend, and have a really positive relationship with you. And if we develop this relationship, we'll have something really great for the rest of our lives."

When I started the book, I wrote to convey my experiences and their messages to others. But as the book progressed, I discovered I was writing for my own enjoyment and learning as well. Now that I've finished, I want others to learn what I've learned. I hope coaches and parents will read this book and learn something about their children. Ultimately, I want children to read the book and recommend it to their parents. If either hope becomes a reality, I'm certain the children and their parents will have some rewarding relationship-building discussions.

The setting for the learning experience was the St. Raphael Football Program, which was founded in 1963 by Ron Baumgartner, Jim Cooney, Lou Jerman, and Jim Davis. The founders' intent was to create a developmental opportunity for all children, coaches, and parents that would be realized while children, regardless of ability level, had fun learning to play football.

Their vision withstood the test of time thanks to Bill and Kathy Kavanagh, John Pulka, and many others, as they developed the original concepts into an excellent youth sports experience for more than 25,000 children over 47 years. From an initial enrollment of 200, the league has grown to 2600 children on 120 teams that entertain over 10,000 fans each Saturday.

This growth was due primarily to high-quality coaching staffs that believed football should be a vehicle for the total development of the child; an administration that made all decisions in the best interest of the children; and a culture where everybody treated one another with respect.

The seventh- and eighth-grade St. Raphael parish team will be the primary focus of the book. It was formed in 1968, with Lou Jerman as its inaugural coach. Coach Jerman selected me as his assistant in 1969. Neither of us would have a child on the team for several years.

Since 1969, we've coached over 1,000 players, and most of them had a defining story or two. For purposes of this book, I have chosen a few of the most memorable stories with learning points. Rather than present these stories and their messages as a collection of short stories, I've chosen to fast-forward them to the present and place all the players on the 2008 team. Their stories are about a series of problems that must be solved in order for the St. Raphael football team to achieve its goal of winning the Chicago Catholic League championship.

To become a championship team: Kyle must overcome a self-centered attitude, a drinking problem, and learn to lead in order to be an effective team member. Jeff must recover from a nervous breakdown caused by parental pressure. Perry, a foster child, must grow and evolve from a juvenile delinquent, who started a fire in his classroom, to a respected member of the team. Brian must conquer blindness in order to contribute to the championship run. Stewart, a ballet dancer, must defeat his fear of contact in order to become an effective running back. Despite his lack of physical talent, Matt must drive himself to excel and contribute. Bobby must display good sportsmanship after taking a beating during a 40–6 loss. Coach Jerman and I lead the team and a coaching staff of eleven. We coach as a team to facilitate learning for our players.

Each of these characters delivers a message to parents and coaches. For instance, children have a huge potential for mischief if there are no consequences for poor behavior. We make a mistake when we defend our children/players when they are wrong just because they're our children/players. Parents and coaches should not let a vacuum of authority develop when it comes to disciplining their children/players.

Each story has been fictionalized slightly to add interest and enhance the intended messages. So open your hearts and minds and let's see if the children of St. Raphael can teach you as much as they've taught me. These children have had a great influence on my life. I hope they'll have the same influence on yours.

1
Coaches' Meeting

Championships aren't won in the football planning room while we party. They're won on the practice and game fields, one game at a time.

THE DOORBELL RANG AT COACH BROWN'S HOME. The coaches had begun arriving for the St. Raphael preseason football meeting. They carried enough party supplies for the entire year of weekly meetings. The staff had grown over the years to twelve coaches. All of them originally joined the staff because their children played on the team. Once they graduated to their high school teams, they stayed, hooked by the simple joy of coaching youth football.

Some of the coaches relived the past as they perused the memorabilia displayed throughout the room. The walls were adorned with pictures of every team since 1969 and plaques accumulated over the 40-year history of the St. Raphael Parish team. The most cherished was the Honoring the Game plaque awarded by the Positive Coaching Alliance to the best youth sports program in the United States. There were also many garish trophies stacked everywhere, with last year's runner-up trophy displayed on the bar with a picture of the team.

The highlight of the room was the south wall. There, a huge poster listed the names of all the St. Raphael starters since 1983, their team record, the high school they attended, and the position they played. There were signed footballs, action photos, and numerous mementos given to the coaches by their players and friends displayed wherever there was room, and there wasn't much of that. This was the "Football Room" where the staff would meet almost every week to discuss the previous week's game and develop the practice plan for the next opponent.

Coach Brown looked around the room, mentally taking roll of one of the best youth football coaching staffs in the country. They enjoyed coaching so much they attended winter clinics and adjusted work schedules to attend practice. As a group, they had reached a competency level equal to most high school staffs. Each coach was dedicated, but also very independent. It was Coach Brown's job to make sure all points of view were considered, but when the game started, there were to be no "minority reports."

The staff consisted of Lou Jerman, co-head coach with 41 years' experience; Jim Brown, co-head coach since 1969; Ed Taylor, defensive coordinator since 1997; Jim Kanis, special teams coach since 1989; Bruce Martynowicz, offensive line coach since 2000; Paul O'Toole, offensive coach since 2001 and a past Redwing player; Bill Aimonette, offensive strategist since 1990; Dale Grosso, offensive coach and team chaplain since 2003; Greg Cook, player conditioning and defensive coach since 2000; Phil Bus, line coach since 2000; Joe Schroeder, offensive line coach since 2004; and Kevin Kelly, offensive coach since 2004.

Phil Bus was going to be a little late as he, Chris Pieroni, and Nick Gatto concluded the administration of the St. Raphael Hitter Camp conducted the week before the first practice. This four-evening, full-contact football camp for St. Raphael Program fifth and sixth graders cost only $100. The coaching staff was unique in that it included about 50 past St. Raphael players who were members of local high school teams.

The camp gave past St. Raphael players an opportunity to give back to the program and sign a few autographs. The players learned, as they taught the high school stars of tomorrow, because the best way to learn something was to teach it to someone else. During the final day of the camp, the coaches were divided into teams by the high school they attended. They renewed rivalries as they coached a spirited scrimmage between the fifth and sixth graders assigned to their teams.

Greg, a 220-pound tight end at Naperville Central, exclaimed during one of the scrimmages, "I can't believe the pressure I'm under to call a play in 30 seconds."

Once Phil arrived, the staff began reviewing the 2008 registration sheet. Last year's team had come within a play of winning the championship, and there were nine starters returning. There were two players missing. Scott, the starting quarterback, had moved, and George, the starting left tackle, had decided to take a year off for some unknown reason. Since the seventh-grade team had gone undefeated, and the fifth sixth-grade team had an 8–2 record, there was considerable optimism about the 2008 season.

As the meeting concluded, Coach Jerman, the dean of the staff, reminded everybody, "Championships aren't won in the football planning room while we party. They're won on the practice and game fields, one game at a time. Let's keep that in mind."

As the coaches rose from their chairs to leave, Coach Brown said, "It's been our practice over the past few years to end this meeting with a reminder of why we coach. As you all demonstrated during this meeting, we are ready to coach. But, I want to read you an e-mail I received recently that emphasizes why we coach. The author wished to remain anonymous. I will only tell you he's currently playing college football."

Coach Brown read the following e-mail.

Thank you for being the best coaches I have ever had. I learned so many things at St. Raphael, I can't fit them on a page. I will first say I have remembered to keep my arm up high when I deliver the ball. You coaches not only made me a better player but a better person as well. You cared about me and everyone else on the team as well. You coaches pushed us just the right amount to make us better and still have fun. This is what made us champions.

When I think back, I see the changes in some of the players which were remarkable. To watch somebody at the beginning of the season who couldn't tackle anybody to taking down other team's best running backs was awesome to watch. It only happened because of the coaches who applied their efforts toward our team. It was incredible how you coaches sacrificed so many hours for this team and didn't get paid. I have good coaches now, but I don't think they could do what you coaches did. We talk about past coaches here and I will tell you, I learned to appreciate St. Raphael all the more. I don't know if I would be able to do what you coaches do, but I want to try someday. I still remember our great season, full of joy and excitement, and the best part, it was fun.

Thank you for being great coaches. PS If you read my letter to the coaches, please don't tell them who sent it. It doesn't matter because we all felt the same way!

When Coach Brown finished reading the letter, the coaches began to file down a long hallway and out the door into another season of St. Raphael Redwing football. But Coach Cook, otherwise known as Dr. Death because he managed the training regimen, said, "Coach, you got to stop reading stuff like that to us. I may lose my toughness and edge and then you guys will go all soft on me."

"No chance!" shouted several coaches in unison as they playfully pushed Coach Cook out the door.

St. Raphael's 40th season was about to begin.

PLAY NUMBER ONE

When we coach your children, we try to find common ground for communication by going to a place close to where they live. They haven't been to our place yet, so we must go to them. We must go there naturally without fanfare. If we say, "Hey, look at me, I am acting like a kid," we'll be displaying insincere behavior the players will not respect.

2
First Day of Practice

He never said, "Hey, look at me." Instead, he said, "Hey, look at you," even though his teams had won 285 games and he had a nation of players who still called him Coach.

THE FIRST DAY OF ST. RAPHAEL FOOTBALL PRACTICE was as it had been for the past 40 years. The players arrived before 5:30 PM, full of youthful enthusiasm. Returning players were getting reacquainted and introducing themselves to the nervous new players from the fifth–sixth-grade team.

During a ten-minute period before each practice, the players were encouraged to just "fool around." This time was scheduled into each practice for teambuilding. It also gave the coaches an opportunity to finish their practice planning and talk to specific players about team-related topics. At 5:40 PM the first practice of 2008 began.

All the coaches except Lou Jerman were present, having planned their work schedules to accommodate opening day. Everybody had anticipated this season since they walked off the field after a difficult loss to St. James in the championship game, just 230 days ago. The coaches were optimistic, but cautious, as they were familiar with the unpredictability of youth sports.

The St. Raphael teams were fortunate to have practice fields that rivaled many college facilities. Thanks to the local school and park districts, their teams enjoyed a twenty-five-acre site with three fully lined football fields, and many smaller practice areas. The grass was thick and green due to fertilization and the summer rains.

Earlier in the day, the fields had been walked by coaches and varsity players to determine unsafe conditions such as exposed rocks or uneven areas. Each stone now removed and uneven spots filled, the fields were ready for practice. The tackling dummies were in place and blocking sleds had been assembled and stood under a line of trees that bordered the south end of the practice facility.

The Prairie practice facility was one of three used by St. Raphael travel and intramural teams. Each of the three major sites had a full-time certified athletic trainer. The trainers were also present at all games and contributed significantly to the safety of the children and the coach's peace of mind.

Mary Ann, a certified trainer at a local high school, volunteered her time to manage a part-time staff of ten trainers. She was the trainer at the varsity site today, and had brought extra water to deal with anticipated dehydration, as it was still over 90 degrees at 5:40 in the afternoon. Each St. Raphael two-hour practice was broken into fifteen-minute segments. The coaching staff believed in fast-paced, efficient practices, designed for the thirteen-year-old attention span. The coaches employed station teaching with an emphasis on fundamentals. The offensive and defensive schemes were not introduced until a week before the first scrimmage.

While Mary Ann discussed her safety concerns with the coaches, Coach Jerman emerged from his car parked in its usual spot and began his trudge to the practice area. He had just completed his one-hour journey from Chicago to Naperville to coach his beloved Redwings. As he began his deliberate 100-yard walk to the practice area at the southwest corner of the complex, all the coaches and players were genuinely glad to see him. Years ago,

Coach Jerman's gait was quicker, but always deliberate, as were most aspects in his life. Today his posture was slightly stooped with age, but if one looked closely, they could see the image of a bruising college fullback of yesteryear.

As Coach Jerman approached the practice area in his baggy tan pants, he placed his sweat-stained 1996 championship hat on his head, with the flat brim up and cocked slightly to the right, as he had done for so many years. He was also dressed in a worn-out red coaching shirt with the insignia "St. Raphael Redwings—CCL Champions—1991." No amount of pressure from his players or assistant coaches could convince him to wear shorts in 90-degree heat, change his opening-day shirt, or be "cool enough" to curve the brim of his hat to shade his eyes. Coach Jerman's focus was not on fashion, but on working harder and smarter than opposing coaches to develop his players and maybe win another championship.

As Coach Jerman approached the 50-yard line, the players donned their shoulder pads and helmets, because tradition dictated they be in their exercise circle before Coach Jerman arrived at the goal line. As he completed the final 50 yards, the captains could be heard calling out "championship jumping jacks," defined by Coach Jerman and conditioning coach Greg Cook as "at least 20% more than our competition." The St. Raphael athletes were conditioned for safety and to outperform their opponents in the fourth quarter, when most games were won or lost.

Coach Jerman was soft spoken, and at times a little long winded, but his players listened out of respect and the value of his message. He never swore or told a joke, but was quick to laugh in good taste. In forty years, he never said an unkind word to a player, but always got his points across. He never said, "Hey, look at me." Instead, he said, "Hey, look at you" even though his teams had won 285 games and he had a nation of players who still called him Coach.

After the 1996 Championship, he nominated Coach Brown for the League's Coach of the Year Award. In 2003, Coach Jerman's players earned him a new hat and shirt by winning the Chicago Catholic League championship. That year, he was chosen coach of the year and elected to the League's Board of Directors.

While the players were introduced to the conditioning regimen by Coach Cook, Coach Brown discussed the practice plan for the week with the rest of the coaches. There had been the usual good-natured bantering about the time allotted for offense and defense.

During this meeting, he read an e-mail from a past player who was about to start his college football career. The message was like many others received from past players. These letters were special, because it was the coaching staff's objective to coach well enough to earn similar letters from every player. Coach Brown chose one letter each year to remind the coaches of the true objective of the St. Raphael football experience ... use football as a vehicle for the total development of the players. This year he selected two because of the quality of the letters received.

This year's second letter was from an exceptionally well-motivated player who started two years at St. Raphael and Naperville Central. He would play college ball at Truman State this fall.

Coach,

Thanks a lot, it was a decision I struggled with for a while but I came to the conclusion that I couldn't hang up the cleats just yet. Football has been in my blood ever since my first practice. The two years I had with you as a coach were by far the most fun and those will stick with me forever. Thanks for everything. You and the rest of the coaches will always be my favorites. By the way I plan to wear a Redwing hitter shirt under my pads every day for college football. I really can't express my gratitude towards you and the rest of the coaching staff through this e-mail, so I'd just like to say again thank you for everything. I hope I can be as good a coach to my guys someday as you were to me.

God bless Dan Martynowicz Red-Shirt Freshman (And always a Redwing) Truman State University

Bruce Martynowicz, the proud father and a current member of the coaching staff, said, "Dan took a lot of time to write this e-mail. He wanted it to be just right. He was a little frustrated he couldn't deliver it in person. He's very emotional when he talks about his St. Raphael experience."

Once the championship conditioning was completed, the players gathered around Coach Brown for team introductions. The coaches introduced themselves first. Once they finished, the players introduced themselves, with the captains going first to set an example. Each player was encouraged to give his name, school, grade, position he'd like to play, and something interesting about his personal life. Since the team was open to sixth through eighth graders from St. Raphael School and Religious Education, the players attended as many as five different junior high schools. The introductions were important and required most of the first practice, because the coaches believed good team chemistry was essential to team success. The introductions went smoothly. As usual, far more players wanted to play skill positions than line positions. Each time a player volunteered to play line, the line coaches cheered.

Stewart was no exception as he introduced himself. "I'm an eighth grader from Lincoln Jr. High, a first-year player, and I want to play running back. I'm also a dancer, who'll perform in the Nutcracker Suite, in Chicago, during the Christmas season."

As Stewart finished, several of the players laughed in a mean-spirited way. Coach Brown held up his hand and stepped to the middle of the group and demanded, "What's that about?" Looking into the eyes of the offending players, he asked again, "What's so funny about Stewart's introduction?"

Brian, the legally blind left tackle, stood and said, "There shouldn't be anything funny about it," as he glared at Kyle, the tailback and one of the primary offenders. "I think anybody who laughed should apologize."

As Brian and Coach Brown made eye contact with each player, there was a series of "sorry, mans" and "didn't mean nothings" and head nods.

Stewart interrupted, "It's okay, Coach. They were just kidding around ... just like at school. I'm sure I'm the only ballet dancer on the team."

This response brought a good-natured laugh as the introductions continued and were completed without further incident.

With the introductions complete, Coach Brown stood to address the team.

"Your coaches are going to instruct you in three main areas to get you ready to compete against some very good football teams in the Chicago Catholic League. This is one of the toughest 7-8th grade football leagues in the country, and we must elevate our performance level well above the norm in order to have a successful season.

That performance level consists of three elements; your skill set, your physical condition, and your mental approach to the game. Coach Cook will condition you to be the best conditioned team in the league. We want to own the fourth quarter, when a lot of games are won or lost. Your conditioning will also contribute significantly to injury prevention.

This coaching staff knows how to play and instruct. They will improve your football skills through instruction, repetition, and positive reinforcement. All you have to do is pay attention, which is something you control. They will work hard with the seventh graders so each of you will play like eighth graders by playoff time.

The toughest part of our preparation and most important, will be achieving the level of maturity and mental toughness required to play at this level. This is most important because the team's ultimate performance level is leveraged significantly by how well we do in this area. The new players may not understand this concept now, but I notice the eighth graders are nodding their heads.

In order to reach the optimum level for this team, we are going to teach you to deal with adversity; to fulfill your commitments to each other at all costs; to do your best; never give up; support each other; play without fear of failure; learn from your mistakes and play with class. All of our championship caliber teams, including last year's, achieved a high level of success in this area. In addition, these skills will also be beneficial in all aspects of your life. So, let's get to work."

As the players stood to resume practice, Billy, a two-year starter at fullback, asked, "Coach, where are Scott and George? Are they on vacation or something?"

Coach Brown gave Billy a pat on the helmet and said, "Billy, Scott's moved to be closer to his brother, who plays for Kansas State, and we've heard George decided not to play football this year. We hoped George would change his mind and be here today. Since he's not, I guess he's decided to take a year off. So, we'll be looking for a new quarterback and right tackle, unless George changes his mind."

Keith, one of the team captains and two-year starter at right guard, was disappointed along with several other players and said, "I'll talk to him, Coach. I know him pretty well. He's been doing a lot of stuff this summer."

As the players moved to their first drill stations, Coach Brown approached Greg, the center and a team leader, and asked, "Why were you and the other players laughing at Stewart?"

"Coach, Stewart's a ballet dancer. He wears tights and acts weird sometimes. The kids make fun of him at school. He'll never be a running back because, you know, he won't be able to take a hit. I don't have anything against him, Coach. I'm sorry I laughed. That wasn't right. You want me to say something to him?"

"I want you to make sure he feels welcome. He's a member of our team. Make sure you and the other players get to know him as a football player and as a person before you pass judgment."

"Sorry, Coach, I'll talk to him and the other guys at the first water break."

At the break, Greg assembled some of the other team leaders and said, "Coach wants us to make Stewart feel welcome. He's a member of our team."

All the players agreed except Kyle, the first string tailback, who said, "I think the dude has to earn team membership. We all paid our dues last year."

"I agree," said Greg. "We all have to earn our positions, but let's give him a chance. The eighth graders gave us a chance last year. Remember, our team needs the new players to step up and get better if we're going to make the playoffs."

Brian, not sensing sufficient remorse, said, "Let's not prejudge him. When I first came out last year, you guys didn't think I could play because of my sight, but I proved you wrong. I earned my starting position, and you guys helped me. Let's give Stewart a chance."

After some reluctant nods, the four boys approached Stewart, who was standing alone, drinking from his water jug. "Sorry about the team meeting," Greg said. "We shouldn't have laughed, man."

Greg looked at Kyle, who had his head down, and said, "Right, guys?"

Kyle responded without looking at Stewart, "Right. Sorry, man."

Then Brian in an exaggerated gesture of support, extended his hand to Stewart and said, "Welcome to the team. It'll be my pleasure to block for you." Brian glared at Kyle and continued, "And, if you have any problems, let me know and we'll work things out."

"That's okay," said Stewart, shaking all four hands as the players ran to their designated stations.

During the initial agility and conditioning drills, Stewart was outstanding. There was no limit to the number of pushups and sit-ups he did, each with perfect form. The coaches walked from player to player teaching proper form and recording their performance.

This data would be used to measure progress at mid-year and season's end.

As Coach Cook approached Stewart, he yelled for all to hear, "Hey, look at Stewart. This kid knows how to do a pushup."

Next, the team ran a series of 40-yard dashes at three-quarter speed for warm-up and then at full speed, with the coaches recording their times. Stewart beat everybody by five yards. Kyle came in second.

As several players complimented Stewart, Kyle grumbled, "Wait until contact drills. I'm not giving up my tailback spot to a dancer."

PLAY NUMBER TWO

Players have to be conditioned before they are ready to learn. Learning to tackle is a good example. We must convince the children they can deal with the discomfort of tackling, and the discomfort is reduced if they're aggressive. We can't rush the instruction because when the child is ready to learn, the teacher arrives. If the teacher arrives too early, there are setbacks.

3
George Retires

He wants to please you, just like most children who participate in any activity want to please their parents. He loves you and sees how much you enjoy his success and how much you enjoy talking about it. And, like most children, he doesn't want to disappoint you.

AS THE PLAYERS FINISHED THEIR STATION DRILLS, the coaches noticed George and his father approaching, with his pads in hand. As they arrived, George's dad, Ben, shrugged his shoulders and said, "I'm as surprised as you are. George, tell your coaches what you've decided, if you're still sure that's what you want to do. You're going to disappoint a lot of people. You're letting the whole team down."

George didn't look at his father. He just handed his shoulder pads to Coach Brown and said, "Coach, I'm just tired of football. Thanks for coaching me. I like the team, but I'm just tired of sports right now."

"I'm sorry to hear that, George," said Coach Brown. "I know you've had a busy summer with your basketball, baseball, and football camps. I had hoped you'd changed your mind about not playing. Do you need a week off?"

"No, Coach, I'm just tired of sports right now."

Thinking there might still be some negotiating room, Coach Brown pointed to a secluded area called "the office" and said, "Let's sit down by the backstop and talk a little."

But George was firm as tears welled up in his eyes. "Coach, I just need time off. Dad, can we go now?" When Ben didn't move, George started walking to the parking lot alone, rubbing either tears from his eyes, or sweat from his brow.

Ben stayed behind to explain. "George played 50 basketball games over the summer and was the star of his team. At the same time, he played travel baseball and was the team's best pitcher. His team lost in the regional finals. George was the losing pitcher because he was just too tired to compete."

Coach Brown interrupted, "Was he upset about that?"

"Yes, he was. And to make things worse, a couple of parents got on him about attending the football camp. You see he'd been at a football camp all day and had to change his clothes in the car on the way to the game. He also won the outstanding camper award for his age group at the football camp. So, he's had a lot of athletic success this summer. This decision to quit the team came out of left field as far as I'm concerned."

"Ben, has George given you a reason other than he is tired of football?" Coach Jerman asked. "I thought football was his favorite sport. Is it anything we did?"

"I've had only a brief discussion with him. But, you can be assured it's not the coaching. He looks up to you guys. He was going to make that clear, but he must've forgotten. You could see how emotional he was. When I tried to discuss it with him on the way here, all he'd say was that he was tired of football and needed time off."

"When did you first suspect he might not want to play?" asked Coach Brown.

"This all started earlier this summer with a few comments. It concluded when I picked him up at the pool today. He was having a good time just fooling around with his friends. He lingered at the pool and looked sad when I told him we'd be late for practice. This was unusual, since he usually can't wait for football practice. I don't know what to do. Do you guys have any ideas?"

Coach Brown turned to Lou. "Do you remember a few years ago when we had an outstanding quarterback named Jordan returning for his eighth-grade season and much to our surprise he decided to quit the team?"

"Yes, I remember all too well. He decided to play fall basketball. I don't believe he ever played basketball beyond his sophomore year in high school, and never played football again. I think the football coaches tried to get him out for football as late as his junior year."

Coach Brown looked at Ben and said, "I believe there are similarities between Jordan and George, and one difference. The similarity is, Jordan played four sports during the summer: baseball, basketball, golf, and football. He had little time to himself, and little time to just hang with his friends. The difference was, during Jordan's seventh-grade year, his dad attended every practice. He was a college quarterback and worked with his son before and after practice. He complained about our coaching and was disappointed his son didn't start. I believe Jordan felt the pressure from his father and was embarrassed about his father's involvement. In order to get some relief, he took the drastic step of quitting a sport he enjoyed, and one in which he had an excellent future."

"Yes, I remember," said Coach Jerman. "Jordan knew he wasn't ready to start. The first-string quarterback, Brian, was outstanding. He went on to play college ball. There were times during the season when we tried to play him early in games for development, but he said he'd preferred to play later. Even though we backed off, I think Jordan was so desperate to get relief from the pressure of the situation, he sustained some questionable injuries in order to avoid practice."

All of a sudden, Ben touched Coach Jerman's shoulder and said, "Wait a minute! Do you think I put that kind of pressure on George?"

"No," said Coach Brown. "Let me finish the story and I think you'll see where we're going. There's a big difference between you and Jordan's father, but the result is the same. Jordan's father put direct pressure on his son with constant coaching, criticism, and never being satisfied. I believe your pressure is more subtle, but it's having the same effect."

Ben interrupted again with a concerned look in his eyes. "Give it to me straight, Coach. Let's not leave anything out. This is too important."

Coach Brown continued, "Ben, this summer you enrolled George in basketball, playing 50 games, and sometimes two and three games a day. He played baseball, regular season and tournament. You enrolled him in a football camp where he played up with the high school players and won an award. You're at almost all of his activities. He gets lots of positive feedback from you and others. Because he's an all-star in all sports, his coaches, teammates, and parents have great expectations. They depend on him and they let him know it, most of the time in very positive ways. The opposing team's coaches and players focus on him. They've got to stop George in order to win. That's a different kind of pressure, but it's still pressure. And I think George feels it."

Ben looked at Coach Brown, puzzled, as he shifted his weight from one foot to the other. "But George has never said anything. I thought he enjoyed all of the sports ... and the attention. Are you leaving something out?"

Coach Brown continued, "Ben, I think George enjoys sports and the attention, but not as much as you think. He's a quiet person. I think you might have enjoyed the attention more he did."

Ben raised his hand and started to interrupt, but Coach Jerman said, "Let Jim finish."

Coach Brown continued, "I think he sees how much you enjoy his accomplishments and that's a big part of his motivation. He wants to please you, just like most children who participate in any activity want to please their parents. He loves you and sees how much you enjoy his success and how much you enjoy talking about it. And, like most children, he doesn't want to disappoint you."

Ben raised his eyes to the sky, exhaled, and said, "Oh, my God, what have I done? If he doesn't play this year, it's going to hurt him in high school. I think he's got a real future in football. He's six feet tall and 180 pounds in the eighth grade. What can we do to get him back? Can you guys talk to him? Should I tell him if he plays football he can take the winter off? Should we have the players tell him how much they need him?"

"No, I've seen this before and I don't think any of those ideas will work with George," said Coach Brown. "Those actions will create the same kind of pressure that caused him to quit. George has to develop the desire to return on his own. What do you think, Lou?"

"I agree. But Ben, if I were you, I'd be more concerned about permanently damaging your relationship with George. You and he are friends as well as father and son. If you force him to return, you could damage a relationship you'll enjoy for the rest of your life. It took a lot of courage for George to quit. But he hit a wall, then experienced relief while playing golf and swimming with his friends. He's taking a big risk to get relief."

"Wow! I don't want to damage our relationship! What should I do?"

"Ben, I believe you have to go to the car and tell George you respect his decision," said Coach Brown. "Tell him you love him and value your relationship. I'd also tell him you're available to discuss whatever led to his decision at any time. I'd make it clear it's his decision to make, and his decision won't have an impact on your relationship. Tell him the coaches said he could come back anytime.

Then, I'd talk about topics other than football and encourage him to do something with his friends tomorrow."

"This is going to be tough," said Ben. "But I'll do it. I hope I can repair any damage already done."

"Let me tell you one more story for emphasis," said Coach Brown. "I know of a father who had two sons. He pushed the first son to be an exceptional athlete. He managed his lifting, coached his youth football teams, and generally pushed him beyond his capability. The child was under so much pressure he never achieved his potential. His second son had about the same natural ability as the first son. One day he went to his mother and asked if his father was going to treat him like he did his older brother. His mother passed this on to his father. The father was shocked. He changed his approach. He became supportive of the younger son and he turned out to be an exceptional athlete."

As Ben turned to make the long walk to his car, Coach Jerman looked at Coach Brown with a sly smile. "Just remember, kids are more resilient than we are."

When the coaches returned to the practice, the players, drenched in sweat, were on a much-deserved water break. The players looked tired as they removed their helmets and shoulder pads for the final conditioning drills.

As the coaches approached, Keith asked, "Is George going to play?"

Coach Brown looked at Coach Jerman and then the other coaches and said, "I don't think so, but you never know. I think we just have to let George decide for himself, and practice as though he'll not be part of the team."

Brian rubbed the sweat from his eyes and said, "Coach, don't worry. He'll be back. In the meantime, I can play right tackle. I'm not worried. He won't be able to stay away."

Then Jeff, who played backup quarterback last year, said, "Even though I wanted to play defense, I'll try quarterback again. I thought Scott was coming back and you'd want to train a seventh-grade backup."

Coach Brown thanked Brian and Jeff, knowing it would be difficult for either to replace Scott and George, but he admired their willingness to try.

PLAY NUMBER THREE

Coaches and teachers have a tremendous advantage over parents. We are often perceived by children to be experts in our field. Once we achieve expert status, the children accept what we say without question. Because a parent has to be an expert in many fields, their job is more difficult. A parent also has to deal with a child's disappointment. This is difficult, but it's also an opportunity to contribute to the child's development.

4
Brian's Long Lap

Still breathing heavily and smiling, Brian responded in a halting voice, "I have to go all out in everything I do because of my condition. I want to be as normal as possible."

THE FIRST TWO WEEKS OF PRACTICE WENT WELL, especially the conditioning, as the players strived to outwork the other teams in their conference. Jeff practiced at quarterback in place of Scott and progressed nicely. His acclimation was difficult since he'd played very little quarterback as a backup. He spent most of his time as a wide receiver and defensive back. His progress had slowed recently because he experienced difficulty taking the snap from center. Jeff had small hands, but the coaches believed he was nervous about the scrimmage with Sts. Peter and Paul on Saturday. Two additional players emerged at quarterback from last year's JV team, but both had trouble adjusting to the speed of the varsity game.

Stewart was progressing, but as expected, had difficulty dealing with contact. He was fumble prone, as were most running backs who shied away from contact. Given this situation, he would see little playing time on Saturday. During practice, the coaches planned to run him outside until he was able to deal with off-tackle contact. They were optimistic about his potential and thought Stewart would learn with time.

Brian had become Stewart's protector and mentor. The two boys became good friends on and off the field. Brian's move to right tackle was progressing, but he had trouble with run blocking due to his impaired vision. When he experienced success, he was elated. But when he experienced failure, he took it hard. The coaches tried to encourage a more consistent motivational pattern, but were unsuccessful because of Brian's determined personality. He also felt additional pressure because he would play against the opposition's best lineman each week.

The players indicated George was enjoying his time away from football and was unlikely to return. That put additional pressure on Brian, who began to experience more trouble with his conditioning due to asthma.

On Thursday night, the team finished practice with the long lap, a run of about 600 yards. Brian insisted on running the full lap even though the coaches advised against it. He pushed himself throughout the run because he wanted to be the first lineman to finish.

At about 500 yards into the run, the coaches saw he was in trouble. Stewart, who finished first, also noticed Brian's difficulty. He ran to Brian's bag, took out his inhaler, and sprinted to his aid. He gave Brian his inhaler and tried to support him while he took several deep breaths. Coach Cook arrived and encouraged Brian to stop, but he refused. Leaning on Stewart, he continued to put one foot in front of the other.

As the team stood in awe, Keith began a staccato clap, then started to run toward Brian and Stewart. The rest of the team followed. Soon the whole team was walking and running with Brian. They continued to clap and cheer. At the 30-yard marker, Brian refused Stewart's support. He wanted to finish on his own. He stumbled and inhaled his way to the finish line, where he dramatically fell to the ground with his arms raised in triumph. He'd finished last, but he'd finished.

Mary Ann, the trainer, hurried to his side and made sure he was all right. She chastised Brian and the coaching staff, and then asked him, "Why would you do something like this? I'm sure you've been told over-activity, especially in these weather conditions, is dangerous."

Still breathing heavily and smiling, Brian responded in a halting voice, "I have to go all out in everything I do because of my condition. I want to be as normal as possible."

As Brian recovered, his "life coach" arrived. Brian introduced Rita to the team. "This is my off-the-football-field coach and the person who helped me learn how to cross the street without damaging any cars."

Rita helped Brian adjust physically and emotionally to being an unsighted person. Last year, she sensitized the coaching staff to the importance of football to Brian's developing self-esteem.

Today, she brought a pair of glasses to practice that simulated Brian's level of sight. The coaching staff donned the glasses and experienced Brian's limitations. Brian, and members of the team, laughed as the coaches tried to play catch wearing the glasses. They soon appreciated Brian's limitations. His only clear vision was about the size of a pinhole in each eye.

After the final conditioning drills, Coach Cook addressed the team. "We practice about two hours a night. We spend about 30% of our time on conditioning. We don't do this to punish you, although you might think so. We do it because we want you to play the game as safely as possible. We also want you to be as strong, quick, and flexible as possible relative to your opponents. We want you to be well conditioned so if a game's close in the fourth quarter, you know it's yours. The fourth quarter is also when most injuries occur."

Coach Cook surveyed the team to make sure he still had their attention and continued, "We also want you to hustle in drills and between drills. You must practice as hard as you expect to play. You'll be given time to rest, so don't pace yourself. Remember, time lost in practice is lost forever. We won't be able to make it up."

Coach Cook paused again and stared down a few inattentive players, then continued, "There's a tradition at St. Raphael. At the end of each practice, your captains will ask, 'Did you practice like Redwings today?' If you did, you'll say yes. If enough players say yes, we'll end our practice by putting hands in and yelling 'Redwings.' If not, we'll put hands in and say 'team,' knowing we must work harder the following day. Last year's team were Redwings every night but one. Any questions?"

The team put their hands in, and Todd the left guard asked, "Did we practice like Redwings today?"

The team gave a resounding, "Yeah!" Then, "Redwings!"

As Keith carried the ball bag and hand dummies to Coach Brown's car, Coach Brown said, "I liked the way you led the players tonight when Brian was struggling with the long lap. Actions like that help unify the team."

"Thanks, Coach. I remembered when Mark did it last year when Todd was having trouble with the run. I thought it was cool ... so I guess I just did it without thinking. No big deal."

After Keith trotted off to his ride, Coach Jerman said, "Isn't it interesting that players can be role models for one another? It reminds you of how important it is for us to be good role models, especially in how we relate to our players. If we treat them with respect, they will treat each other with respect."

PLAY NUMBER FOUR

Once a conversation begins, we try to participate as much as possible in the child's environment through a series of questions and comments that indicate we understand content and how the child feels. If we don't understand, we ask a question that does not put the child on the defensive. Asking the right questions affirms the child. Think about how good you feel when somebody asks you a question and listens to your answer. If you ask questions, your child may ask you additional questions. Of course, when this happens, take the time to answer them completely and thoughtfully. Don't be offended by follow-up questions. They are part of a normal conversation. Be careful not to answer questions that were not asked. This happens when we're thinking of our answer before the question is completed.

5
Story of Matt

*If Matt could have verbalized what he knew instinctively,
he might do it as Stephen Covey did in his book* The Seven
Habits of Highly Successful People. *Covey wrote, "Proactive
people believe they are responsible for their own lives. They
believe their behavior is a function of decisions they make and
not conditions beyond their control. They take the initiative
and make things happen in theirs and others' best interest."*

THE ST. RAPHAEL VARSITY PROGRAM WAS DIVIDED
into two levels. The Red team played on Sundays. The White team,
comprised of sixth and seventh graders plus non-starting eighth
graders, played during the week in lieu of practice. The White team
played a six-game scrimmage schedule against White teams from
other suburbs. All the players on both teams practiced together,
dressed on Sunday, and played if game conditions permitted.

During the first two weeks of practice, the players were evaluated physically and emotionally to determine which team was best
for them. After the evaluations were completed, Coach Brown discussed the staff's recommendations with each player and his parents.
All of the discussions went smoothly this year with the exception of
a boy named Matt.

Shortly after this discussion began, Matt interrupted and said, "Coach, I want to be on the Red team. Last year you said you needed me. I told you I'd play on the Red team on the way home from the championship game. Don't you remember?"

"Yes, Matt, I remember," said Coach Brown. "But I think you'll gain more experience playing on the White team."

Matt's parents tried their best to support the coaching staff's recommendation, but Matt was adamant. "Please don't worry about me. I can handle it. I realize I won't play much, but I think I'll learn more on the Red team and become a better football player. I want to become as good a player as my brother, Sean. He's going to start for his high school team this fall."

The final decision was always left with the parents and their child. The coaches believed no child should be cut from a team at this age. Most families accepted the coaches' recommendation, but a few decided the Red team was best for their child. Since Matt couldn't be convinced of the merits of White team membership, he was assigned to the Red team.

When Matt chose the Red team, he made an unqualified commitment to do something that was important to him. He had no idea of the difficulties he'd experience or how he was going to handle them. He made no conditional requests such as joining the White team if things got too tough. Matt was fully committed to his goal. He knew a breakthrough was required to achieve his goal because he lacked the natural athletic ability of his brother, Sean.

Playing on the Red was hard for Matt. He had difficulty with conditioning and drills even though the coaches tried to match him with boys of comparable size and aggressiveness. Matt experienced more than his share of minor injuries primarily due to his willingness to go all out against everybody in drills and scrimmages. Whenever Matt sensed he was being specially treated, he sought his own drill partner before one could be assigned.

During the second week, Matt injured two fingers when they were caught between helmets during a scrimmage. The coaches tried to comfort him. As he unsuccessfully held back tears, he said, "Don't worry about me. Injuries are just part of football."

Matt was back at practice the following night with three of his fingers crudely taped together, proclaiming, "My mom said it was okay to practice if I can deal with the pain."

Two days later, Matt was again helped to the sidelines with an injured ankle. The scrimmage continued while one of the coaches prepared an ice pack. The offensive team ran a sweep left with a pulling tackle that went wider than anticipated. Matt stood up to get out of the way, but Garrett, a 170-pound tackle, mistakenly knocked him down. Matt jumped to his feet and instead of yelling something colorful at Garrett, yelled, "Nice block!"

The next day, Matt brought a note from his doctor. It said Matt could not practice for a couple of weeks. He had a sprained ankle and a broken finger. In spite of his injuries, Matt continued to attend practice every night to learn what he could. He missed only one practice all season, and that was because he promised his dad he would be a "designated screamer" at the Jaycee haunted house.

During each scrimmage, Matt was one of the last players to participate, but he never complained. Instead, he was overheard bragging about his playing time in practice because it had increased each of the last two scrimmages.

Matt had set exceptionally high goals that required several discoveries. First, he concluded he must think outside of his normal frame of reference to develop the plan required to achieve his goals. He also learned he would need breakthroughs, not just incremental improvements, over his current level of performance.

To achieve a breakthrough, he discovered he must commit to difficult plans that were not definable when he established his original goal. He realized breakthroughs required an unconditional commitment to his plan. He also discovered commitments were personal, and once made, he alone could fulfill them. And finally, he experienced true commitment as a state of mind. He could feel it and it felt good.

Matt did not understand the formal definition of a breakthrough, but there was no question he was committed to one. As Matt became fully committed, he became more confident and proactive about his plan. He began having proactive conversations with his teammates, which helped him build his commitment and clarify his plan for the achievement of a goal that sometimes seemed unachievable.

Matt was the personification of this final principle. His conversations with his coaches and teammates were non-stop as he encouraged others, told them of his accomplishments, and asked his coaches for feedback. He also gave unsolicited suggestions for team improvement. Those included everything from practice procedures to game strategies.

Matt's effort were addictive and contagious. His proactive conversations served to reenergize him around his commitment as he slowly became a role model for others on the team. The team began to notice Matt's effort and even model their behavior after his.

Each year, the coaches strived to reach this state of team as the year progressed. This year, their job was made easier as the team coalesced around Matt and his struggle to achieve a breakthrough.

One night Matt noticed Mike, another seventh grader and one of his frequent drill partners, was discouraged, and he began to miss practice occasionally. Mike had been a starter on the JV team and was one of the top candidates for a starting position at the beginning of the season. The coaches tried to find a solution to Mike's subpar performance by listening, encouraging, and even moving him to positions of indicated interest. Nothing worked, including discussions with his parents, who were concerned because Mike had become uninterested in other aspects of his life as well.

One night Mike approached Matt before practice. They had an engaging conversation. During practice, they continued their conversations, usually at Mike's initiative. These conversations continued after practice, and throughout the week.

After the week's final practice, Mike approached Coach Brown and asked, "Can we talk, Coach?"

Mike hung his head uncomfortably and began. "I know I haven't done as well as I should've this year. I don't know why. I hope the coaches haven't given up on me. Matt and I think we can start next year. I'd like to play defensive end next year instead of guard. So Matt thought I should let you know this year, so maybe you'd let me play my new position as soon as possible. He said I should go after what I want. That's what he does."

Coach Brown smiled and said, "Mike, sounds good. We've been worried about you. I'll talk with Coach Taylor about working with you on Monday. How's everything else going?"

Mike smiled, "Fine, Coach. I've got to go. My dad's waiting."

As Mike hurried to his car, Coach Brown caught up with Matt. He told him about his discussion with Mike, then asked, "What've you and Mike been talking about? Mike has a renewed interest in football."

Matt replied proudly, "Coach, our discussions were private. Let's just say we've got a lot in common. You catch my drift?"

As the preseason practices ended, an interesting phenomenon had occurred. The team members had changed their opinions of Matt. They went from wondering why he was on the Red team to expressing respect and encouragement.

Matt improved his football skills significantly and became an integral member of the team, especially from a social standpoint. This encouraged him, and he became increasingly confident about his involvement with the team. Matt became famous for a sideline dance he did only after important touchdowns.

Finally, at Mike's encouragement, Matt joined the White team. He explained to Coach Brown, "The White team's struggling a little and could use my help."

If Matt could have verbalized what he knew instinctively, he might do it as Stephen Covey did in his book *The Seven Habits of Highly Successful People*.

Covey wrote, "Proactive people believe they are responsible for their own lives. They believe their behavior is a function of decisions they make and not conditions beyond their control. They take the initiative and make things happen in theirs and others' best interest."

Covey illustrated these concepts with his concentric circles of influence and concern. He wrote, "Those who are committed and proactive concentrate their activity within their inner circle of Influence, where they have control. They work at expanding their circle of Influence, thereby reducing their circle of concern where they have little influence over outcomes."

By being committed and proactive, Matt controlled the outcomes within his circle of influence. He didn't worry about what others thought because their thoughts were outside his circle of influence. As he followed this practice, Matt became responsible for what he was, what he did, and what he was to become. Once he accepted this responsibility, he began to achieve things he never thought possible on the football field and in other aspects of his life. In three weeks, Matt had made a significant impact on the team. Nobody thought this was possible at the beginning of the season and Matt was not finished yet.

PLAY NUMBER FIVE

We try to make sure our players know we understand how they feel. Once children believe you understand how they feel, you have established the broadest of communication links. Once established, this link has to be nourished by empathetic listening and mutual respect. Parents and coaches have a lot to share with children that impacts their development.

6
A Father's Pressure

Doug was not satisfied. "Don't baby my kid," he said with a scowl. "He has to grow up. What he needs is a good kick in the butt. I was at practice last week and you guys are way too soft on these kids. This whole team will be in trouble when they go to the city to play. I'm from the city. I know city kids and they're tough. They're going to eat this team alive."

THE SCRIMMAGE WITH STS. PETER AND PAUL WENT well. The offense scored several times, while the defense held the Trojans to a single score. Jeff had difficulty with the snap from center, but this was of little concern to the coaching staff.

After the scrimmage, the players, coaches, and parents enjoyed hot dogs, beverages, and conversation. The party, however, was interrupted for Coach Brown when he noticed Jeff and his father having an animated discussion near the goal post on the practice field.

Doug had attended several practices last week. The coaching staff encouraged the parents to attend practice whenever they could to show support for their children. Their attendance also gave the coaches an opportunity for informal discussions about the team and their child's progress. They also believed an informed parent group added to the cohesiveness of the team. However, in Doug's case, the coaching staff sensed his disapproval as he paced the practice area and initiated private discussions with other parents.

Sensing a potential problem, Coach Brown approached and overheard Doug screaming at his son, "What the hell's the matter with you, Jeff? The snap from center is the simplest part of playing quarterback. If you can't even do that, how do you expect to do the hard stuff on Sunday when the pressure's on? This was only a practice game. What are you going to do when the whole team's depending on you? Let's get with it. Concentrate! This is embarrassing."

Doug might have said more, but Coach Brown interrupted as he stepped between father and son. Coach Jerman arrived shortly thereafter, and escorted Jeff toward the far end of the practice field.

As Jeff moved away, he stopped to listen as Coach Brown told his father, "The quarterback position is difficult to learn. Jeff was doing fine until last week. The learning process has its ups and downs. I'm not concerned, but talking to Jeff like that will impede his progress. Jeff will be okay on Sunday. It's a practice game and we'll keep things simple. We never intentionally put our players in a position to fail."

Doug was not satisfied. "Don't baby my kid," he said with a scowl. "He has to grow up. What he needs is a good kick in the butt. I was at practice last week and you guys are way too soft on these kids. This whole team will be in trouble when they go to the city to play. I'm from the city. I know city kids and they're tough. They're going to eat this team alive."

With that, Coach Jerman moved Jeff out of earshot as Coach Brown and Doug continued their animated discussion. Before they finished, Jeff's mother, Kathy, arrived and ushered Doug to the car. As Doug walked to the car, he shouted a few last comments. Coach Brown didn't hear these comments as he moved briskly to the other end of the practice field, where Jeff was pleading with Coach Jerman for help.

Upon reaching his side, Coach Brown put his arm around Jeff, who was sobbing uncontrollably. He held Jeff until he stopped crying. As Coach Brown continued to comfort Jeff verbally, he noticed he was sweating profusely and his hands were shaking.

Jeff looked up at Coach Brown with pleading eyes, held out his hands, and said, "Coach, I'm so sorry. This happens all the time, sometimes at school, sometimes at home. I don't know what to do. I feel so bad. What's wrong with me? Coach, can you help me?"

Coach Brown looked at Coach Jerman for any help he might give, then said, "Do your Mom and Dad know how you feel?"

"No, I'm afraid to tell them because ...," sobbed Jeff. "Well, you saw my dad."

Coach Brown thought for a moment and said, "Jeff, we need to tell your parents and get you some help."

Jeff paused, wiping away his tears, then pleaded, "Coach, we can't tell my parents. That would make things worse. Can't you just help me?"

"Jeff, I'll do all I can, but I'm not qualified. You need help from somebody who has experience dealing with what you're feeling. There are people who are really good at that."

"You mean like my counselor at school?" Jeff murmured, clasping his hands to reduce their movement.

"Yes, and there are others who specialize in helping kids, too," said Coach Brown. "You remember when Matt had to get his broken finger treated the other day? He needed a specialist. Well, you need a different type of specialist. But first, we must tell your parents. Maybe I can help with that."

Jeff paused, tears still evident in his eyes. "Coach, I'll have my mom call you. Maybe you can tell her what you think. Then she can tell my dad."

Jeff thought for a moment, and then said, "Coach, I don't think I can play quarterback right now. I know we have a game next week, but I think I'll hurt the team. I think Joe and Harrison look good. Can I go back to defense until I feel better?"

"That's a great idea," Coach Brown said with a sigh of relief. "Let's see how you feel. Your health is our first concern. We'll have you play defense for now."

"That's okay, but I don't want my dad to think there's anything wrong." Jeff paused and nervously asked, "What are you going to tell my dad? He wants me to play quarterback."

With a wink of his eye, Coach Brown said, "Jeff, I'm going to tell him you're such a gifted athlete you're going to play both sides of the ball, and you need some defensive practice."

Jeff smiled. "Good luck, Coach. I don't think he'll buy it."

After he walked Jeff part-way to his car, Coach Brown returned to the party. As he enjoyed his hot dog, he kept one eye on Jeff and his father as they were engaged in another conversation near their car.

After a few minutes, Doug started walking and trotting toward the party area. Coach Brown, sensing trouble, dropped his hot dog on the picnic bench and moved quickly to intercept Doug before he could reach the rest of the parents. "Why aren't you going to play Jeff at quarterback on Monday?" shouted Doug as he approached. "Have you given up on him?"

After making the agreed-upon response, Coach Brown paused, trying to control his anger. He then said, annunciating every word, "The bottom line is, if you'd cut your son a little slack, he'd be fine. We've not given up on him, but his health is our number-one concern."

Doug wasn't in the mood to listen. He moved close to Coach Brown and said, "I told you guys before you're too soft on these kids. Football's a tough game, just like life. Nobody cut me any slack. I don't expect it and I don't want my kid to expect it. I want to see him at quarterback on Monday or I'm taking him off the team. He can play for his grade school."

Before Coach Brown could answer, Coach Jerman stepped in and took Doug by the arm, turning him toward his car. Doug ripped his arm from Coach Jerman's grip, threw his hands in the air in frustration, and walked quickly to his car.

Coach Jerman turned to Coach Brown. "What are we going to do? That's one angry man."

"Thanks for intervening," stammered Coach Brown. "I think I was about to lose it. That guy really ticked me off. He has no idea what he's doing to Jeff. Can you believe that? You wonder how kids survive. I don't know what to do. Let's just go try to enjoy the party ... and thanks again. I was almost out of control. Can you believe that? I can't believe I let that guy get to me."

As they walked back to the party of horrified parents, Coach Jerman said, "I'd call Kathy in the morning."

"I will, Lou. Let's enjoy the party, everybody. Lou has everything under control ... including me."

PLAY NUMBER SIX

Ignoring a child shows a lack of respect. We try to be attentive even when questions are untimely. We try to treat our players like we want to be treated. Commitment and trust are essential to teaching. Mutual respect reduces the need for a formal hierarchy that can impede the communication required for learning.

7
A Critical Meeting

Coach Brown looked uncomfortably into a set of pleading eyes,
reluctant to give an unprofessional opinion about something
as important as a young boy's mental health. The silence
was deafening, interrupted only by the roar of passing cars
on a nearby highway. Both Kathy and Coach Brown were
oblivious to the noise which could have drowned out most
conversations. Kathy steadfastly waited for an answer.

THE NEXT MORNING COACH BROWN CALLED
Kathy. They briefly discussed the events of the previous day, and
agreed to meet at a coffee shop on Monday morning.

When Kathy arrived, she hurried to the booth Coach Brown
had selected near the back of the restaurant. It was 10 o'clock. The
breakfast crowd had cleared, so there were only a few customers sip-
ping coffee, engaged in business meetings of various types.

As Kathy slid into the booth she said, "I'm so sorry about Saturday. You shouldn't have to put up with that type of behavior. You
guys are there to coach the kids, not deal with dysfunctional families. I'm so sorry."

Coach Brown smiled and said, "That's okay. This is not the first meeting I've had in this booth. It's reserved for me every Monday morning ... just kidding."

Kathy did not react, but came straight to the point. "Let's talk about Saturday and what caused it."

Coach Brown and Kathy discussed the events of Saturday and the previous two weeks. Coach Brown included Jeff's request that his father be uninvolved initially, and gave Kathy an overview of his exchange with Jeff's father. He also told Kathy he had introduced the concept of obtaining professional help. Jeff knew something was seriously wrong, and wanted somebody other than his father to help him.

Kathy listened intently, then said, "I sensed there was a problem, but I had no idea it was this serious. You're scaring me. What do you think we should do? Have you seen this before when parents put too much pressure on their kids?"

"Yes, I've seen it before. Quite often, kids try to hide it because they're embarrassed. Their condition gets worse and they become more difficult to treat. I think we're fortunate Jeff's condition surfaced with something as insignificant as a few dropped snaps from center."

As Kathy wiped away a tear she said, "Do you think playing football is the primary source of the problem or is it something else? I've seen some of these same symptoms at home."

Kathy paused to collect herself, then leaned forward and whispered, "I've seen Jeff avoiding us, especially his father. He spends a lot of time in his room and at his friend's house. He eats dinner quickly and doesn't have much to say. When Doug gets on him, he doesn't say anything. He just goes to his room. When I go to his room to comfort him, he's asleep, sometimes by eight o'clock. His grades have gotten worse. He used to be an A student. That's one of the reasons Doug's been on him, in addition to football. I just don't know what to do."

Kathy paused again, with tears now streaming down her cheeks, and said, "Poor Jeff. He doesn't understand what's happening to him. He thinks he has no place to go for help. Can we get out of here?"

After paying the bill, Coach Brown and Kathy walked to Kathy's car at the back of the parking lot without saying a word. When they arrived, she turned and said, "Coach, I know it's not fair to ask, but I need your help. You've had a lot of experience with kids. I know Jeff's my son, and I'll make the decisions. But I need to know what you think. Jeff respects you. I hope I'm not asking too much. What do you think I should do?"

"Kathy, I had a situation like this once before. It worked out well, but it took time."

Coach Brown looked uncomfortably into a set of pleading eyes, reluctant to give an unprofessional opinion about something as important as a young boy's mental health.

The silence was deafening, interrupted only by the roar of passing cars on a nearby highway. Both Kathy and Coach Brown were oblivious to the noise which could have drowned out most conversations. Kathy steadfastly waited for an answer.

Sensing nobody was going anywhere until he said something, Coach Brown took a deep breath, and just let go. "I'll give you my opinion, but you have to promise to get professional advice."

"Okay! Okay! I promise to get professional help," said Kathy. "I'm listening."

"First, I'd go home and talk to Jeff before he goes to practice. I'd tell him you talked with me, that you're going to help him solve his problem, and you will talk to his dad about the problem when the time is right. Then I'd arrange professional help."

Kathy, knowing Coach Brown had more to offer, said, "Go on, ... please, ... I promise to get professional help."

Coach Brown looked away for relief from Kathy's intense eye contact, then continued. "Next, I'd make an appointment with his school counselor. I'd get his opinion, but I'd also ask for the name of a professional outside the school who's worked with teenagers. I'd interview the therapist and see if it's someone who'd relate well to Jeff. Then, I'd talk with Doug about the treatment and the family commitments required."

"Thanks, Coach. Is there anything else? What about practice and games?"

"I'll talk to Jeff at practice and tell him we talked. I'll tell him I think he should concentrate on defense in scrimmages for the rest of the week until he and his family determine what to do. Jeff will continue to participate in quarterback drills to the extent he's able. I'd also recommend you keep me informed to the extent necessary, so we can use football as one of the vehicles for solving his problem."

Coach Brown paused, then said, "I don't know if this is a good plan or not. It needs to be evaluated by professionals as we go. I'm open to whatever they suggest."

Kathy reached over and gave Coach Brown a hug and said, "Thank you, Coach. I've only got one more question. Are you sure I should tell Doug right away? What if he says no to therapy?"

Coach Brown smiled and said, "I think telling Doug will be a little difficult. But in my opinion, since Doug is part of the problem, he's got to be part of the solution."

That evening, Jeff arrived at practice a little late, accompanied by Kathy. He walked slowly to the practice field and then trotted to where Coach Brown was conducting a passing drill. Jeff looked at his coach apologetically and said, "Coach, I'm sorry I'm late. My mom and I talked and she said to tell you we're going to do what you suggested. Thanks for talking to my mom."

"Jeff, you're welcome. How do you feel tonight?" asked Coach Brown.

"Coach, to be honest, I don't feel so good right now. Do you think I could work with the defense tonight? I talked to Ryan, the kid that plays end, at school today. He said he'd try quarterback until I feel better as long as he could still play end when I return."

Coach Brown smiled, patted Jeff affectionately on the shoulder pads, and said, "Jeff, that's great. I'll talk to Ryan in a few minutes. Do you feel up to participating in quarterback drills this week?"

Jeff looked up the hill to where his mom was standing watching the discussion and said, "Coach, I think I should concentrate on just one thing until I feel better."

"That's great!" said Coach Brown. "I know that's a tough decision. I admire your courage. You go practice with the defense. You let me know when you're ready to play quarterback again."

Jeff nodded, made a small wave to his mom, and was off to defensive drills and hopefully his recovery. Kathy unclasped her hands long enough to wave back and walked slowly to her car.

At the water break, the other coaches were informed of Jeff's condition and the plan. Next, the team was informed of the changes. The players didn't understand much about Jeff's problem, but they knew instinctively it was serious. The players welcomed Jeff unconditionally to his new position with the traditional slaps on the shoulder pads and helmet.

After the players left for their drills, Todd, the defensive captain, approached Coach Taylor and said, "Coach, I can help Jeff catch up. I live in his neighborhood. I don't understand what's bothering him, but I'm sure he could use a friend."

* * *

The next day, Jeff and his mom went to his counselor, who recommended Jeff get professional help. That evening, after interviewing the therapist, Kathy informed Doug of Jeff's condition, the discussion with the counselor, and her subsequent discussion with the recommended therapist.

Doug responded as expected, "I believe this is an exaggeration of a problem we could've avoided if we hadn't babied Jeff. If we continue to pamper him, he's going to need psychological support for the rest of his life."

Kathy did not argue during a long one-sided conversation. She only asked Doug to attend the first family session, which would take place next week. Doug reluctantly agreed and said, "I'll go to one session and that's it. From then on you're on your own. I think this is a waste of time."

* * *

During the first meeting with the therapist, Doug was combative as expected. However, as the meeting progressed, he became more interested as he became aware of the severity of Jeff's illness and his role in its creation. Kathy was relieved as Doug's attitude turned from combative to concerned.

Coach Brown was asked to participate in the third family session, during which they developed the role of football in Jeff's recovery. Jeff enjoyed playing defense and his condition slowly improved as he contributed defensively in White team games. He also participated occasionally in quarterback drills, but did not play quarterback in games or scrimmages.

One night Jeff approached Coach Brown and said, "I think I'm getting better, Coach. But I'll know I'm back when I can take a snap from center in a game, even a White team game."

PLAY NUMBER SEVEN

Create an environment where children can just "wade in"—trust in themselves. Achieving exceptional performance requires focus, structure, and stability. Encourage children to seek for themselves. They shouldn't wait for others to do this for them. As you coach, keep your senses—your sense of history (learn from the past—keep doing what went well—change what didn't).

Keep a sense of balance between all aspects of your coaching —work, play, and the relationships that are the building blocks of communication with your children. Help children be, and discover who they are, and help them become who they want to be. Then, give them the support and space to grow and flow into that person athletically, socially, and intellectually.

8
Head Coaches' Meeting

It's important to recognize an environment is conducive to learning when it's supportive, proactive, risk free, and where everybody treats one another with respect. The extent to which this environment is achieved and maintained determines the ease and speed at which learning takes place for the players, the parents, and the coaches.

ASIDE FROM COACHING HIS BELOVED REDWINGS, Coach Brown had served as president of St. Raphael Football for the past twenty-five years. Monday, following the second week of the season, he didn't attend practice. Instead, he spoke to the 107 head coaches of teams that comprise the intramural division of St. Raphael Football.

The head coaches' meeting was important because the league relies heavily on them to manage the assistant coaches, the parents, and the total team environment. After Coach Brown's remarks, the division commissioners met with their coaches in separate rooms to develop a rapport, distribute teams, and answer all questions.

Tonight, there were 97 head coaches and ten assistants in attendance. After Judy, the program's business manager, handed out and explained the contents of the coaching packet, Coach Brown began his remarks. "First, I'd like to congratulate last year's coaches of the year, picked by their peers. The criterion for selection was:

"Coach conduct during games relative to players, referees, parents, and opposing coaches and players. This conduct should be consistent with the St. Raphael definition of "How We Coach." The quality of this behavior might be most obvious in defeat, the quality of the parental culture at games, or the apparent improvement of the team during the season.

"Since 1963, the participants of St. Raphael Football have strived to make it one of the best youth sports programs in the United States. The achievement of that objective was confirmed by the Positive Coaching Alliance as they awarded us their Honoring the Game Award. Lou Jerman and I went to San Francisco to accept the award and participate on a panel. I got to receive it, but you were the ones who earned it, and the children of St. Raphael Football were the ones who benefited from it."

Coach Brown held the plaque up for all to see and said, "The reason we won this award is simple. We have an excellent coaching philosophy and coaches who endorse the philosophy by the way they coach. 93% of our families gave positive grades to last year's coaching staff. 160 of 205 respondents rated their coaches excellent. We believe the seven percent unfavorable ratings were directed toward three or four coaches. Those coaches were appropriately managed by the commissioners.

"Our coaching philosophy, which we will discuss tonight, constitutes the cornerstone of our program's culture. Our culture is created by all participants acting from the program values to ensure coaches and parents have fun using football as a vehicle for the total development of our children.

"The key to achieving this higher-level football experience lies in the creation of an environment that's conducive to learning. The head coaches are the keys to creating this environment, and our most successful coaches are excellent teachers. We also must understand that, although the coaches have the leadership responsibility, the creation of this environment is the joint responsibility of the coaches and parents, led by the head coaches.

"It's important to recognize an environment is conducive to learning when it's supportive, proactive, risk free, and where everybody treats one another with respect. The extent to which this environment is achieved and maintained determines the ease and speed at which learning takes place for the players, the parents, and the coaches. If you're able to achieve this environment, you're assured your teams will perform at the highest possible level, everybody will have fun, and the child/parent/coach developmental experience will be optimized.

"This level of coaching is difficult to attain, as many coaches in this room will attest. However, this approach has proved very successful over the years. Coaches who've adopted it have been very successful; those who have not are at a competitive disadvantage. There will be additional meetings for your assistant coaches, but I'm relying on you to present this material and manage their performance as you develop an effective coaching team.

"Judy, our business manager, has included some of my thoughts on how to achieve the desired environment in your packet. As indicated before, the responsibility for creating the required environment lies with the coaches, the parents, and the players, but you must provide the leadership.

"Remember, you all have an opportunity to teach and learn life's skills that will be leveraged over a lifetime. Once a coach, always a coach. I'd like to close by reading an e-mail I received this summer from my 38-year-old son."

Dad,

I need to tell you the most interesting event that occurred. I recently bought a "book on CD" related to leadership. I listened to the CD in my car to and from work and whenever I drove by myself. I found the book to be very good right from the beginning. As I listened to the narrator, I kept thinking "This is how I manage things at work ... these are things I believe in"... so naturally I kept listening and enjoying the book ....Then he mentioned something that was kind of incredible ... he started talking about the "circle of influence"... If you recall, you had told me about that concept ... and I have been teaching it to my employees, and they have been practicing it with success. The book also constantly referred to working with integrity and working based on "values".... Once again these are things you have taught me for so many years. It was tremendously rewarding to know that I have been trained by you in these great concepts. Then it really hit me .... In 1993 you gave me a set of tapes. I recall listening to just the beginning, but not finishing them. However, I kept the tapes in my dresser since then and had said "I really need to listen to those"... but I never had a chance ... so I went upstairs and I opened my drawer and there the tapes were with the card you wrote .... It said, "AT&T was using these tapes to drive their change".... it was by Stephen Covey ...THAT IS THE BOOK I JUST FINISHED!!! I instantly felt bad for not listening to them in 1993! The material was great ... However, I was instantly reassured when I realized you have been training me on these concepts for all these years! So I have to thank you Dad for giving me all this knowledge and leadership skills over these years ...You were teaching me one conversation at a time!

Love Mike

"One final thought. I can't remember who said this to me. ... But remember, ... kids don't care what you know until they know that you care. ... Have as much fun as your players. It's going to be a great year."

PLAY NUMBER EIGHT

Children have a huge potential for mischief if there are no consequences for poor behavior. We make a mistake when we defend our children/players when they are wrong just because they're our children/players. Don't let a vacuum of authority develop when it comes to the disciplining of a child. It's important to give children as much positive feedback as they deserve and maybe a little more. When children are affirmed for doing well, they stop doing some of the "dumb" things designed to get our attention.

9
Leadership

*Remember, leadership is bestowed, not claimed, and is given
in recognition of actions taken that benefit those being led.
A leader must adjust his leadership style to those he's leading.
So, the bottom line is, just step up and make contributions for
the good of your teammates and you'll be their leader. Take
charge of what you do. Some say knowledge is power, but
that's not entirely true. Character is power. Character is the
great differentiator in leadership.*

DURING THE FIRST WEEK, THE TEAM FOCUSED ON
fundamental instruction and drills. After evaluation, the players
were divided into two groups by ability and experience. Kyle was
placed in the first group and Stewart in the second. The players
tested Stewart as he took some good hits, often fumbling the ball.
Initially, he was timid, but did not back down. As the week progressed, he became more confident within his group. But Stewart's
trials were just beginning.

Midway through the second week, Stewart ran a sweep and
jumped in the air to avoid a tackler. His body went completely

horizontal, but he still managed to land on his feet and ran to the endzone.

Coach Kelly exclaimed, "I've never seen that kind of agility, ever." After he recovered, Coach Kelly moved Stewart to group one.

During an inter-squad scrimmage, Stewart was moved from defense to run a few plays at tailback with the first unit, replacing Kyle. Kyle stood in the background for a few plays as Stewart used his speed to make several good runs against the second team. As Stewart's success continued to rave reviews, Kyle grew impatient and asked Coach Taylor, "Coach, would you let me play a little defense since Stewart's in my position?" Middle linebacker was Kyle's normal position as he was a two-way player.

On the first play, Kyle blitzed and hit Stewart hard just as he took the handoff. The ball flew up in the air, and Stewart hit the ground hard, and started to squirm in pain. The coaches ran to his side. As the coaches administered to him, they discover he only had the wind knocked out of him. Once Stewart recovered, Kyle was banished to the sidelines because it's against the rules to blitz during inter-quad scrimmages unless part of a planned drill.

After a few plays, Coach Jerman approached Kyle and said, "Kyle you know there's no blitzing in inter-squad scrimmages. Did you intend to make a point?"

"Yes I did," replied Kyle defiantly. "I wanted to show the dancer what it's like to play on Sunday."

"Kyle you're in no danger of losing your position. You should know we need to find a second tailback. You won't last the season in the Chicago Catholic League playing middle linebacker and tailback the whole game. You're one of our captains. You should be contributing to team unity, not ripping it apart. Do you think anybody on this team respected you for what you did?"

"No. I guess not, Coach," Kyle said with considerably less attitude.

"I want to get together with you after practice," said Coach Jerman. "I want you to think about what you did and tell me how you plan to make it right."

"Okay, Coach. Can I return to practice?"

"No, Kyle! I want you to reflect on what you did, and how to fix it."

As practice ended, Coach Jerman approached Kyle and asked, "Kyle, what did you decide?"

"Don't worry, Coach," Kyle replied as he tried to walk away. "I'll make it right."

Coach Jerman called Kyle back and said, "Kyle, I'm worried about three things. First, I'm concerned about your development as a team leader, Stewart's development as your backup, and team unity. We can't win the championship without all three. Do you understand?"

"Coach, that's a lot of stuff. Honestly, I don't know what to do. I just want to play hard. Isn't that enough?"

"Kyle, we need more than that from you," said Coach Jerman, with unyielding eye contact. "The players on this team look up to you."

"Yeah, that's because I'm one of the toughest kids in my class, not because I do all that stuff required to be class president or something."

"Kyle, there's a big difference between natural and developed leadership. You're a natural. But let's not go into that. Let's keep it simple."

"Okay, Coach. What do you want me to do?" he said as he nervously looked toward the team assembling for end-of-practice sprints.

"Kyle, I want you to teach Stewart to be your backup. If you do that, you might achieve all three things this team needs from you."

Kyle shrugged his shoulders and said, "Coach, I don't get it. How's teaching Stewart going to do that other stuff?"

"Kyle, you'll understand it better as you teach Stewart to be a tailback. In order to teach Stewart, you'll have to develop a positive relationship with him. If other players see that, it'll help create team unity and they'll see you as a more effective leader. So, just teach him and let's see what happens on the other fronts."

"Okay, Coach. All I have to do is teach him to be a tailback. Right? That's it?"

There was a pause, and Kyle said, "How do I get started ... like just go over and tell him I've been assigned to teach him to play tailback? Won't he think that's pretty lame? Isn't that your job?"

"Kyle, before you leave practice tonight, let him know you've been a little rough on him. Maybe you could apologize for the mugging. Tell him the team needs him to step up and you want to help him."

"Coach, I'd like to start tomorrow night. It would give me a chance to think about it a little and maybe talk it over with Todd and Keith."

"That's okay," Coach Jerman replied. "But tell the other captains Coach Brown and I want to meet with them before practice tomorrow night to talk a little more about leadership. They might learn something from your situation as well."

* * *

Before practice the following night, Todd, Billy, Brian, and Kyle met with Coaches Brown and Jerman.

Coach Jerman opened the meeting. "We have a number of players from several schools with different backgrounds and personalities on this team. We need to come together as a team in order to reach our potential. The coaches have the main responsibility for leadership, but you guys play a major role as well. For example, I've asked Kyle to help Stewart become a better running back as a way of developing his leadership skills. Since Kyle was unsure of how to do this, I thought we'd all benefit from a discussion of leadership. Coach Brown's going to tell you a story about a similar situation a few years ago. While he's telling you the story I want you to think about how we might apply the lessons learned by Mark to our situation." Coach Brown asked the captains to take a knee as he began.

"Several years ago, we had a quarterback who was a terrific athlete. We'll call him Mark. Mark also had the potential and desire to lead, but he didn't know how. There was also a boy on our team who desired acceptance named Tom.

"Tom looked up to Mark and wanted to be his friend. Tom was strong and a very good lineman, but he had a personality that irritated Mark. Tom did strange things to get attention. He also had a limited attention span. He had difficulty paying attention during instruction periods and going offside during games at the worst possible times. His actions were due to the self-imposed pressure resulting from the competitive environment and his desire to be recognized positively by his teammates.

"One day, Mark called Tom a name. Neither of them knew what it actually meant, but they knew it was a popular derogatory term of the times. Mark also told Tom he drove him crazy.

"After practice, I took Mark aside and told him Tom has tried very hard to make big plays and to protect him. He wants to make a contribution and gain your respect. Without him, you would not be having the season you're having. He's protecting your back. I asked Mark what it is about Tom that irritates him.

"Mark indicated Tom said weird things. He was always hanging around, talking, and he interrupted Mark all the time.

"I told Mark he was a leader of this team of the best type. I told him not to make people into something they can't be for your own personal gain or comfort. Enjoy other people for who they are and who they want to be. Remember, leadership is bestowed, not claimed, and is given in recognition of actions taken that benefit those being led. A leader must adjust his leadership style to those he's leading.

"For instance, some need a lot of attention, others need little. Tom needs a lot, so try to give him what he needs. I told Mark, 'Tom desperately wants to be part of the group, and you are his ticket in. Just give him your endorsement and see what happens to his performance. You could help him build his relationship bridge to the team.'

"Mark was concerned if he complimented Tom, he'd want to hang with him and he said he couldn't take that.

"The team had a tough game on Sunday. Mark completed a pass late in the fourth quarter for the win. As the players huddled before the extra point, Mark reluctantly pointed across the huddle and complimented Tom on his block.

"That's all it took. The offsides went away. Several games later, Mark took a late hit. As he got up to defend himself, Tom stepped in, grabbed the player, and told him never to do that again. This was his quarterback and he was his bodyguard. And if you mess with him, I'll kick your—"

The four captains laughed.

"That may sound a little strange," said Coach Brown. "But that was Tom's way of developing self-esteem from a job he took very seriously. It was his way of expressing himself. He believed if he protected Mark, the team would win games, and he would've done his job."

"Each of you has a similar opportunity on this team," continued Coach Brown. "There are plenty of Toms here, especially among the seventh graders. Brian, you've adopted Stewart. It's been very helpful. But Stewart's stuck on the contact issue. Kyle, it would be helpful if you'd help get him through it. You know what to do because you dealt with it last year."

Kyle said, "Yeah, you're right, Coach. I think I know what to do with Stewart, but I have two questions. Did Tom hang with Mark? ... and, was I as bad as Stewart about taking a hit?"

"No! The recognition he got for doing his job was enough. Tom made the all-star team and had an excellent high school career. Don't worry. I don't think Stewart will want to hang with you at school. He's got other interests and friends. Football is not his primary sport. ... And Kyle, you learned how to take a hit early in the season, when you were leveled in front of our bench. Do you remember? I think it was the St. Ann game."

"Yeah, I remember. It hurt, but I didn't want to show it, I guess."

Brian asked, "What happened to Mark? Did he understand leadership later, like with his high school team?"

"Yes, he did," said Coach Brown. "He was selected captain of his high school football team. I ran into him the other day and he told me he's studying leadership in college. He's going to send me a paper he wrote on leadership. I can't wait to read it."

Coach Brown paused, then said, "To help you understand leadership, I want each of you to select a leader and observe him or her. I want you to write down some of the things this person does to lead. It could be a teacher, a parent, a coach, or a friend. You don't have to show this to me. As you observe, I'd like you to emulate this person."

Kyle interrupted, "Coach, what does emulate mean?"

Brian raised his eyebrows, sighed, then answered, "Do as that person does. You just do what I do and you'll do well, Kyle."

Kyle shoved Brian playfully and said, "Yeah ... sure."

With that, the meeting was over and the boys geared up for practice. Coach Jerman started to walk to the practice area.

When Coach Jerman was out of earshot, Coach Brown called the boys back together and said, "I'll give you a hint. We don't have to look far for the leader I try to emulate. Coach Jerman has always been my role model for leadership. As you might guess, Coach Jerman is a coaching style of leader. He creates a supportive environment in which all of us can work to our full potential. This is the same way we coach you. We build a relationship with each of you based on mutual respect. Then, we teach you how to play. We don't criticize you when you make a mistake. We just teach you again. We don't want you to fear failure, because fear will limit your performance and growth. Why would a person want to follow Coach Jerman? What are the characteristics that make him a leader? I have written them down for you. I want each of you to determine which of these things you can do to improve your leadership skills. You'll not be able to do them all, so just act from your strengths. First, he always has a good plan. He always knows what's good for our team. He's honest with us. He says the right things to our players in any situation. Sometimes he's supportive; sometimes he's firm when you guys are messing around. But he never gets angry. Coach Jerman works harder than the players. He never misses a practice even though he travels over an hour to get here. He gives us all he's got. He has a lot of enthusiasm and knows just what to say to us when things are good or bad. He pulls us together as a team. He never says anything bad about our coaches or players even when they may be driving him nuts. He gives us a lot of encouragement and positive feedback. He never has a negative word or gets angry. He thanks us for doing something well. Because he does all these things, you always know he's the coach. You know he's in charge.

"So, the bottom line is, just step up and make contributions for the good of your teammates and you'll be their leader. Take charge of what you do. Some say knowledge is power, but that's not entirely true. Character is power. Character is the great differentiator in leadership."

The captains joined the team for the final week of practice, before their first league game with St. James. At the end of conditioning, the captains called the team together to remind them of last year's championship game and its outcome.

The coaches smiled as the captains led for the first time.

PLAY NUMBER NINE

We have found children to be more observant than you might think. They would like to say to us sometimes, "What you do speaks so loudly that I can't hear what you're saying." We believe we must be open and honest with players by our actions. Once we reach the field, coaches must be consistent in what they do and say because players are always watching. Remember, personal relationships based on what you do are very important to children. Develop those action-oriented relationships and you will be teaching children constantly by what you do.

10
Team Goal Setting

The primary purpose for volunteering is to contribute your time to a worthy cause. If people didn't volunteer their time, our country would be severely limited in its ability to provide the standard of living to which we've become accustomed.

EACH YEAR BEFORE THE FIRST PRACTICE GAME, THE coaches and players meet to establish their goals and objectives for the season. During this meeting, the coaches and players are on equal footing because they are all members of the team and must fulfill their commitments if the team is to be successful.

Coach Brown opened the meeting. "Tonight we're going to establish a realistic set of goals for our season. Then, we're going to develop a plan for achieving them. In order to create an effective plan, we must first define our assets and liabilities. Next, we must define the barriers to be overcome. Once we develop our plan to overcome these barriers to success, we must make an unqualified commitment to work on our plan."

Coach Brown saw limited interest, but continued anyway. "It's most important to define the right plan, because if the plan's wrong, no level of performance will achieve our goals. Sometimes goals and plans have to be adjusted for changing conditions. So we'll evaluate our goals and plans throughout the season. For instance, if we lose our first four games, making the playoffs would be unrealistic."

Brian interrupted. "Coach, has St. Raphael ever lost its first four games?"

"Yes, we have. It was one of our favorite teams. We'll tell you about it sometime."

Coach Brown continued. "Once we set our goals, develop our plan, and commit to it, we'll concentrate on working on the plan, because that's the only actionable item. For example, working hard in practice should be part of our plan. Getting excited about the goal is of little value unless it motivates us to work the committed plan. We will celebrate interim successes because that's the fuel for our fire for working the plan. This group should do well in the area of celebration." As expected, there was limited laughter at Coach Brown's lame attempt at humor.

After this brief introduction, the coaches showed a highlight video of the previous year. This helped the players visualize what their team should look like on Sunday afternoon. Then, the players were asked to visualize what their video would look like at the end of the season. The players were then asked to define realistic team goals. They were cautioned about setting unrealistic goals as they would be sources of dissatisfaction and discouragement.

The players had trouble getting started, but after a few suggestions from the coaches they did an excellent job. The team decided since there were nine starters returning from a team that was 9–2 the previous year, they would set a goal of winning the Chicago Catholic League championship. They also set two interim goals of winning their division, which would qualify them for the playoffs, and winning with class. The players defined winning with class as:

- No trash talking under any conditions
- No late hits

- No referee complaints
- Complimenting teammates and opponents on good plays.

One player suggested setting a goal for shutouts. After some discussion, the team decided shutting out an opponent, after the game was won, was the same as running up the score. Therefore, it would be winning, but without class.

The players set two final goals. First, they'd give 110% as a team and individuals. They also wanted to be judged as good as the 2003 team that won the Catholic League championship. They asked the coaches to judge them at the end of the season.

After the goals were set, the players were asked to define where they were, and where they had to be, in order to win the Chicago Catholic League championship. The players made the following assessment.

1. We're not as strong or as tough as the city kids. We have to develop the stamina to create margins and play the fourth quarter better than our opponents. Last year we lost two games in the fourth quarter. 2. We have to improve our passing game so teams can't put eight players in the box. 3. We have to help the seventh graders become eighth graders fast because there are only thirteen eighth graders returning. 4. We need to develop some defensive "tricks." We cannot overpower the city kids. 5. We have to improve more than St. Genevieve does. We heard they practice twice a day before school starts. They beat us last year and almost beat us as sixth graders.

Next, Coach Brown asked the players, "What's our plan for moving from where we are to where we need to be to achieve our goals?"

After much discussion, the players defined the following plan. Each player set, in conjunction with the coaches, personal conditioning goals for speed, endurance, and strength. Each player would be tested against these goals every three weeks. When the players exceeded their goals, they contributed their excess to a conditioning bank. These deposits could be loaned to any player not reaching his goal. All players must reach their goal (with loans) to play in the divisional championship game. Each player set skill goals depending on their position. Each eighth grader would be assigned a seventh-grade buddy to mentor. The eighth graders would help the seventh graders get acclimated and contribute to their skill and conditioning progress. The coaches would contribute M&Ms when a seventh grader and his mentor reached all of their individual goals without using the banking system. The team decided two-a-days were not necessary if every player agreed to focus for two hours at practice. There was to be no fooling around. After each practice, if the team decided they met that goal, they would yell, "Redwings." If they had a bad practice, they would decide how to make it up. The players also decided they would get their homework done before practice and do well in school so nobody would get grounded and miss a practice. The coaches agreed to develop and implement some stunts for the defense and a passing offense with a caution from Coach Cook. And finally, the players asked, if they won the championship, would Coach Brown write a rap song about the season and perform it at the banquet like he did for the 2003 team? Coach Brown agreed, under considerable pressure from coaches and players.

At the end of this session, which lasted about two hours, the coaches helped the players understand the importance of commitment to the achievement of their goals. The players were encouraged to talk to the coaches, their buddies, or other players if they were having trouble fulfilling their commitments. The team agreed, if somebody asked a teammate (including coaches) for help, it would become that person's number-one priority to give it.

Coach Brown asked the players if they would make a commitment to the team goals and the plan for their achievement. They all said, "yes," even though they were not sure about the full meaning of their commitment.

In closing the session, Coach Brown announced that the team would do a community service project on Labor Day weekend. They would be responsible for cleaning up during the Last Fling Charity Concert. There was some moaning and groaning as the players recalled their experience last year.

Coach Brown raised his hand for quiet and said, "The primary purpose for volunteering is to contribute your time to a worthy cause. If people didn't volunteer their time, our country would be severely limited in its ability to provide the standard of living to which we've become accustomed.

"For instance, if people didn't volunteer their time at professional golf tournaments, the PGA would not be able to donate as much money to the charities benefiting from each tournament. The other day, I figured out that it takes almost 100,000 hours of volunteer time to run St. Raphael Football. If we had to pay these volunteers $20 per hour, it would cost $2,000,000 to run this program. Since we have 2,500 children, it would cost each family $800 per player. That is a small indication of the impact of volunteerism in the United States."

"There is a second reason we're doing this," added Coach Jerman. "We want each of you to understand the value of volunteering and be inclined to volunteer throughout your lives. There are a lot of people who just take what they can without giving. We want you to always give more than you receive. This will be hard to do because, I believe, the more you give the more you receive."

"But Coach, that's the day before our first game with St. Mark," said Kyle. "I was kind of tired last year when we finished. Are we doing four hours again?"

"Four hours will be required. If anybody wants to do more, it's up to them. The game is a practice game, and Coach Cook has you ready for both. If we're unprepared to do both, I'll ask him to increase your training a little. I see him smiling over there in the corner."

Kyle looked at a smiling Coach Cook and said, "All's good, Coach. Put me down for eight."

As the room cleared, Kyle approached Coach Brown and asked, "Can I mentor Stewart even though he's an eighth grader?"

"Yes, you sure can, Kyle."

"Coach, I'll do my best at this leadership stuff. I don't understand a lot of the stuff you're talking about like Brian does. But I think if I help Stewart learn to take a hit, we'll have a better team."

Coach Brown nodded his head in agreement and Kyle started to jog to his car. Part-way there, he was stopped by Brian. They had a short conversation that ended with Brian banging Kyle on the shoulder pads as an expression of approval.

As Coach Brown turned and walked to his car he said, "Yes!" He knew this was a big step forward in the development of the required team chemistry.

PLAY NUMBER TEN

We had a player several years ago named Devin. He always had an excuse for non-performance. We had to convince him that excuses shielded him from the truth. If he was the reason for non-performance, then he was in control of the solution. If he thought, incorrectly, that the problem belonged to somebody else, he was probably wrong, was working on the wrong problem, and was not in control of the solution. He experienced a serious season-ending injury, but came to practice every night. He learned to accept the responsibility for his actions by observation of others. He had an excellent eighth-grade year.

11
St. Mark Practice Game

This is an exhibition game. But let's play it like a league game. Let's get used to playing St. Raphael Football today. Remember, we do our best, we never give up, we support each other, and we have no fear. Let's put our hands in.

ON SATURDAY, THE TEAM ARRIVED EARLY AND excited for their preseason game with St. Mark of Aurora. St. Raphael had beaten the Mustangs five years in a row, but this year their athletic director said they had their best team ever.

As St. Raphael began their warm-up exercises, the St. Mark team arrived by bus. This was unusual, since most teams carpooled to games. As the Mustangs filed off their bus, the St. Raphael players and coaches were impressed with their size and numbers. St. Mark dressed 47 players for the game. The coaches counted 15 players with striped helmets, which meant they weighed over 140 pounds. By comparison, St. Raphael had six players over 140 pounds.

As warm-ups progressed, the Mustang coach crossed the field to shake hands and issue a challenge. "I understand you've beaten us five years in a row. Well, I'm the new coach and we have a new attitude. This is the best team we've ever had, and they can't wait to avenge five years of frustration. I've told them this will be their biggest challenge of the season and they're ready."

Coach Brown was a bit surprised and could only respond, "Hope we have a good game."

With warm-ups completed, the team assembled for their team prayer and a final message from Coach Brown. His message was short and to the point. "You've practiced hard. Every day you've gotten better as players and a team. Coach Cook has conditioned you to play two games if you had to. This is an exhibition game. But let's play it like a league game. Let's get used to playing St. Raphael Football today. Remember, we do our best, we never give up, we support each other, and we have no fear. Let's put our hands in."

As the team started to put their hands in for a final "Redwings" before the prayer, Coach Grosso and several other coaches moved to the center of the team huddle.

Coach Grosso addressed the team. "Each practice and each game for the eight years I've heard Coach Brown talk about our code of conduct. Do your best, never give up, support each other, and have no fear. We want you to remind each other of that code when you look at each other on the field and in practice."

With that statement, an inquisitive look came over the faces of the players, including Coaches Brown and Jerman. The Redwings were a throw-back team in that they were all about football and its value as a vehicle for development. They didn't get individual award stickers for their helmets, because football was considered a team game. For the same reason, they didn't award team balls or publish team statistics until after the season. They didn't pick an MVP and reluctantly picked players for the All Star game because it was a league requirement.

Their uniforms had been the same for years. They wore scarlet jerseys with white numerals and TV numbers, white pants with two red stripes, and a white helmet with a red stripe and Seahawk emblems on each side. The coaches wanted the players to focus on football and its potential for growth, not superficial trappings.

Coach Grosso and the other coaches reached in the bags they carried and displayed stickers for each helmet. Coach Grosso said, "There are four stickers for each of you. You've all earned them by the way you've practiced over the past few weeks. Many of you have already achieved some of your performance goals and made performance bank deposits. The stickers say: Do Your Best, Never Give Up, Support Your Teammates, and Have No Fear."

The players were excited, and pushed and shoved as they got in line for their stickers. Once properly adorned, the players grew quiet for the team prayer, and one more "Redwings" cheer. They were ready to play some football.

Coach Brown said, "That was a good idea. I wish I could think of things like that."

Coach Martynowicz laughed and said, "It was such a good idea, we decided to act first, then beg forgiveness."

The season started badly for the Redwings, as St. Mark took the opening kickoff and marched 60 yards in eight running plays for a touchdown. The Redwings could not move the ball and punted to the Mustangs. St. Mark, utilized their superior size and strength again as they moved the ball relentlessly down the field for a second touchdown in 10 plays. They missed the extra point, to make the score 13–0 at the end of the first quarter.

The Redwings battled, but couldn't sustain a drive. They took a physical beating, but lived up to their helmet insignias.

The teams played scoreless football the rest of the half as St. Mark incurred several drive-stopping penalties. The 90-degree heat and humidity had started to take its toll on the players. Three Redwing players sustained minor injuries which would keep them on the bench during the second half. One of those players was Ryan, the quarterback who had replaced Jeff after the first week of practice. Coach Brown looked briefly at Jeff, who had his head bowed to avoid eye contact. Ready or not, Joe and Harrison would have to split quarterback duties in the second half.

At halftime, Coach Brown addressed a team of tired, bruised Redwings. "When a game is not going well, we don't panic. Everybody relax, take a deep breath, and realize it's a long game. Let's just come back with what we do best and don't get down on one another. Encourage one another. This is when we have to do what the coaches stuck on your helmets before the game. Let's stay upbeat … one play at a time and see what happens."

While the players relaxed, the coaches decided to employ a nothing-to-lose blitzing defense with everybody in the gaps and a short passing offense to be run by Harrison and Joe. Because of their inexperience, Coach Brown planned to send the plays in with alternating quarterbacks.

As the players returned to the field, Kyle approached Coach Jerman and asked, "How can you coaches be so calm? We are getting our butts kicked out there. They've got overweight kids playing linebacker. That one kid must be 180. He's killing us."

"Kyle, when leaders panic, it's all over," replied Coach Jerman. "That's why you have to stay calm and execute what you know best. We want you to be focused but at ease so that you'll play with a 'just let it happen' attitude. If you panic, the other players may give up. Then, we're finished. Do you understand?"

"Yeah, Coach, but it's hard to stay calm. I just want to go off on a couple of their trash talkers."

"Kyle, if you punch one of their players, you're taking the easy way out. If you think you're going to do that, we'll just take you out of the game and save ourselves a 15-yard penalty. Do you understand?"

Coach Jerman paused, waiting for an answer, then said, "Kyle, it's even okay to compliment an opponent during a game for a good play. Doing so reduces the feeling of failure by transferring the responsibility where it belongs ... the exceptional play of your opponent."

Kyle paused, as his sweat-drenched facial expression turned from frustration to focus. Coach Jerman knew he understood without extracting an obligatory yes.

The Redwings took the second-half kickoff and marched 70 yards in 12 plays for a touchdown; six of them completed passes. The extra point was good on a pass from Harrison to Garrett, the left end. The St. Raphael blitzing defense confused and frustrated St. Mark. They were able to gain yardage on most plays, but lost enough yardage on other plays to prevent them from sustaining drives as they had in the first half.

Late in the fourth quarter, St. Mark moved the ball to the St. Raphael 25-yard line on their way to a clinching touchdown. But on fourth and three, the Mustang running back was met head-on by Kyle and Todd, a yard short of a first down. There were three minutes left in the ball game.

A Redwing touchdown was improbable on this hot muggy afternoon, especially when the first two Redwing passes fell incomplete. On the next play Joe was sacked for a 10-yard loss to the 15-yard line. The parents started packing their chairs for the trip home.

After a time-out, Harrison replaced Joe and completed a 21-yard pass to Mathew, the right end, for a first down. On the next play, Joe completed a pass to Sean, and Harrison found Riley for short gains. Then, Joe hit Mathew for his fifth catch of the afternoon at the 50-yard line. Mathew got out of bounds, stopping the clock with one minute left in the game.

Coach Brown was calling his next play when he heard the vociferous St. Mark coach threaten his players with excessive physical conditioning if they allowed number 49 (Mathew) off the line of scrimmage for the rest of the game. His exact words were, "next week, you'll run until you drop."

Coach Brown had an idea! He called a time-out and called a play that had run only a few times in practice. Mathew was to line up at left end instead of his usual position at right end, with Garrett at right end. He sent Stewart, who'd played sparingly, in at a flanker to the left side of the field.

The Mustang coach noticed Mathew at left end and yelled to his players, "Remember, don't let 49 off the line of scrimmage. He's gonna get the ball."

Joe took the snap from center, faked a handoff to Kyle running left, then rolled right.

Mathew fought his way off the line of scrimmage and ran a crossing pattern to the right side of the field. No fewer than three Mustangs followed him. They were certain the pass would be thrown his way. Garrett ran a sideline pattern to the right, followed by two St. Mark players.

That left Stewart all alone with one defender, who was distracted by all the action on the right side of the field. Joe stopped, and threw the ball across the field to Stewart, who bobbled it, then caught it, and ran down the left sideline with the St. Mark coach running alongside him. For just a second, Coach Brown thought the frustrated coach was going to tackle Stewart.

Only one defender stood in the way. Stewart slowed as the defender was knocked off his feet by Kyle, who had moved left after the fake handoff to form a one-man screen. Stewart scored to make the score 13–12.

Matt went crazy on the sideline doing a dance of unknown origin. The others tried to imitate him without success. Matt declared, "It's my dance. I'll do it after every important touchdown for the rest of the season."

An extra point running or passing would tie the game. A kicked extra point was worth two points and would win the game. The Redwings decided to go for two and the win. They had come too far to settle for a tie, especially in a practice game.

Santos, a seventh grader who'd never played in a football game, would be called on to win the game. He had spent several weeks this summer at a national "invitation only" soccer camp. He had kicked 30-yard field goals in practice, but could he do it in a game?

During a time-out taken by St. Mark, the Redwing special teams coach, Jim Kanis, could be seen going over what seemed to be an elaborate set of instructions. He was pointing and waving as though he was designing a fake kick.

Coach Cook was worried, as he muttered to nobody in particular, "What's he doing? All he has to do is kick it THERE," as he pointed to the uprights. He could see Coach Kanis's actions didn't go unnoticed by the Mustang coach.

The Redwings took the field. The line positioned themselves foot to foot to block for the extra point. Greg, the center, looked to see that Harrison was in position seven yards from the line of scrimmage. He then pointed to the linebacker, who was planning to blitz up the middle.

He bent down slowly. Harrison moved his hands, and the ball came back perfectly on line. The ball was fumbled briefly, then placed down. The kick was high into a slight wind. It seemed like the ball took forever to reach the goalposts. Then, it dropped through with little room to spare. The Redwings had won 14–13.

Mysteriously, the huge Mustang line did not rush. They played for a fake that never materialized. Coach Kanis's antics must have convinced the St. Mark coach that St. Raphael was going for a tie.

After a brief celebration and handshakes, the tired Redwing team gathered around the coaches for a postgame review. Coach Brown addressed the team, "Before the game their coach told me this was of the best teams St. Mark had ever had. They expected an undefeated season, and I think he was right from here on. You all earned your decals today. Did any of you notice them during the game?"

The team responded, "Yeah!"

Kyle added, "I thought it was kind of hokey when we got them before the game. I couldn't believe how often I looked at them during the game. I even noticed them when my man Stewart went by me on his way to a touchdown. Damn, that kid's fast ... er, sorry, Coach."

"Kyle, did you know your man Stewart almost dropped the ball? Were you a little nervous, Stewart?" Brian said with a sly smile.

"Guys, I don't even remember catching the ball. My heart was pounding before the play started. I'm just glad it's over and there was nobody there to tackle me."

Brian asked, "Do you get that nervous before you dance?"

"No way! ... er ... a little ... sometimes," Stewart responded. And all the players laughed. But this laughter differed greatly from the laughter on the first day of practice. The team was coming together.

Coach Brown announced practice plans for the next week, and a parents' meeting Tuesday night during practice. He asked that at least one parent from each family attend. He then asked if the other coaches wanted to address the team.

They all said no except Coach Cook, who said, "You guys played hard today under very tough conditions. You were physically and mentally strong. I hope you understand now why we spend so much time on conditioning. Your opponent today was sucking wind physically and mentally by the end of the game, while you were ready to play another game, even after your strenuous garbage retrieval effort yesterday ... right?"

"Yeah, Coach ... Right ... maybe half a game," said Matt. "By the way, Coach, how do you suck wind mentally?"

"Hey," responded Coach Cook with a rare smile as everybody laughed. "That will cost you."

After the players left, Mary Ann, the trainer, reported Ryan had sprained his wrist on his throwing hand, and Trevor and Sean had a sprained ankle and bruised back, respectively. "We'll have to see how they feel on Tuesday. Trevor's going to get an X-ray."

As the coaches were leaving, Todd caught up with Coach Brown and said, "Coach, did you notice George was at our game? He was sitting on his bike up on the hill during the first half when we were getting killed. Want me to talk to him? We could sure use him."

"Todd, let him know he's welcome, but it has to be his decision to return. Also, please don't tell the other players, because they'll get their hopes up. We're doing fine without him. "

"Okay, Coach. He's welcome, but don't talk him into it. We're doing fine without him, but would be a little better with him. I got it!"

Coach Jerman looked at Coach Brown and said wearily, "I feel like I've coached a whole season already. Are we getting old?"

"Naw ... You go home and have a cup of tea with Nancy and you'll be ready to go on Monday. Right?"

"Right ... A cup of tea with Nancy would be fine if I knew we had things under control for the rest of the season."

"We do, Lou. Have faith and some tea," said Coach Brown with a sly smile.

 PLAY NUMBER ELEVEN

We get only so many shots at the basket with our players ... only so many opportunities to deal with the important things that have the largest impact on their development. For instance, if we had a choice of allowing long hair or being more influential in the areas of drug use, playing hard, never giving up, and classroom performance, which should we choose? Our son Mike wanted to have long hair and wear black clothes in high school. We told Mike his hair and clothing color were his choice as long as he got good grades, stayed drug free, and continued to do his best on the varsity tennis team.

12
Happy Returns

It was obvious he was never going to contribute to your championship run his eighth-grade year. Yet the staff invested its time with no apparent desire for an immediate return. I want you to know your investment has been leveraged many times throughout Marty's life. If he hadn't played football, he might have been forced in another direction.

THE REDWINGS WERE PREPARING FOR PRACTICE Tuesday before their first league game of the season. The coaches were going over their practice plan, which would include a run-through of a relatively simple game plan for St. John the Baptist. The coaches had just gotten a report from Mary Ann that Ryan had broken a small bone in his hand. He would be able to play defense later in the season, but his career as Redwing quarterback was over. Trevor's ankle was badly sprained, not broken, and Sean's back was badly bruised. All three boys would miss several games, but would continue to attend practice and learn until they were ready to play.

The rest of the players were gearing up, when a boy in an Augustana College letter jacket and his father approached. The boy said, "Hi, Coach Jerman. Hi, Coach Brown. Do you remember me?"

Both coaches looked at this 6'3, 230-pound man-child and then at his father, who was smiling ear to ear, and said, "Marty?"

"Yeah, Coach, it's me. I almost fooled you again. You remember the last time you saw me was at St. Francis. After the game, I told you I'd come and speak to your team someday. Well, I decided to come today, if that's okay."

"That would be great," said Coach Brown. "Let's do it right after conditioning. It's really great to see you again, Marty."

After conditioning, the players, sweating profusely, water bottles in hand, took a knee to hear the plan for the week. They looked curiously at the player standing next to Coach Brown.

Matt, the jokester, said, "I hope that kid standing next to you is George's replacement." A couple of players pushed Matt to the ground and good-naturedly told him to be quiet.

Coach Brown began, "Several years ago, a seventh-grade boy by the name of Marty came out for the team. He was overweight, out of shape, and had an asthma problem that required an inhaler. As I recall, during the initial weeks of practice, Marty could not run a complete lap. Each day, he pushed himself and by midseason he had proudly completed his first lap. I think I'll leave it to Marty to tell you the rest of his story."

"Thanks, Coach," Marty said. "I was watching your guys do conditioning. They're doing a lot more than we did. Maybe I shouldn't say that, Coach, but it'll help you guys win ball games."

Marty laughed nervously as he pulled a wrinkled piece of paper from his pocket. "I played here several years ago, right on this field. Now I'm starting guard for Augustana and we almost won the Division III national championship last year. I learned a lot here and I just wanted to talk to you guys about it."

Marty rocked back and forth nervously as he referred to his notes. "I played in every White team game when I was in the seventh grade, where I improved my running, arm strength, and blocking technique. I lost 15 pounds during the season. That made my mom happy. I got into a couple of Sunday games, but the White team was where I had fun. My goal was to return and start for the Red team my eighth-grade year."

Marty paused and took a deep breath. "Well, I returned the following year, about 5 inches taller, able to run my lap, and able to do pushups correctly. I thought I was ready to start for the Red team.

"However, as hard as I tried, I couldn't crack the starting lineup. We had a good team and won the championship that year. Three players from the team are playing Division I. So, I decided to be the only eighth grader on the White team. I became captain, we were undefeated, and I improved a lot, but never started a Red team game. Who's captain of the White team this year?"

Matt and Mike raised their hands proudly.

"Well, the rest of this story is for you guys."

Marty paused to see if he still had the team's attention and continued. "I grew that summer, lifted weights, and went through puberty. Coach will tell you about that later."

Marty laughed, looked at the coaches, and continued, "By my sophomore year, I was 6'3, weighed 220, could bench over 300 pounds, outgrew my asthma problem, and earned starting guard on the varsity, at St. Francis High School.

Marty paused again, then asked, "Coach, whatever happened to Charles, the other kid who never started for the varsity, but started his senior year at Central? I couldn't believe it when I played against him in college at North Central."

"He's doing fine and so is his mom," said Coach Brown. "They came to practice late last year to check on us. He was a lot like you. He worked hard every day. He told me he developed a 38-inch vertical."

Marty shook his head as he reached in his pocket and took out a pad of helmet stickers and said, "I planned to give these to you guys today, but I see somebody beat me to it. So, I'll just give them to Coach. But my message to you guys is the same ... you should never give up. These coaches didn't give up on me or Charles, so don't ever give up on yourselves. If I had given up, and believe me I thought about it, I would not be playing in college today."

Marty handed the stickers to Coach Brown and said to all the coaches, "Thanks for all your help and support. I hope this helps the team a little. I just wanted to give something back."

Coach Brown said, "Thanks, Marty. I'm sure your talk helped the team. Let me add something to what Marty told you." Coach Brown paused and looked at Marty proudly.

"Marty finished his high school career all-conference, all-area, and got a football scholarship to Augustana. He's started for his college team for two years and this will be his senior year. I bet he makes all-conference this year even though he's the smallest lineman in the league."

As Marty walked around and shook hands with each player, Matt asked, "Coach, can we have Marty's stickers for the White team? He's our most famous player."

Before Coach Brown could answer, Brian suggested, "I think we ought to put them on all of our helmets. We've got plenty of room."

Coach Brown handed the stickers to Marty and said, "Marty, why don't you do the honors, okay, Matt?"

Matt, in the interest of always having the last word, said, "Okay, if Mike and I can help. Marty was one of us."

After Marty's talk, his father asked to speak to the coaches while Marty talked to the team as he, Matt, and Mike placed the stickers on each helmet.

Marty Sr. said, "I've always wanted to talk to you guys about Marty and the impact St. Raphael football had on him. It would have been real easy for you guys to discourage Marty. It was obvious he was never going to contribute to your championship run his eighth-grade year. Yet the staff invested its time with no apparent desire for an immediate return. I want you to know your investment has been leveraged many times throughout Marty's life. If he hadn't played football, he might have been forced in another direction."

Marty Sr. paused for a second, then said, "Let me tell you one more thing. I think you ought to know. I ran into big Mike the other day. You remember, the big kid that started as a sixth grader and I think plays Division I. He told me he still remembers Marty, because he was his role model. He told me he couldn't understand why a kid with so little talent didn't quit. And a lot of other kids felt the same way. So, maybe you and the team got more out of Marty than just the good feelings that come with what you do."

Coach Brown pointed to Matt as he and Marty continued to paste each sticker carefully to the back of each helmet and said, "That boy is Marty the second. I'm sure he benefited greatly from Marty's talk today."

As Marty and his father left the practice area, Todd approached Coach Brown and said, "Coach, I think George might be here today. I saw him at the movies last night. I think he might ride his bike to practice. He's worried you won't let him join the team. If he comes and does extra conditioning and stuff, can he still join the team? I think the other players want him to join. I think he's getting tired of golf and swimming. We think it would be good for George and the team."

"Yes, he can join if he wants to," responded Coach Brown. "I think it would be good for everybody."

"Coach, if he comes, I don't think we should make a big deal of it. Some of us know what happened. If he comes and wants to talk, I'll tell him what you said. I'll tell the team not to go crazy if he comes. I think we should make him sweat a little. You know what I mean?"

"I do, Todd."

The team was about a half hour into practice when George appeared at the top of the hill sitting on his bike and leaning against the tree. During one of the water breaks, Todd walked to the top of the hill, and he and George had a brief discussion. After returning,

Todd motioned Coach Brown to "the office" and said, "Coach, I told him what you said. He misses the team, is a little embarrassed about quitting, and is afraid of what the team will say if he returns. I told him everybody needed a break sometimes and the team would not say anything, because they want him back. I said Brian really wants him back because he doesn't want to play against the opponent's biggest player each week. He said he wanted to watch practice for now and we should not tell his dad he was here."

* * *

The following night, as Coach Brown arrived, he saw George dressed for practice sitting alone under a tree near the parking lot. Coach Brown reached into his trunk, took out George's shoulder pads and the football practice bag, and walked toward the field. As soon as George saw Coach Brown, he got up and trotted toward his coach. When they met, Coach Brown extended his arm with his pads and said, "Welcome back, George."

George took the pads and said, "Thanks, Coach. I think I just needed some time off. Can I carry the bag?"

As the rest of the team arrived, they talked with George. There was some good-natured kidding, which made George feel at home. Just before stretching began, Todd approached the coaching staff and said, "George has insisted on extra sprints after practice each night this week as his price for rejoining the team. Brian and I will run with him since we ride together."

"Insisted?" said Coach Jerman, laughing. "I think I understand what insisted means."

Later that evening, Ben appeared and said, "I can't give you much insight into his change of heart. I did as you suggested and stayed off the topic. I know he had some discussions with his mom and some kids on the team. This morning he told me he wanted to rejoin the team. Then, his mother told me it would be a good idea if I worked a little more and watched practice a little less. That's going to kill me. But, I've learned a lot in the past two weeks. I guess you do what you gotta do for your kids."

Ben paused and then said with a sly grin, "Wait until you guys see my six-year-old. His mother's going to let him play Mighty Mite football this fall and I'm going to coach his team. Do you have any plays for six-year-olds? ... Just kidding."

PLAY NUMBER TWELVE

We don't have rules we cannot enforce. If there are too many rules, the players will lie because they don't want to upset us and be punished. We believe too many rules poison a relationship. The reason we focus on values is because we would like to have our players do the right things and show good judgment without a lot of rules and supervision.

13
Parents' Meeting

The more we use a values-based learning methodology, the more internalized and defining it becomes. As this occurs, the players become more natural and instinctive as they act from their values to learn. As the players learn, they role-model proper behavior and become influential with one another. The relationships created in this process are similarly grounded and therefore more substantial, lasting, useful, and enjoyable. Most importantly, this becomes the basis for the all-important team chemistry.

BEN AND COACH BROWN WALKED TO THE GRADE school where the parents were assembled. Margi and Terri, the team moms, had already handed out a letter which described their role and all the events planned for the year. This letter included the schedule for the Red and White teams, and an assignment of volunteers for various functions such as after-game refreshments, videotaping, down markers for home games, etc. Margi and Terri recorded all the volunteers and answered other questions before Coach Brown began his remarks.

"The bottom line is, we want the parents to have as much fun as their children and I guarantee you your children are going to have a great time. The best way to do this is to assume your child will do his best. So, sit back and enjoy whatever happens. One of their primary reasons for playing is to please you and gain your respect.

"Many years ago, my children played tennis at Naperville Central. I attended almost every match and was a volunteer coach. I hung on every point and was exhausted by the end of a three-set match. I took satisfaction from the outcome and a good effort, but took little satisfaction from the match in progress.

"My wife, Marcia, who is a tennis professional, was able to sit back and enjoy the whole match regardless of the outcome. She knew, as did I, our children were doing their best and appreciated their effort. But, unlike me, she was able to enjoy the entire match, win or lose. This is what I hope you'll do, so you'll all enjoy this wonderful experience.

"Your children have been taught to do their best and not feel bad if they lose as long as they did their best. Our coaches will be using football as a vehicle for the total development of your child. There will also be a special emphasis on values.

"The coaching staff believes children who are grounded in a good value system will have the stability and consistency of decision making required to enhance their learning. The sooner our players are able to develop emotional skills, such as self-discipline, goal setting, social skills and acting from sound values, the sooner they'll be able to learn.

"Making an investment in their value system is like putting money in a savings account early; it maximizes the impact of compound interest. That's why opposing coaches say, You'd better play St. Raphael early if you want to beat them. We make our investment in a child's emotional skills and football fundamentals first, then work off that platform as the season progresses.

"The more we use a values-based learning methodology, the more internalized and defining it becomes. As this occurs, the players become more natural and instinctive as they act from their values to learn. As the players learn, they role-model proper behavior and become influential with one another. The relationships created in this process are similarly grounded and therefore more substantial, lasting, useful, and enjoyable. Most importantly, this becomes the basis for the all-important team chemistry.

"Too many people today let their actions define their values because it's convenient. At St. Raphael, we want our values to define our actions.

"In addition, as they grow to enjoy this environment and who they are, they open themselves up to additional development. This state of mind helps us teach, because our students are open and confident about the learning process. They focus on what's really important, which helps them deal with learning and change.

"If you have any questions or concerns about anything, please talk to us at any time. Feel free to attend practices. Your children will view this as being supportive. Please do not complain about your impressions of our coaching to your children. If you do, they'll lose confidence in us and it'll have a negative impact on their development. If you've got concerns, please talk to the coaching staff. We'll always be available. Quite often concerns are based on incomplete information. We'll be honest with you. We'll not, however, make decisions in the interest of the vocal minority at the expense of the silent majority. We need to have parents team with us to optimize the development of their children. We'll be effective as a team if we speak honestly with each other.

"You'll be close to the field during some away games. In forty years, we've never won or lost a game because of the referees. Never! So, please don't say anything negative to a referee. It sets a very bad example for our players and affects their performance level.

"Get to know the parents on the team. Youth sports can be a vehicle for enhancing your social life. It can be a source of new relationships and some great parties. And ... don't forget your coaching staff likes parties too.

"Over the years, the coaching staff has learned a lot about communicating with children. I have included some of our observations in the handout in front of you. Maybe some of this will be helpful to you.

"So in conclusion, please enjoy the season. Your coaches will. Let's get some refreshments and then I'll take questions."

PLAY NUMBER THIRTEEN

We encourage our players to take responsibility for their own development as soon as possible. Players who are focused on their development leave fewer voids for others to fill. We look at your children's problems as opportunities for growth. We must allow children to make some of their own decisions in order to stimulate growth. There are also times when we must make decisions for them in their best interest. We had a boy several years ago who quit the team when he didn't make running-back weight. The parents both worked, and initially let the boy make his own decision to quit. In a call to the parents, one of our coaches blurted out, "There are times when you have to step up and make the right decision for your children." The boy reluctantly returned, had a great season playing line, and made the all-star team.

14
Perry Joins the Team

We expect you to do your best in practice at all times. In the beginning it'll be hard to keep up because you haven't played before and we've just finished the third week of practice. The coaches will spend extra time with you. When they do, it means they care about you, and are interested in helping you become a better football player. Please don't think we're picking on you. We have assigned Blake and Bobby to help you catch up. How does that sound?

PRACTICE WENT WELL ON WEDNESDAY. THE TEAM was energized by George's return. He was quiet, but determined to make up for lost time. He was focused in drills and did his extra conditioning without urging from the coaching staff. Brian was pleased with his move to left tackle, where he would share the position with Garrett, a seventh grader with a lot of potential.

The seventh-grade quarterback tandem was working well. The two quarterbacks complemented each other. Harrison was a better passer, while Joe ran the option well.

Jeff's therapy was going well. He practiced with the defense, and played well in his first White team games. He participated in passing drills, but plans to take a snap from center in a game would be delayed until his doctor thought he was ready.

Kyle was making progress with Stewart. His mentoring contributed to Stewart's confidence and improvement. Kyle learned the importance of patience in effective leadership, as Stewart continued to disappoint him with his fumbles and a reluctance to run hard inside the tackles.

Matt returned to full practice and continued to develop due to a super-human effort. He continued to sustain minor injuries as he went all out on every play and every drill.

Wednesday night, as Coach Brown walked to his car, Matt caught up with him and asked, "Coach, what should I do in the off-season to improve so I can be a starter next year? I know this will be tough because we've got a lot of seventh graders coming back. I even recruited a kid who's better than me to be on the team next year."

It had been a long practice and Coach Brown responded half-heartedly, "Matt, you've made a lot of progress this season. I've seen it in your White team play. I guess I'd do some running to strengthen your legs so you can increase your speed and quickness."

Matt stared at Coach Brown and said, "Is that it?" Then, before Coach Brown could answer, Matt continued. "Coach, I need to know everything. You won't be doing me any favors if you don't tell me everything."

Matt stood fast, his feet firmly planted, blocking Coach Brown's path to his car. His eyes were the eyes of a person who had just asked a question, but wasn't sure he wanted to hear the answer.

After thinking a few seconds, Coach Brown responded, "Okay, Matt. You should try to improve your upper-body strength by doing pushups and situps. You should also lose some weight around your waist. I would get your brother to help you with technique, and go to a football camp during the summer."

Matt was satisfied and smiled. "Now that wasn't so hard, was it, Coach? I thought that was about what you'd say. So, I already planned to run a mile every day including sprints until next season. I will also do the situps and pushups. Maybe you could talk to my parents about the rest of the stuff."

On the way home, Coach Brown thought about the parents' meeting at which he'd stressed the importance of listening and giving open and honest feedback. In his rush to get home, he had almost violated his own principles. All Matt wanted was to tell his coach he wanted to pay the price for a chance to start and help the Red team next year. He wanted to be heard and he wanted the benefit of his coach's opinion.

He knew the feedback he would receive would be in his best interest. Matt expected Coach Brown to give him honest feedback because he cared about him. Coach Brown decided he would look for an opportunity to give Matt more thorough feedback in the near future.

* * *

Coach Brown arrived early for practice on Thursday. It would be a light practice designed to review the game plan for Sunday's opener with St. John the Baptist.

In addition, all the players were weighed to make sure they met the league weight guidelines. Danny was the starting cornerback. He was fearless, and a hard hitter at 80 pounds. He was nicknamed the ankle-biter because he tackled so low. His teammates had convinced him he'd have to weigh 85 pounds in order to play. He had discussed this with Kyle, who suggested he put rocks in his pocket for the weigh-in.

Coach Brown came early for another reason. Several nights ago, he got a call from Susan, a teacher at one of the junior high schools. Her son Bobby played on the team. He had played in the St. Raphael

Program since the second grade, and was an excellent player and person. His parents were outstanding supporters of the program.

After some small talk, Susan nervously got to the point of her call more quickly than usual. "Coach, I have a huge favor to ask of you. If you say no, I'll understand."

Susan paused to collect her thoughts, and continued. "Coach, there's a boy in my class named Perry, who's a foster child waiting to be placed in a permanent home. He's a good kid, but is very disruptive in class, has few friends, and gets in fights at school. Recently, he got himself in more serious trouble. His temporary foster parents are good people and are trying to help Perry all they can. They had a son in the football program about ten years ago. They said you drove him to practice when his mother was unavailable. He was also disruptive. They said football was good for him, and he turned out to be a fine young man."

Coach Brown replied eagerly, "Yes, I remember Blake. Football turned out to be good for him. He became a very good player in high school, and went on to play a little in college. He came by the other day to check up on the team and give us a little advice."

Susan interrupted, fearing Coach Brown would tell her more than she needed to know about Blake. "Did he say anything about Perry?"

"No. But we did reminisce a little about what a problem he was, and how glad he was we didn't let him quit."

"Coach, I think he was going to ask you about Perry, but lost his nerve. He was the one who suggested his parents give you a call. They called me instead, so here we are."

After a pause, Susan continued, "Remember, Coach, you can say no and I would understand."

Before Coach Brown could respond, Susan continued, "Coach, this boy started a fire in my classroom last weekend because he was angry about a disciplinary action I was forced to take. I don't think he meant to burn the school to the ground, but he's in a lot of trouble. Did you read about it in the newspaper?"

Coach Brown said, "Yes, I did, and ..."

Susan interrupted again, "Coach, here's the request and remember I wouldn't blame you if you said no. If we can keep him out of juvenile, would you take him on the team? He's Catholic, and I think we can get him into religious education. I know that's a requirement. The court social worker thinks this would be good for him. So do I, and so do his foster parents."

Coach Brown asked, "What does Perry think?"

"Coach, Perry doesn't know about it. We wanted to check with you first. And Coach, if it makes a difference, Blake says he'll help coach, kind of help with control and communication, on a kid-to-kid level. In addition, I think Blake wants to give something back. And Coach, if this proves too disruptive to the team, we can end it at any time. I'm sure you want some time to think about it. Please call me back when you decide. And remember ..."

Coach Brown interrupted Susan, "Yes, we'll do it. I think it'll be good for our team and good for Blake. I think he'll feel good about giving something back. And, of course, good for Perry for many reasons. Maybe we could get Bobby involved doing a little mentoring. How should we introduce the idea to Perry? Is there a way I can help with that?"

Susan paused, collecting herself emotionally, and then managed to say, "Thank you so much. I don't know how to thank you. I'll talk with the court, the foster parents, and our school counselor and get back to you."

* * *

Susan called back in a couple of days and said, "Everybody involved is on board. The court allowed Perry to stay with his current foster parents until his case is resolved. They want regular reports, which you may have to sign."

Coach Brown asked, "How does Perry feel about being on the team?"

"We're not sure. My son thinks he's playing because it'll help him stay out of the juvenile facility. He's never played football before and has no idea how hard the players work. He did ask my son why we're letting him join the team. I think he wonders if this is a trick or something. He probably wonders what's in it for us. What's next, Coach?"

Coach Brown responded, "Why don't you have his foster parents bring Perry to the field tonight about six, with Blake? I'll speak to the team about him. Let's have him observe a practice and meet his teammates. Then we'll get him his equipment over the weekend and he can start on Monday. Our equipment supplier, Steve, wants to supply the helmet and all the other stuff he needs, and of course he'll be on scholarship."

"Thank you so much," Susan said with a smile. "I thought I'd pick up the expense. Maybe my husband's company can sponsor a team or something. One more thing, Coach, I think you ought to give the team the whole story on Perry. Most of the kids already know about him."

* * *

That evening, Coach Brown talked to the team about Perry. The coaching staff had discussed the situation earlier in the week. After a short discussion, Coach Brown asked the players if they had any questions or concerns. All the players were quiet until Brian said with a sly smile, "What's the big deal? We know Perry. This could be good for him and besides, he could help the team."

As they were about to start their exercises, Bobby raised his hand and said, "This is not going to be easy. He's had a lot of disappointments and has a chip on his shoulder. He doesn't trust anybody. Some of you guys know him. I think we should treat him like any other kid that joins the team. I think we should help him catch up.

As the season goes on, he could help us. I can tell you one thing, he's one tough dude."

At six, Perry, his foster parents, his probation officer, and Blake arrived at the practice field. They all seemed to have different expressions. The foster parents, Mike and Marie, were happy to see the coaching staff again. Blake had a sheepish look, knowing he'd been the instigator of what he hoped would be a good experience. Perry was expressionless, even a little defiant.

Blake introduced Perry to the coaching staff. Coach Taylor shook Perry's hand and said, "We're going to start you off playing defense. I'll be one of your coaches." The coaching staff had decided to start Perry on defense, since it relied more on natural instincts than learned skills.

A few minutes later, the team finished their warm-up exercises and trotted over to meet Perry. As planned, Bobby introduced Perry to each player. Through all of this, Perry said little, as did most of the players on the team.

As practice started again, Blake took Perry around to each drill and explained its purpose. While Blake conducted the tour, Mike and Marie and Coach Brown reviewed some ground rules intended to make this a successful experience.

Coach Brown asked Mike and Marie, "Please tell me anything you think might contribute to Perry's success in the program."

Marie started by saying, "Perry's a good boy with a lot of potential, but he's very bitter. His father and mother were divorced early, and he was taken from his mother because she was declared unfit. I think she lives in Chicago, but has had no contact with Perry for several years. He doesn't say much. He watches a lot of television, rides his skateboard, and listens to that heavy rock stuff in his room. He's been with us for about three months. He was with his previous foster parents for two years, but they had to give him up for financial reasons."

Coach Brown asked, "What does he like to watch on TV?"

Mike responded, "He likes MTV best, but he likes sports too. He and I watched some Cubs games, and he enjoyed going to the Cubs games a couple of times with Blake and me."

"What do you think are the keys to his success or failure with the team?"

Mike thought for a minute and said, "His temper. It could be an asset, but most likely it'll be a detriment to his success. If you push him a little, he gets angry and very defensive, especially at school. He just lashes out as a way of defending himself or not letting you get too close. I think he likes sports, and I think he has good coordination and balance. You ought to see him ride a skateboard. I also think he responds well to positive reinforcement. We've tried to familiarize ourselves with what he likes, and work off that to expand his horizons."

Coach Brown asked Mike, "Why do you think he agreed to play football?"

"Coach, I hate to say it, but I believe he thinks he has to play in order to stay out of the juvenile home. His background has taught him good survival skills, and I think he's operating in that mode right now. In addition, I think he's concerned that setting the fire will severely jeopardize his chances of permanent placement."

Marie added, "I think he's in the same spot as Blake was several years ago. I think you should do whatever you did with him because he turned out great. I'm so proud of Blake and the fact he wants to help. It makes me cry every time I think about him and the problems he had."

Coach Brown responded, "Marie, you and Mike should be proud. Blake has turned out great, and you had a lot to do with it. I hear he'll be attending College of DuPage this fall. Here come Blake and Perry. Let me spend a few minutes with Perry, and then you can take him to the sports shop and get him equipped. Steve and Barb are expecting him."

Coach Brown took Perry aside and walked to an area under a small tree at the far end of the practice area. The coaches refer to this area as "the office." Once there, Coach Brown asked Perry to sit down and said, "What'd you think of the tour?" Perry nodded his head in approval.

Coach Brown continued, "Perry, the coaches call all the players by their first names and we ask that the players call us Coach or Coach Jerman or Coach Brown. What do you think about football so far?"

Perry thought for a few seconds and said, "Coach, It looks like these guys are pretty good. You know I ain't never played football before."

Coach Brown responded, "That's okay. There are several players who've never played, and a few who've played a lot. We rely on the experienced players to help those who are just starting. I expect a couple of the new kids will be contributing a lot by midseason. What else do you think about your first day?"

Perry squirmed a little and said, "The guys get along with each other. They beat on each other pretty good, but nobody gets mad."

"That's one of the rules. We don't get mad at each other, because we're a team. One of the reasons we play hard in practice is to get better and make our teammates better. We need to be as good as we can be in practice so we'll play that way on Sunday. We play kids from Chicago and they're tough."

Perry responded, "Coach, did you know I'm from Chicago?"

"Yes, I did, Perry. Being from Chicago might help you play football."

Coach Brown continued, "Perry, we only have a few rules here. First, you need to be on time for practice unless you have too much homework or have to attend religious education. Do you drive?"

Perry looked at Coach Brown in disbelief and said, "Coach, I'm only thirteen."

Coach Brown said, "Perry, I was just kidding." Perry smiled for the first time as Coach Brown continued. "We expect you to do your best in practice at all times. In the beginning it'll be hard to keep up because you haven't played before and we've just finished the third week of practice. The coaches will spend extra time with you. When they do, it means they care about you, and are interested in helping you become a better football player. Please don't think we're picking on you. We have assigned Blake and Bobby to help you catch up. How does that sound?"

Perry responded with a little enthusiasm, "That sounds good. Blake said he used to be pretty good."

"That's right, Perry," Coach Brown said with a smile. "When you watch football on TV, which position looks like the most fun?"

Perry responded without hesitation, "Defense! Someday I'd like to make some big hits like on TV."

Coach Brown concluded the conversation by saying, "Perry, welcome to the team. We're glad to have you. Go with Blake to the equipment truck and he'll fit your shoulder pads. Then go with Mike and Marie and they'll help you get the rest of the equipment. I'll talk to Marie about getting you signed up for religious education and we'll see you on Sunday at our first league game. We'll take you to the weigh-in next weekend after all the paperwork's done."

Perry, much to Coach Brown's surprise, extended his hand and said, "See you Sunday, Coach."

As he walked away, Coach Brown pounded his fist into his hand and said, "I think that went well." Little did he know, this conversation would represent the pinnacle of success with Perry for a while.

PLAY NUMBER FOURTEEN

We believe if we listen to our players they can teach us a lot. Sometimes the teacher has to become the student to enhance learning. Then, with a new perspective, the teacher becomes more effective. Think about the discovery that takes place during two-way conversation as people work off one another's input. When listening to our players, we try to look beyond the obvious for the real meaning of the conversation. Due to limited vocabularies and shyness, we may have to listen very carefully to obtain the true meaning of a conversation.

15
First Game—St. John the Baptist

As Coach Grosso said at the beginning of the game, we're coaching you to be exceptional. Being exceptional only requires a little more work than being good. We hope to convince you it's worth it now, and for the rest of your lives. Believe me, if you work hard, you won't have to scramble for success. It will come to you and you'll wonder why you're so fortunate.

THE WEIGH-IN WENT WELL ON SATURDAY. THERE were several boys on diets designed to lose five pounds or less in order to make the weight required for their position. Each time a boy made weight, there was a rousing cheer of relief from the rest of the squad. The cheer was accompanied by laughter when Danny weighed in at a rocks-aided 92 pounds, and Coach Kelly asked for a reweigh. The players laughed as they told Danny there was no minimum weight requirement. Danny charged Kyle and took a playful swing at his teammate, who outweighed him by 50 pounds.

The loudest cheer, however, was reserved for Tom, a seventh grader, who tipped the scales at 184.5, one-half pound under the required weight for participation. On opening day, he had weighed in at 195 pounds.

After the first practice, Coach Cook had discussed the league weight limits with Tom's parents. He made a few healthy dietary suggestions and promised he'd take care of the exercise required at practice. Tom's parents saw this as an opportunity to help Tom and themselves lose some weight and make some basic lifestyle changes. They committed to change the family diet and exercise to the same degree suggested for Tom. They cut out sweets, soft drinks, and excessive carbohydrates, and practiced portion control. The family joined a health club, and for five weeks followed a diet and exercise program they had designed. Tom and his father bet a Cubs game versus additional family chores to increase their incentives.

After Tom made his weight, he requested the administrator to weigh his father. His father, who weighed in originally at 252, had made a 22-pound drop. Tom lost the bet, but his dad was so proud, he promised him a Cubs game anyway.

* * *

Sunday dawned a beautiful day. At game time the temperature was 85 degrees with a slight wind from the southwest. There was usually a confident crowd on hand ready to cheer another Redwing team. This year, however, the mood was slightly different because of the uncertainty caused by the first practice game against St. Mark and the myriad problems experienced by the team thus far.

John the Baptist was expected to have a strong team, since they returned several seventh-grade starters from 2007. The Redwings would have a tough game each week, because they were seeded number three for the season. This seeding resulted from their cumulative five-year record of 45–7. Schedules were determined based on seeds to affect parity.

The players were anxious. They had practiced hard for five weeks and wanted to see how they would perform in their first league game. There was no fooling around as they went through warm-ups. A few dropped passes and fumbled handoffs were testimony to their nervous frame of mind. Even the experienced coaching staff had a case of first-game jitters. Coach Brown had left his laminated play card in the car. As Coach Kelly volunteered to retrieve it, he said, "I don't know why I prepare the card each week, you never use it. Next week, I'm going to prepare a defensive card and see if you'll recognize the difference. "

Coach Brown responded, "I need it. It's like the blanket I chewed on as a child. Besides, I think the opposing coaches are intimidated by my organized appearance. You notice, I always flash it during the coin toss."

"Why bother with a defensive card, Kevin?" injected Coach Grosso. "All you need to call defensive plays is a blank sheet of paper."

"Since it's so simple, we won't need any defensive dabbling from the offensive gurus today," said Coach Cook.

There were three unwritten coaching rules at St. Raphael. The offense and defensive coaches called their own games. Each "dabble" from the defense was an invitation for a return dabble from the offense and vice-versa. Coaches Jerman and Aimonette were allowed unlimited "dabbles" because of their stature and objectivity.

Coach Brown shook hands with Coach Jerman, as had been the custom before each game for forty years, and said, "Feels the same every year, eh, Lou?"

"The excitement never grows old," responded 73-year-old Coach Jerman. "When it does, I'll know I'm getting old."

The players gathered for their prayer. The young faces usually full of joy and mischief were now taut with focus and anticipation.

For each game, Lou Rotta, a father of three past St. Raphael Redwings and a current player, composed a prayer connecting the Sunday Gospel to the message for today's game. The impact of the special prayer was unknown, as most of the players were lost in their own thoughts. But, the coaches knew the prayer was important. Last year, the prayer was omitted on opening day because of a late start time. Several players asked about it after the game as they considered it unique to the Redwings. Each Sunday, Coach Grosso led the team prayer.

> My brothers, take a moment and put yourselves in the presence of the Lord: In the Name of the Father, the Son, and the Holy Spirit. In the book of Romans there is a verse that reads "I raised you up for this very purpose, that I might display my power in you and that my name might be proclaimed in all the earth." Lord, you have given all of us talent. If we use that talent, we are displaying your power that is in us. It's a tremendous challenge and opportunity to have your power within us. It's a challenge to recognize our talent and gifts and aspire to use them. It's a challenge to do the right thing, which is to use every bit of our talent and gifts. This is something the Lord has placed totally within our control. Our gifts vary, Lord, but if we use what was given us, we'll succeed in displaying your power. The one ingredient, Lord, which gets us to maximize our talent and gifts is DESIRE. It separates one player from another, and one team from another. We can play with desire or not. It's our decision and at the end of the game each player will know if he used every bit of talent granted him by the Lord. Today, Lord, it's our desire to display your power on this field. We have prepared well. Let's see how much we have improved. Let this be our test today. It is within our control. Amen.

Coach Grosso said, "Let's have hands in. Let's remember. If we're going to do something, let's do it right. Doing it right takes very little additional effort, but it results in excellence and the margins needed for success. Remember what's on your helmets ... Support Each Other, Do Your Best, Have No Fear, and Never Give Up. The team responded, "Redwings!"

As the kickoff team took the field, Kyle called the team together and said, "Now that we have prayed, let's go kick some butt!" Coach Brown and Coach Jerman were just close enough to overhear. All they could do was shake their heads and smile.

St. John the Baptist Bobcats took the opening kickoff and scored in ten plays, running the ball inside the tackles. They concentrated their attack on the right side of the Redwing defense where Brian, Garrett, and Drew from the White team were sharing playing time. They apparently scouted St. Raphael, because they only ran at George once and were stopped cold.

The Redwings were also successful on offense as they scored on eight plays with Kyle and Billy running primarily over George and Keith on the right side. Santos kicked the extra point for an 8–7 lead. There was no more scoring during the first half, as both teams made defensive adjustments.

St. Raphael took the second-half kickoff and was driving until Billy sustained a leg injury and was replaced by Stewart. On his first carry, Stewart sprinted around right end with a big block from Keith, for a 12-yard gain. Kyle was the first to his side with con-gratulatory bangs on the helmet. Stewart raised his hand in the air as he bounced back to the huddle.

Two plays later, Coach Brown called the same play, but with a much different result. Stewart got outside, but fumbled at the 13-yard line, when he was hit hard by a cadre of Bobcat defenders. John the Baptist recovered the fumble. Kyle again was first to his side as Stewart slowly got to his feet and stared at the jubilant Bob-cats running and jumping in celebration as they left the field.

Stewart looked at Kyle, expecting the worst. But Kyle put his arm around Stewart, pointed to his chest, and said, "My fault, man. I missed my block. Let's go. That was a nice run. We'll get another chance."

Stewart looked at Kyle in disbelief and said, "Yeah ... right, man," as he trotted off the field.

Stewart approached Coach Brown and said, "Sorry, Coach. I just can't hang on to the ball."

"Don't worry about it. You made a couple of good runs. It won't be long before you do something special out there. Next time, when you get to the contact area, put both hands over the ball and protect it. Don't worry about getting extra yards. Okay?"

As Coach Brown patted him reassuringly on the shoulder pads, Stewart muttered, "Okay."

"Get some water, because as soon as we get the ball back, you're in. Billy's hurt and we need you."

The Redwings held on defense as Garrett, Brian, and Kyle, who had been moved to the right side, made several hard tackles. The Redwing offense came back on the field.

Joe, the quarterback, called, "48 with the works with Stewart at tail." Stewart's eyes rolled back in his head. He looked to the sideline, and made eye contact with Coach Brown, who nodded his head once.

Kyle looked at Coach Brown, then Stewart, and said loudly for the team to hear, "Don't worry, dude. Nobody's gonna touch you."

The team broke the huddle and came to the line of scrimmage, determined to make Kyle's forecast a reality. Joe started his cadence and Kyle went in motion right. The ball was snapped. Nick put a crushing crack-back block on the defensive end, knocking him off his feet. George and Keith pulled right with Matt, the right end, blocking down on the tackle. George sealed inside, Keith stampeded the outside linebacker, Kyle screened the corner, and Stewart went to the end zone untouched. Stewart handed the ball to the official, just before he was mobbed by his teammates. Stewart trotted off the field escorted by Brian gasping for breath.

Coach Kanis yelled to Brian, "Get back in there. You're on the point team."

"I can't, Coach. I guess I'm so excited for Stewart, I need my inhaler." The extra point was blocked and the Redwings led 14–7 at the end of the third quarter.

Bobby replaced Stewart on the next series as the Redwings pounded the ball inside for ten plays and another score. Santos kicked the extra point for a 22–7 victory.

An elated Coach Cook met the team as they came off the field at the end of the game and said, "Now do you guys understand why we condition you? That was beautiful. That's St. Raphael Football. Who needs to pass the ball ... Yeah!"

Coach Grosso, the quarterback coach, countered, "Wait until we get a little further into the season. You'll be begging for the passing offense."

Coach Cook waved his hand and said, "No way. We've got the horses and the backs ... and they're in shape," as he walked to the center of the field for the postgame talk.

Coach Brown began, "Nice game ... Great effort! You were in midseason form. Few mistakes ... and yes, Greg, they were in shape. I have just a couple more thoughts.

"As we've discussed before, success requires hard work and it's defined differently for each of you. Today's success for Kyle was improving his leadership skills; success for Stewart was scoring after he fumbled; for George, it was his return and his block of the middle linebacker on Stewart's run; Brian, Drew, and Garrett got stronger on defense and wouldn't let St. John pick on them, and so on. You all had success today because you earned it, and those of you I didn't mention can recognize your own success because you all experienced it today. And I bet it felt good.

"You experienced success because you pushed yourselves for five tough weeks. For many of you, your original definitions of success have been surpassed. Just look at how many of you have achieved your individual performance goals. We want you to play football so you'll develop the means for success; however, you must define and redefine success for yourselves.

"As Coach Grosso said at the beginning of the game, we're coaching you to be exceptional. Being exceptional only requires a little more work than being good. We hope to convince you it's worth it now, and for the rest of your lives. Believe me, if you work hard, you won't have to scramble for success. It will come to you and you'll wonder why you're so fortunate.

"Hands in ... Who's the Redwing, Kyle?"

"Stewart!"

Stewart smiled, "One, two, three, Redwings!"

PLAY NUMBER FIFTEEN

We try to approach our players openly and honestly. If there's something wrong, we go to them. This demonstrates we care about them and have set no preconditions for communication. When we make a mistake with our players, which we seldom do, ... eh ... we go to them, admit the mistake, and make sure they understand why it was a mistake. We do this quickly to avoid the development of a barrier to the communication required for relationship development in the future. We don't always tell them what they want to hear, because the transparency will diminish the value of future conversations.

16
Perry's Practice Problems

Blake called Coach Brown later that evening and reported,
"Perry was at first reluctant to talk about missing practice.
But I wouldn't let him off the hook. He didn't say much, but
I think he was surprised that somebody cared enough to check
on him. He was also relieved we took him at his word about
his homework. He went to his room right after we talked to
do his homework."

ON MONDAY, PERRY SHOWED UP ON TIME TO
mingle with the players before practice. The team went out of their
way to include him in their conversations and horseplay.

Once practice started, Perry fell behind even though Blake and
Bobby coached and encouraged him during warm-up exercises.
Upon completion of the stretching and strength drills, the players
started the long lap. Perry fell behind again and finally started walking. After completing his lap, Bobby went back to encourage him
to finish the half mile any way he could. Perry ran and walked alter-
nately, with Bobby at his side until they finished the run.

Next, the team ran ladders in groups of three. These conditioning exercises were continuous sets of 10-20-30-40-yard sprints run

at about three-quarter speed. Perry finished these, but with considerable difficulty. After sufficient rest and some water, the players ran six 30-yard sprints with one-minute recoveries, during which Perry demonstrated good speed.

During the remainder of the practice, Perry showed good coordination and modest progress during skills training. Perry was paired with Todd during the contact drills. Todd varied his intensity as Perry was introduced to contact. Perry initially enjoyed contact, but as the intensity increased, he backed off and did a little shoving after the drill.

Blake took Perry aside at the first water break and said, "There's no shoving allowed after a play or in practice. Our team could be penalized for this in a game and you could be ejected. If somebody gets the best of you, as Todd did, just try a little harder the next time."

As practice ended, Coach Brown asked Blake, "How'd you like your first night of coaching?"

"It was frustrating. It took a lot of patience. Was I a lot like Perry?"

"I don't think so," laughed Coach Brown. "But you had some of his characteristics. It'll be interesting to see if you can deal with yourself of a few years ago."

"What!"

"Just kidding, Blake. How'd Perry do tonight?"

"Fine," said Blake. "He had trouble with conditioning, but we all did our first week. He got into it with Todd when Todd turned it up a little. But he popped him back, and Todd told him nice job. He's got quite a ways to go, but I think he had a good first practice. I told him to stay out of the final sprints because his feet hurt. I think he's being truthful. Did you see those shiny red shoes? While the kids were sprinting, I asked him to pick up the gear and move the blocking sled to the storage area. I'll bet he runs sprints tomorrow even if his feet are killing him. I also told him he did a good job today. It is tough to join this team five weeks into the season."

"It sure is," said Coach Brown. "It sounds like he's off to a good start."

Blake continued, "Having Perry pick up the equipment instead of running reminded me of the Masterson kid. Do you remember him, Coach? He was on my team and was always looking for a way out of running. One day, he said he couldn't run the long lap because he'd pulled a hamstring as he obviously faked a limp. He said he did it running up some stairs at school. So, one of the coaches told him to run back and forth between two telephone poles about 20 yards apart until the players came back from their half mile. He didn't understand, until one of the players told him he was running the same distance regardless of where he ran. Then, all of a sudden, the hamstring got better. Coach, did you know he played in college?"

"Yes, I did," said Coach Brown. "He grew to be about 280 and played at Harvard. Today, he's a consultant for a major accounting firm. He came to practice last year."

"Did he remember the incident?" said Blake.

"Yes, he did. He said he'd never forget it. He said he laughs about it all the time, but he never told anybody at Harvard about it."

On his way to his car, Coach Brown caught up with Perry and asked, "How'd practice go?"

Perry responded, "Coach, it was tough. Coach Cook said I did good and if I made it through the first week, I'd be okay. He also said I should weigh in tonight. If I weighed 140 or less, I could play more positions. I weigh more than 140 now."

Perry got on the scale and with adjustments for his equipment weighed about 145.

Coach Brown asked, "Do you want to try to lose five pounds before the supplemental weigh-in three weeks? That just means you can't play in league games until you weigh in. We can play you in White team games."

Perry anxiously answered, "I think I can do it, Coach. I must've lost weight today."

"You'll have to give up sweets, potato chips, Big Macs, and soft drinks. Can you do that? You'll have to eat more salads, cereal without sugar, chicken, and vegetables. I'll talk to your foster parents," said Coach Brown.

Coach Brown called Perry's foster parents to discuss the first night of practice and the weight-loss proposition. Marie said, "Perry didn't have much to say other than he was tired, he wanted to lose weight so he could play more positions, and the coaches said he did good."

Mike and Marie thought losing weight would be a good vehicle for teaching discipline and improving Perry's eating habits. They reminded Coach Brown that Blake had to lose weight and it was good for him. He's watched his weight ever since that experience.

The second and third nights of practice went well. Perry still lagged behind in some of the drills, but he made progress skill-wise and socially. He was still quiet, and got a little frustrated in drills, especially those that involved physical contact.

On Thursday, Perry didn't show up for practice or call. Blake, who had come directly from work, called home.

He reported to Coach Brown, "I just talked to my mom and Perry said he didn't want to come to practice because he was tired and had a lot of homework. She thought some of the newness had worn off and Perry was reverting to some of his old ways of taking the easy way out. Do you want me to force him to come?"

"What do you think we should do, Blake? You know him better than I."

Blake responded, "Coach, I think Perry needs a little space. I can remember how I felt. He's way behind in everything. If he doesn't do better in school and stay on this team, he probably thinks he'll go to juvenile. He's on a diet. That's tough. I think he's a little overwhelmed."

Blake paused, waiting for Coach Brown to give him the answer, then continued, "I think I should tell him his homework has priority and he's done well the first three practices. I'll find out how his diet is going and make sure he's at the game on Sunday. He has to be at the game or we might lose him."

Blake called Coach Brown later that evening and reported, "Perry was at first reluctant to talk about missing practice. But I wouldn't let him off the hook. He didn't say much, but I think he was surprised that somebody cared enough to check on him. He was also relieved we took him at his word about his homework. He went to his room right after we talked to do his homework."

"Do you think he'll show up Sunday?" asked Coach Brown

Blake responded, "Yeah, no doubt. I think he knows we care about him. He hasn't had too many people like that in his life. I also told him he'd get his uniform and could dress for the game. Is that okay, Coach?"

"Yes. He just can't wear his shoulder pads," replied Coach Brown. "By the way, I think you're doing a good job with Perry. This isn't easy."

"Thanks, Coach. I have to admit I'm not sure what the hell I'm doing sometimes ... er, excuse me, Coach. I didn't mean to swear. I remember what you said about that."

Coach Brown laughed, "That's okay. I'll take it as a measure of your enthusiasm."

"Right, Coach!"

* * *

Sunday arrived and so did Perry. He ran directly across the field toward Coach Brown as if on a mission. Upon arrival, he blurted out, "Coach, I'm sorry about missing practice. I told Coach Blake I had too much homework, but the truth is I was just tired and sore. I didn't feel like practicing. Do I have to run some laps or something?"

"I appreciate your honesty, Perry," responded a somewhat surprised Coach Brown. "Telling the truth was probably harder than running laps. We'll call things even if you give it your best in practice next week. Next time, call me if you have to miss practice. How are you doing making weight?"

"Coach, I have lost two pounds. I was 143 this morning," said Perry proudly. Giving up all that stuff is harder than I thought. My foster dad said I'll have to lose more than five pounds to make weight because I am adding muscle and that weighs more than fat. My foster dad is going on the same diet with me."

After Perry excused himself, he sprinted to where the team had started stretching. A few of the players, including the captains, asked about his absence. This was probably a good and bad experience for him. The bad was the explanation to his peers. The good was, the team missed him and cared enough to ask where he was.

Prior to the start of the game with St. Thomas, Blake gave Perry his jersey and pants. Perry immediately went behind the stands and changed into his uniform and proudly took his place in the pregame huddle with the rest of the team. His abruptness and his body language announced his arrival. The team acknowledged his appearance with either a smile or nod of the head.

After the team prayer, Coach Brown addressed the team.

"We've worked hard and had excellent practices. The reason we strive for excellence in practice is because we want to achieve excellence in our games. You don't hear the coaches talking about more of this and more of that, with the possible exception of Coach Cook."

The team laughed as Coach Cook mumbled. Coach Brown continued. "That's because we're not looking for more of what we do, we're looking for excellence in what we do.

"Practice must be excellent in order to achieve excellence in a game or sport. A player must know the fundamentals, constantly strive to improve, have a good attitude every day, every practice, every hour of every day in order to excel. A desire to excel must come from inside. It's far better for a player to push himself rather than being pushed by the coaches. This has been the case so far. We initially pushed you, but when you started pushing yourselves we supported you. Excellence depends on continuous improvement, one step at a time. This is what you've done. Achieving excellence requires only a little additional effort, if it's the right effort. You have given this, so let's see it today."

Todd called, "Hands in, one, two, three, Redwings." With the loudest "Redwings" coming from Perry, several players smiled and patted him on his helmet as a symbol of inclusion.

The game with St. Thomas went very well. The Redwings played their best game of the year, as they cruised to a 32–12 victory. Kyle led the team on offense with 180 yards on just ten carries. Bobby, filling in for Billy, whose ankle was still injured, ran hard for over 100 yards. Stewart carried three times without a fumble and caught four passes for 60 yards. The defense played great, shutting out St. Thomas for three quarters. George, Brian, Todd, Drew, and Garrett were dominant on the defensive line. St. Thomas scored twice in the fourth quarter against the White team. These were their first touchdowns of the year, as they were shut out in their previous game.

Several players from the White team played well, as the seventh graders continued to grow into eighth graders. Most notably, the twins Brian and Brendan, and Matt registered his first tackle of the year in a Red team game. The White team players had improved significantly and were undefeated in their first two games.

However, the most entertaining play came late in the fourth quarter, when Vince from the White team took what the coaches called the hardest hit in the history of St. Raphael Football, as he ran back a punt. Consistent with his macho-man image, he bounded to his feet, started running off the field as if to say, "Is that all you got?"

but gladly accepted support from the trainer as he stumbled to the sideline.

Jeff played well on defense, as he had in White team games. More importantly, he enjoyed the support of both parents as they walked to the car.

* * *

On Monday, the White team won their third game of the season over All Saints Academy. Matt and Mike both played well, as did the twins Brian and Brendan. They were especially motivated by their brother Donnie who had returned from Northwestern, where he was a member of the varsity squad. Donnie started for the Redwings his eighth-grade year, and through hard work, became a starter on Naperville Central's state championship team.

Several other players emerged with fine games, among them Mark, Jimmy, Mitch, Big Mike, Dan the beast, Chris, Heyden, and the brothers Will and Andy.

Frank, the founder of the All Saints program, laughed and said after the game, "Coach, everything appears to be going so smoothly for the Redwings. You'd better not get too comfortable."

Coach Brown smiled, "You're right, Frank. It's not a matter of if, but when, the unexpected will occur in youth football."

PLAY NUMBER SIXTEEN

We try to enjoy the relationship with your children. The quality of that relationship will be based on how we view each other. One of our parents told me about a child who participated in show and tell about his father's occupation. When it was his turn, Jake told the class his father was a great coach. The teacher knew Jake's father was not a coach, but did not say anything to embarrass the child. After class, the teacher asked the boy why he told the class his father was a coach. The boy started to cry and insisted his father was a coach. After comforting the child and developing a little trust, the boy admitted that his father traveled a lot and did not spend much time with the family. The only time the two were together was when the father coached his football team. The boy said he was a good football player and his father said a lot of nice things to him about that. Since the boy had contact with his father only when coaching, that was what he wanted him to be and therefore he was. Parents need to make enough time to support their child by attending their games, and an occasional practice.

17
Perry, Matt, and Mrs. Philips

I'm sure parents have asked you, "Why do you coach? You don't have any children in the program." I think we know Coach Peterson's answer. We give so little compared to what we get back. Makes you realize how mundane X's and O's are in comparison to what these children learn about life ... and they can teach us a thing or two.

ON WEDNESDAY, MATT RODE HIS BIKE TO PRACTICE as usual. He showed up late and without his shoulder pads. He also had a skinned elbow and scrape on the right side of his head. When asked about his tardiness, he explained some bullies from school knocked him off his bike and took his shoulder pads. He explained he knew who they were and he'd handle it. Regardless of Coach Jerman's persistence, Matt would not reveal their names. After getting a spare pair of shoulder pads from the equipment bag, Matt participated in practice.

After practice, Coach Brown interrupted Matt's discussion with his teammates. He asked him to have his parents call him that night to discuss the incident. Matt tried to convince Coach Brown he could handle it, but to no avail. Coach Brown also told the team, itching for revenge, to stay out of it. He, Matt, and his parents would deal with it.

That evening, Matt's parents told Coach Brown Matt would not reveal the names of the kids involved. He insisted, if parents got involved, it would only get worse. He said he'd pay for the pads from his allowance if he didn't get them back. The last part of this statement, "if he didn't get them back," concerned Coach Brown.

* * *

On Thursday, Matt rode his bike across the field to practice, with Perry perched on the handlebars. Perry carried two sets of shoulder pads, triumphantly raised in the air. As they approached, the team began a staccato applause. They knew what had happened before Matt could launch into his story of how he and Perry "took care of business."

Coach Brown, fearing the worst, took Matt and Perry aside and demanded, "Tell me what happened and I want the truth."

Matt laughed and said, "Nothing, Coach. That's what makes this so great. I told the kids at school I wanted my pads back and safe passage to practice. I also told them I'd be giving my friend Perry a ride to practice on my bike. That's all it took. They all know Perry, and I guess they didn't want to mess with him. Perry lives near me so I gave him a ride to practice. One of the kids was waiting for us at the scene of the crime. So it's over, and Perry never said a word. He just got off my bike, went over, and took the shoulder pads from the kid."

"Matt, you may have gotten Perry in a lot of trouble," Coach Brown said firmly. "He's gotten into trouble in the past and is on probation. I'll have to discuss this with his case worker tonight. No more rides for Perry, and I want your parents to call me tonight."

Turning to Perry, who had his head down, Coach Brown said, "Perry, have Marie call me tonight."

"Sorry, Coach," said Perry. "But what's the big deal? That's the way we handle things in the city. Those kids shouldn't have messed with Matt."

"The big deal is that you're on probation and about this far from juvenile. You have been doing so well. You can't afford to do things like that even though you thought you were helping a teammate," explained a concerned Coach Brown.

That evening, Coach Brown talked with Matt's parents and Marie. They agreed Matt would carpool with Perry to practice for a while until this incident was forgotten. Coach Brown also scheduled a meeting with Marie and Perry's case worker, Sue, for the following evening at practice.

* * *

The following evening, Coach Brown gave Sue a detailed account of the incident and an assessment of Perry's progress with the team. Then, Coach Brown speculated, "I think Perry's intention was to make a contribution so he could gain acceptance from his teammates. He realized he doesn't play football as well as the other players, so he thought he'd employ what he mistakenly considered his strong suit to gain acceptance."

"Do you think the kids involved are going to make an issue of it at school?" asked Sue.

"I don't think so, because they've been told by some of the other players that stealing the pads could get them in a lot of trouble. Tonight, one of our captains said the kids have called a truce. Matt and Perry have been told to stay away from these kids and the area where the problem occurred."

"Perry has made considerable progress over the past two weeks, both here and in school," said Sue. "I also think Perry's desire to be accepted and his nonviolent approach to solving the problem are both positives. I think everything is fine if we keep a lid on this at school and Perry continues to make progress overall. A couple of weeks ago, Perry might have beat on those kids just for the fun of it."

Sue extended her hand with a smile and said, "Thanks for being straight with me. Let's keep working together. We might have a real success story here. I could sure use one."

* * *

Practice for the remainder of the week didn't go well. The players had grown tired of the routine and were a little overconfident as the result of their three wins without a loss. Attendance was spotty because of homework, illness, and an annual school retreat.

The highlight of the week came in the form of a letter to Coach Brown from Mrs. Philips, who had registered her child for the in-house program for the first time in 2007. Coach Brown gave the letter to Coach Jerman. After reading the letter, Coach Jerman decided to read it to the coaching staff on Thursday night during conditioning.

Before reading the letter he said, "I know you guys are a little disappointed with practice this week. Tonight there's only 19 of our 30 players present. In order to put things in perspective, I want to read you a letter from the parent of a boy in our in-house program. I know all of us coached there in the past.

Dear Coach Brown,

I am not sure you remember me. My name is Mrs. Philips. My son is named AJ. He is 10 years old. He could not be mainstreamed at school without a full-time county social worker. I called you last September to see if you would allow AJ to join your football league after a very dis-satisfying experience in another league, in another city. His social worker thought this would be good for him. Without hesitation, you said yes, assigned him to a team, and discussed AJ's special needs with Coach Peterson, Melissa, the social worker, and me. Because of my financial situation as a single mom, you also gave us a scholarship. I hope you remember. It was difficult for AJ at first, but because of Coach Peterson and the special attention of his teammates, AJ is a different person today and everybody involved has called it a miracle. AJ will be mainstreamed on a trial basis this week and we are all optimistic, including AJ. The school has also determined that AJ is actually quite smart. I am not sure because Coach Peterson is so modest, but I think he made AJ's rehabilitation a team project. I wanted to come and thank you personally, but this would be way too emotional for me. So, this is the best I can do for now. Maybe someday AJ and I will both see you and thank you properly. With over 2,000 kids, I still can't believe your program cares this much about a single child who will probably never play beyond St. Raphael Football. Next year, I plan to volunteer since I have a new job. I want to give something back.

Thank you, Mrs. Philips.

After listening to the letter, Coach Kelly said, "Jim, I'd like to hear the rest of the story."

"Okay," said Coach Brown. "This is a good example of what our football program is all about.

"The players from AJ's school knew him as a boy who was always in trouble, and he had very few friends because kids were afraid of him. Coach Peterson explained football would be good for AJ and he hoped the kids would treat him like a teammate both on and off the field."

"Shortly after AJ joined the team, he didn't show up for practice. Instead, his mom came to practice in tears. AJ had been suspended from school for fighting.

"Coach Peterson talked to the kids from AJ's school. They knew about it. Apparently, a group of boys taunted AJ and got him to fight a kid after school. Coach Peterson asked the boys if they did anything to stop the fight. They said no. He then reminded his players that when one teammate had a problem, all the 49ers had a problem. Coach Peterson told the boys, 'Next time AJ has a problem, make sure he has your support, so there will be a non-violent solution.'

"It wasn't long before Coach Peterson's players had an opportunity to show their colors. When AJ returned to school, the same boys taunted him again. It happened on Friday when the boys wore their jerseys to school. It happened in the lunch room and soon the taunters were surrounded by his teammates. The proper words were spoken and the problem went away.

"AJ returned to the team. He was never a star player, but he became a star relative to his previous performance in school. Mrs. Philips believes football raised AJ's self-esteem, his attitude, and his performance.

"I'm sure parents have asked you, 'Why do you coach? You don't have any children in the program.' I think we know Coach Peterson's answer. We give so little compared to what we get back. Makes you realize how mundane X's and O's are in comparison to what these children learn about life ... and they can teach us a thing or two. When I hear about how open AJ was to change, it makes me realize how closed I can be at times. It seems like we have to give so little to get so much back. Let's get to work."

PLAY NUMBER SEVENTEEN

We believe the quality of performance is affected by how we view our players. They sense how we feel about them because their antennas are always up. This is so important to them. If we want our players to feel valued, we must tell them why we value them. We must believe in our players especially when they don't believe in themselves. This has a significant impact on performance and more importantly the relationship required for development.

18
Overconfidence

From now on, we have to start fast and develop the margins that ensure victory. No more close games left in the hands of others. I'm sure you all thought we made that first down near the end of the game." The players nodded their heads as Coach Brown continued. "I think we made it, too. But we didn't lose because of that call. We lost because we didn't build the margins throughout the game required to make that call irrelevant. Let's come to practice ready to work both physically and mentally on Tuesday."

THE REDWINGS' FOURTH OPPONENT, ST. ANN, HAD also won their first two league games of the season. They came to Benet Academy, the Redwings' home for over 40 years, ready to play.

The game-time temperature was 89 degrees and very humid. Several Redwing players were late for warm-ups and the team showed little enthusiasm during their pregame preparation. Even inspirational talks by Brian, Todd, Billy, and the coaching staff had little impact.

The Redwings were physically superior to St. Ann, but had only a 6–0 lead at halftime due to foolish penalties, dropped balls, and fumbles. St. Ann was still in the game and the coaching staff was worried.

The second half began with a bang as Bobby ran the kickoff back 70 yards for a score, but the touchdown was nullified because of a clipping penalty on Kyle behind the play. St. Ann held the Redwings on the first series, and they were forced to punt. The punt was blocked and a St. Ann player picked the ball out of the air and scored. They had only two first downs but led 7–6 after a successful extra point.

St. Raphael moved the ball on the next series, making four first downs on their way to the St. Ann 25-yard line. On the first play, Brian missed his block. Joe threw a pass just as he was hit. It was intercepted by St. Ann.

St. Ann couldn't make a first down and punted to Stewart at the 50-yard line. Stewart was hit immediately, fumbled, and St. Ann recovered. Kyle yelled at Stewart, "Hold on to the ball." Brian pushed Kyle and they were both removed from the game by the coaching staff.

Late in the fourth quarter, the Redwings moved the ball to the St. Ann 11-yard line. But, on fourth down, St. Ann held on a questionable ball placement by the referee.

St. Ann attempted to run out the clock, but fumbled, and Todd recovered for the Redwings at the 7-yard line. The Redwings moved the ball to the 2-yard line. On third down, Bobby ran a sweep, was hit at the goal line, and fumbled. The ball popped up in the air. It was caught by a St. Ann player, who ran 100 yards for a touchdown. St. Raphael had gained over 200 yards to 40 for St. Ann. They had 15 first downs to two for St Ann, but lost the game 13–6.

After the game, the players were upset as Coach Brown addressed the team. "We were physically superior, we outgained them, they had two first downs, but they beat us. They beat us because they were motivated to play and we were not."

Holding a player's helmet in the air, Coach Brown continued. "They did all the things we have plastered on this helmet, but we didn't do. We must remember today for what this loss should teach us. We have to practice hard and we must play hard every down. Any team on our schedule can beat us. And they will enjoy doing it because everybody likes to beat the teams on top. We did not practice well last week. We did not coach well last week either. We must all change if we are to achieve our goal of conference champions."

Coach Brown paused, looked at Kyle, then continued. "We must get along as a team. We must support each other, not criticize each other. Our strength is in the team, not individual players. I never want to see negative words spoken between players again, only positive encouraging words. Kyle, you and Brian get together and work things out. If you need help let me know."

"Okay, Coach," said Kyle as he nodded his head toward Brian, then Stewart.

Coach Brown continued, "The teams in this league are gunning for us because we're on top. Teams dread coming to our house to play, but not anymore. They'll gain confidence from St. Ann's win.

"From now on, we have to start fast and develop the margins that ensure victory. No more close games left in the hands of others. I'm sure you all thought we made that first down near the end of the game."

The players nodded their heads as Coach Brown continued. "I think we made it, too. But we didn't lose because of that call. We lost because we didn't build the margins throughout the game required to make that call irrelevant. Let's come to practice ready to work both physically and mentally on Tuesday. We're a very good team and can still achieve our goal of conference champions. Always remember, what really matters most is how you finish."

Coach Brown didn't ask for the usual comments from the other coaches. He wanted to put this game behind the team quickly before it affected their confidence. It had served its purpose in their championship quest. Brian called the team together and said, "Hands in ... TEAM!"

As Coach Brown walked to the car, he was confronted by Pat, the mother of a first-year White team player by the name of Dewayne. "Why didn't Dewayne get in the game today? He's come to practice every night and deserves to play in the Sunday games."

"Dewayne has worked hard in practice," said Coach Brown, "and has improved a lot. He has started every White team game and played well. But, he's a first-year player and will have to improve a little more before we can play him in a contested Sunday game."

"I don't care about the score of the game," Pat said angrily. "He's worked hard and is very upset because he didn't get in today. He'll quit if he doesn't get in the Sunday games."

"Pat, we would be doing a disservice to Dewayne and the team if we put him in a game before he was ready. He's improving, but he's not ready. Sometimes when you put players in over their heads, they fail and this can impede their progress. The Sunday team is different than the White team in that there are no 'must-play' rules because we are playing the best players from each parish."

"That's a lot of bull. I've watched all the games, and he is certainly better than some of the players who lost the game today."

Coach Brown could feel his anger rising from Pat's last statement and decided to end the conversation. "Pat, I'd like to ask you to do two things. Please come to practice this week and watch Dewayne in drills. Then, have a discussion with him about where he fits in the team hierarchy. Then, let's talk again."

"Okay," responded Pat. "But I don't see what that'll prove."

* * *

Tuesday was a cold rainy night as the St. Raphael varsity football team began practice for their key game against St. Francis. It was one of those nights when Coach Brown wished it would either clear up or rain cats and dogs so the practice decision would be easier.

Halfway through warm-up exercises, he got his wish. The skies opened and he announced to a disappointed team, "Practice will be moved to the school classroom."

This was an unpopular decision because most football players love to practice in the rain, especially when the alternative is listening to the coaches talk. However, this was an opportunity Coach Brown had hoped for since last week's practice and the loss to St. Ann.

Several years before, Coach Brown led a team that designed and implemented a process for changing the culture of Lucent Technologies to high-performing teams and a coaching leadership style. This process required several week-long developmental sessions which included a module intended to define high-performing teams. This evening, he wanted to see if he could successfully condense the exercise from half a day to an hour with his St. Raphael seventh- and eighth-grade team.

Coach Brown began by announcing to a somewhat uninterested team and coaching staff slouched in their seats, "I have written ten characteristics of high-performing teams on the easel facing the blackboard. I'm going to show a highlight video of the 2005 championship team in which almost all of those characteristics are visible. After the video, you'll be asked to identify the characteristics you observed. The purpose of this exercise is to teach you how to perform as a high-performing team, able to achieve the goals you set at the beginning of the season."

The players watched the video with great enthusiasm as they cheered touchdowns and big hits. The coaches made no effort to curb their enthusiasm or redirect it to the point of the exercise. The players were having fun, together, and that was an important part of the exercise.

At the conclusion of the video, Brian said, "Can we see it again, Coach?"

"Maybe later in the season we'll look at this team's highlight video. But now I'd like to have you identify seven of the ten characteristics of a high-performing team. There are seven visible in the video. If you get them, there'll be a packet of M&Ms for each player … and yes, the coaches too."

Todd was first. "A good team must have team spirit. They have to get along. Every time this team did something good they banged helmets, high-fived, low-fived, hugged, and did stuff like that."

"That's right. Number nine is BE FOR ONE ANOTHER— SUPPORT AND INVEST IN ONE ANOTHER'S GROWTH AND SUCCESS."

Next, Billy said, "Listen to the coach and other players like the captains. I saw the players listen to you, Coach, and a couple of the other kids."

"Yeah, Billy. I knew a captain would get that one. We still ain't going to listen to you," Kyle said with a big smile, almost pushing Billy out of his chair.

"LISTEN GENEROUSLY AND EMPATHETICALLY. That's number six. There are five more until M&M time," said Coach Brown.

Next, Joe said, "You have to put the team first. I mean you can't be thinking about your stats. I saw the quarterback pitch the ball to another kid on the option, when he could have kept it for a score."

"That's great, Joe. That's number three. PUT TEAM GOALS AHEAD OF INDIVIDUAL GOALS. Now, we've only four to go. You guys are doing great."

Once again Kyle interrupted. "No, Coach. There are seven more. We can get 'em all. Hey, can we have the coaches' help?"

"We don't need the coaches, Kyle. We can do this," responded Brian.

Next, Greg, the very quiet but reliable center who had not missed a snap in two years, said, "Everybody has to play their own position and do what they're supposed to do even if it's tough. I saw the center getting banged around pretty good by the nose, but he never gave up and never missed a snap. I mean, if you're getting beat up, it is easy to quit out there."

"Great point, Greg. That was numbers eight and four. FULFILL YOUR COMMITMENTS AT ALL COSTS—NEVER, EVER GIVE UP and BE ACCOUNTABLE FOR YOUR OWN RESPONSIBILITIES AND COMMITMENTS SO EVERYBODY CAN TRUST ONE ANOTHER."

Next Matt stood and said with a sly smile, "Coach, I didn't see it in the video, but I did see the result. You told us at the beginning of the season you'd always be honest with us when you gave instructions and feedback, because it was in our best interest. I think everybody has to respect their teammates and give and take honest feedback even from other players."

"Very good, Matt," said Coach Brown, pointing at Matt and shaking his head, as he recalled their previous feedback session." That's number five. BE COMPLETE WITH ONE ANOTHER—OPEN AND HONEST." With that Coach Brown shook his head in admiration and said, "I can't believe how quickly you're getting these. It took my class at Lucent all morning."

Kyle interrupted again. "I can't believe it either. Except for Stewart and Todd and maybe Brian, these guys aren't that smart in school."

With that, Brian looked at Kyle disapprovingly and said, "Never give up. Always have a positive attitude in dealing with problems. I saw that in the game. When they were behind 6–0 with two minutes left and had not scored, they still thought they could win and they did."

"Brian, somehow I knew you would get that one. That's number seven. BE PROACTIVE WHEN DEALING WITH ADVERSITY."

After a several-minute pause, Coach Brown said, "Come on, guys. There are only three left. One is easy. You guys do one of these very well during all of our practices and games, and only the result of the other two are in the video."

With that Kyle's hand shot up and he blurted out, "Have fun! The guys in the video were really having fun. They celebrated every tackle and every good run. They were going crazy out there. They were free spirits. Kind of like me! They didn't let anything get in their way."

"That's right. You got number ten, CELEBRATE TEAM AND PERSONAL SUCCESS—CELEBRATION OF TODAY'S SUCCESS FUELS FUTURE SUCCESS."

After another silence, one of the quietest members of the team, named Riley, said, "Coach, have we done either of the last two?"

"Yes, we have done them both, Riley, and they are connected."

Without hesitation Riley said, "Set team goals and work hard to achieve them. That's what we did at the beginning of the season when we set our goal to be champions and agreed to do extra conditioning each night including extra running."

"Yes, number one is DEVELOP GOALS, OBJECTIVES, AND A PLAN TO ACHIEVE THEM. And number two is PAY THE PRICE REQUIRED TO EXECUTE THE PLAN."

"Congratulations! You guys did it! I really didn't think you'd get them all. My class at work had more difficulty than you did. They would've been impressed. Let me show you what's on the easel." Do you think we can apply these concepts in the future?"

To that question there was a resounding "Yes!"

"That's it. See you tomorrow night."

Kyle cleared his throat and said, "Coach, aren't you forgetting something?"

Coach Brown went to the ball bag. He withdrew the prizes and started tossing them to the team and coaches. "I just wanted to see if you were paying attention, Kyle."

"Yeah ... sure, Coach ... whatever," responded Kyle with a smile.

With that Keith stood and asked, "Did we practice like Redwings tonight?"

The team responded, "Yes ... Redwings!"

PLAY NUMBER EIGHTEEN

Being involved with your children in an activity like football has the potential for being a rewarding experience. This can be an excellent way to spend quality time with your children, and their friends, doing something they like. This experience has great developmental potential if it's recognized for what it is. Parents should not try to relive their youth by living vicariously through their children. This puts too much pressure on the child, affects his performance, and more importantly his enjoyment. If a child is doing something they like, it is a good time to communicate with them. Quality conversations with a child are often stimulated by successful participation in a sporting event.

19
The Rebound

I want all of you to remember how you played today and how it felt. This is our standard for the rest of the season. We will not slip back from here for any reason. We will only build on this to ensure future success. Today, we demonstrated the faith and trust we have in each other.

ON WEDNESDAY AFTERNOON, COACH BROWN MET with Kathy and the therapist for a status report, and to update their plan for using football as a vehicle for Jeff's rehabilitation. During their meeting, Kathy indicated Jeff thought he might be ready to practice some at quarterback, but didn't feel he was ready for a game.

Jeff had played defense in three White team games. He played well and was comfortable with this role. He also gained considerable confidence, which transferred to other aspects of his life. His grades had improved and he had even made some new friends.

His relationship with his father had improved to neutral. Doug had changed, but was uncomfortable with his supportive role in the family. He suffered a minor setback at a White team game.

Jeff tackled a boy near the sidelines and appeared to have a head or neck injury. Kate, the trainer, examined Jeff and declared him unfit to play as a precautionary measure.

Doug confronted Kate, and declared Jeff was okay to play and he would take the responsibility. Kate reminded Doug of the St. Raphael policy which stated, "when a player was placed in the care of a trainer, the trainer's decision was final regardless of the medical qualifications of the parent." Doug objected only mildly, which Coach Brown viewed as progress.

At the end of the meeting, the therapist made the following recommendation. "First, Jeff should continue to play White team games on defense. Second, Coach Brown should find an opportunity for Jeff to play defense in a Red team game when the game was still in doubt. Third, Jeff should take a few snaps from center in quarterback drills. Fourth, if there were any negative signs resulting from any part of this plan, it should be adjusted immediately without fanfare. Fifth, make Doug aware of the plan, and the necessity of his continued support."

The therapist said in closing, "We've observed the impact of the pressure a parent, a coach, a peer, a teacher, or the child himself can inflict. Sometimes, we don't know we're doing it. People in positions of power and authority must be aware of their ability to create stressful situations. When these situations are created, they have a severe negative impact on relationships and performance, whether at work, school, or play. Most kids are relatively fragile and have a great need for recognition and positive reinforcement. In fact, we all do. I think Jeff is making great progress."

* * *

On Wednesday night, the line coaches decided to follow up on the goal-setting session with a drill the players loved called "Bull in the Ring." Coach Bus, with tongue in cheek, invited the backs to participate, if it wasn't too tough for them. The backs and their coaches took the challenge.

In this drill, all the players stood in a circle and were paired initially with players their own size. When a pairing was called by a coach, the players came to the center of the ring created by the other players. At the sound of the whistle, they began to block each other until one player blocked the other out of the ring.

Matt made a great effort, but lost in the first round. George was eventually declared King of the Ring.

To complete the drill, any player could challenge the champion to determine the ultimate King of the Ring. On this day, there was only one challenge, issued by none other than Matt. George, who outweighed Matt by 40 pounds, looked at the coaches to validate this challenge, or force a withdrawal for humanitarian reasons.

The coaches tried, but Matt was not to be dissuaded as he looked at George, gestured, and said, "Bring your best, George."

The two players were purposely lined up very close to one another in order to minimize the initial impact. The whistle blew and for a short time, Matt was doing better than anybody anticipated. As the drill continued, the team's reaction changed from a quiet concern to raucous cheers as Matt continued to hold his own. The cheers grew louder as George, who was performing with restraint, finally blocked Matt out of the ring.

All the players, including George, descended on Matt and tried to lift him onto their shoulders and began to chant his name. Matt fought his way to the ground and said, "This is what we need on Sunday from you guys. So let's save it."

As he walked away, he caught Coach Brown's eye, winked, raised his arm and said, "The rest is up to you, Coach."

All Coach Brown could do was shake his head as Matt walked away seemingly unimpressed with his impact on the team.

As Matt trotted away to the final conditioning drills, Dewayne's mom, Pat, approached Coach Brown and said, "Coach, I need to talk to you."

Coach Brown, fearing the worst, said, "Okay, Pat. Lets step over here away from the players."

"I'm so sorry about my outburst after the game on Sunday. I showed poor timing and poor judgment. Thanks for listening and not getting upset. I talked to Dewayne and watched him practice. He's doing his best but he's not ready for Red team games. You know what he said when I talked to him about it?"

"No, Pat. What did he say?" said a relieved Coach Brown.

"He said what are you trying to do, Mom, get me killed? That's the toughest football league in the world. The world? ... That's funny, don't you think?"

"Dewayne has a great sense of humor," laughed Coach Brown. "... and some good survival skills, too."

Pat smiled and said, "You won't have any more trouble with me, unless you put my kid in before he's ready. Then, we'll have to talk again."

* * *

Sunday dawned a beautiful day for football. The temperature at game time was 75 degrees without a cloud in the sky. By contrast to the prior week, the team showed up early and enthusiastically cheered the JV team to a 21–7 victory over St. Francis.

As the kickoff approached, the players were somewhere between tense and focused. Adrenalin was flowing. The coaches wondered if the contents of a great practice week could be transferred to the football field this afternoon.

After warm-ups, the team took a knee, placed their right hand on the shoulder of the player next to them, and were led in prayer by Coach Grosso.

My brothers of St. Raphael Football, take a moment and put yourselves in the presence of the Lord. In the name of the Father, the Son, and the Holy Spirit.

Do you have faith, my brothers? The blind man in today's Gospel heard Jesus coming and called out to Him. Jesus responded, saying your faith has healed you.

So again I ask you, my brothers, do you have faith? You have come here today to play a football game with faith in your abilities and your teammates. If you do, you will prevail and continue your journey to a championship.

Lord, we know it takes hard work and preparation to accomplish most things in life. But without faith we're nothing. We can be the biggest and strongest, but without faith, we may lose to a smaller, less talented team as we did last week.

Lord, sometimes we allow too many things to distract us. We think of size, speed, talent, win-loss records. These things are irrelevant if we have faith.

Faith means belief without evidence. Lord, we need your presence in our lives to battle all that tears at our faith in you. Be with us today, as we throw away the evidence and firmly grasp our faith.

We need to look each other in the eye and have faith in each other. Our faith will heal us. Our faith will bring us victory. AMEN!

The captains returned from the coin toss. "We got the ball, Coach."

Coach Brown looked at Todd curiously. "Did we win the toss?"

"Yeah, Coach. We did. But the guys didn't want to defer. They want the ball. We really want this game. Okay?"

Coach Brown shook his head in admiration, smiled, and said, "Good choice."

After the kick-receive team got their instructions from Coach Kanis and broke for their positions, they were called together again by Billy. Coach Kanis, wondering what was wrong, wandered out to the huddle. Just as he arrived, he overheard Billy say, "Hands in. Now that we've finished our prayer, let's go kick some butt. Let's show the coaches this week's practice was for real."

Coach Kanis walked to the sideline and said to Coach Brown, "They're ready."

After running the opening kickoff to the St. Francis 25-yard line, the Redwings scored in four plays as Bobby went to the end zone untouched. Santos kicked the extra point and the Redwings led 8–0. St. Raphael held St. Francis without a first down, then scored their second touchdown in six plays as Stewart caught a swing pass out of the backfield and took it to the end zone. The Redwings looked like a different team.

At the beginning of the second quarter, Coach Taylor sent several White team members into the game while the game was still in doubt. He wanted to get them a quality-time growth experience. This experience and others like it would promote the improvement required for late-season success.

Jeff was one of those players. When selected, Coach Taylor could see the uncertainty in his eyes. He looked at Coach Brown, who nodded his head in the affirmative, and Jeff trotted on to the field for his first Red team experience. He was welcomed enthusiastically by his teammates. Kathy reached for Doug's hand and squeezed it tightly. Doug surprisingly squeezed back.

The first two plays were uneventful as St. Francis got positive yardage on both plays and were close to a first down. On third down, the Cougars ran a counter play which Kyle and the team overplayed. The St. Francis running back had a big hole on the left side. Only Jeff stood between him and a big gain and possibly a score. This was it, Jeff's moment of truth.

At first Jeff hesitated. He didn't move to fill the hole close to the line of scrimmage. The back got through the hole and sprinted to the sidelines. Jeff moved with him, shadowing his prey. Then, he charged forward and hit the St. Francis back hard and dropped him to the ground. The ball popped into the air and out of bounds. Jeff leaped to his feet and was mobbed by his teammates. To most observers, it was just another good tackle, similar to those executed by most Redwing players. But those close to the team knew this tackle was Jeff's most significant step across his bridge to recovery.

The whole team played well. Everybody got significant minutes in a 31–7 victory. After the game, Coach Brown addressed the players in the middle of the field. Today he invited the parents to form a circle around the players and participate in the postgame meeting.

"I want all of you to remember how you played today and how it felt. This is our standard for the rest of the season. We will not slip back from here for any reason. We will only build on this to ensure future success. Today, we demonstrated the faith and trust we have in each other. That's what Coach Grosso talked about in our pregame prayer.

"Last year, we had a boy on our team named Ryan. Some of you remember him for his hard work and being a team player. I talked to his dad the other day about faith and trust and how it relates to team performance and I'd like to read what he said.

"Trust is at the very heart of productive relationships, whether they be in business or a youth football team. When forming a team, it simultaneously takes trusting the person behind you while proving trustworthy to the person in front of you. If one person doesn't fulfill their responsibility, there's a chance the team will fail. If you can trust, you don't have to build contingency plans to compensate for possible teammate failure."

Seeing he still had the attention of the team and parents, Coach Brown continued.

"Ryan's dad said, when actions are aligned with honesty and integrity, we usually find trust. Honesty is simply telling the truth. Integrity is doing what you say you'll do. It takes both to create an environment of trust. If you expect others to trust you, you have to trust them. You have to role-model trust."

Coach Brown paused, then continued. "Today, we had many examples of trust, but one stood out. The whole defense got fooled by a St. Francis counter play in the second quarter except for one player. How'd you feel, Kyle ... Todd ... Brian, when you saw your teammate, Jeff, stay home and make that tackle?"

The boys looked at Jeff and mumbled, "That was great, man."

Coach Brown continued, "The trust level on this team will be developed every day, every game, by what we do for each other. Enjoy the win, but more importantly enjoy the faith and trust you displayed in winning. Practice at five on Tuesday. It's getting dark earlier."

That day, few people noticed Jeff's proud parents holding hands as they walked off the field with their son.

PLAY NUMBER NINETEEN

Coaches should put themselves on the child's turf where he's most comfortable as you and he initiate your relationship-building activity. You should begin by telling the kids something about yourself. Make this something they can understand. They are not interested that you're the CEO of a very powerful company and make lots of money and were a great football player. They will be interested that you were an average youth football player, who found football difficult to learn, but had a lot of fun. You don't have to tell them how much you know about football. They will determine that for themselves based on what you're able to teach them.

20
Redwings Win Their Fifth

George, you're a gifted athlete and everybody knows it. You could start by talking less about your accomplishments. The less you say, the more likely it is that somebody will say something good about you. Second, you could compliment some of the players when they do well. That would mean a lot to them coming from you. And third, you could help the other players by coaching in the way I suggested.

OVER THE YEARS, ST. RAPHAEL FOOTBALL HAS HAD players who became bored with practice because of their exceptional athletic ability. George was one of those players. As the year progressed, George began to lose interest and became disruptive and often critical of the other players. George would relieve his frustration by abusing other players both physically and mentally. In addition, he was constantly bragging about his abilities and his individual statistics. Several players grew to dislike George, and this had a negative impact on the team's cohesiveness. George's father compounded the situation when he threatened to remove him from the team and have him play for his grade school, where he could play any position.

This situation came to a head Wednesday night when Kyle told George, "I'm tired of listening to you. Go play junior-high ball. We'll be fine without you." Several players supported Kyle as they were also tired of George's antics.

After practice Wednesday, Keith made Coach Brown aware of the situation, then said, "Coach, we need to fix this. It's messing with our team chemistry."

* * *

The following night, Coach Brown was riding to practice listening to a Stephen Covey tape about learning. Covey said, "One of the best ways to learn a concept is to teach it to somebody else." This was the same concept Coach Brown used to teach cultural and leadership style change at Lucent Technologies. The top executives at Lucent were first taught the new cultural and leadership concepts. They were then organized into faculty teams and were coached to teach these concepts to their organizations.

After discussions with the rest of the coaching staff, Coach Brown decided to try this with George. It was decided Coach Bus, George's line coach, would approach George with the idea.

After warm-up exercises, Coach Bus took George to "the office," and said, "George, you're clearly the best lineman on the team. You're probably one of the best we've ever had at St. Raphael. Since you're not being challenged at practice, you're losing interest, not improving as you should, and that's hurting the team. Therefore, we have to find a way to make use of all of your talent at practice for the good of the team."

At this point George was curious, but uncertain, and said, "Okay, Coach, what do you want me to do?"

Coach Bus continued, "In order for us to be champions, several of the less experienced linemen have to improve. We can't continue to run most of our plays behind you and Keith because teams are beginning to overload the right side of our line."

George agreed and said, "What do you have in mind, Coach?"

"George, I'd like to have you help Coach Martynowicz and me coach the linemen. When we feel you're ready, we'll assign you to tutor a different lineman each week. What do you think of that?"

George dropped his eyes and said, "Coach, I know what to do, but I don't think the other players will listen to me. Some of them don't like me."

"What do you think we can do about that?" asked Coach Bus.

George said sadly, "Coach, I don't know. I don't have a lot of friends at school either."

Then, after a pause, George looked up and asked, "What do you think I should do, Coach?"

Given the opening, Coach Bus asked George to sit down so they could talk.

"George, you're a gifted athlete and everybody knows it. You could start by talking less about your accomplishments. The less you say, the more likely it is that somebody will say something good about you. Second, you could compliment some of the players when they do well. That would mean a lot to them coming from you. And third, you could help the other players in the way I suggested."

George stared at the ground as if hoping it had the answer or at least would give him the courage to say yes. After a long pause, George raised his eyes and said, "Coach, I think I can do the first two. But do you think you could ask Todd to help me with the third? The other players like Todd. They'll listen better if we both do it. You know Todd is very good. I'm just a lot bigger."

Coach Bus extended his hand and said, "It's a deal, George."

George pumped Coach Bus's hand and said, "Thanks, Coach."

"One more thing, George … I'd like you to get straight with Kyle regarding your little exchange Tuesday. Can you do that?"

"We already did, Coach. Todd got us together before practice. Everything's cool. I'm not bragging anymore."

"Sounds good, George. This is going to be fun."

George trotted back to practice with a spring in his step. He proved capable of solving his own problem. Involving Todd was the key to making it work for George, Todd, and the team. None of the coaches thought of that approach, but George did. Next, Coaches Bus and Martynowicz discussed the project with the parents, who gave it their full support.

As this project progressed, George had some rough days, but he and Todd got better with time and experience. By the end of the season, George and Todd had improved their playing ability significantly and their students became "their kids." They even coached "their kids" in White team games on Monday night. As George got recognition for helping others, he had less to say about himself.

Once George knew what was expected, he was able to deliver with a little help from his coaches. Previously, his inconsistent behavior was due to his inexperience. He lacked the confidence for consistent behavior. When Coaches Bus and Martynowicz provided guidance, both boys leveraged the guidance, and delivered beyond their coaches' expectation. In addition, George's parents believed the experience contributed significantly to his overall sociability.

* * *

The practice sessions went well the week following the St. Francis game. The idea of "slipping back" became a mantra for high performance. If the players perceived a lack of effort, they would yell, "Are you slipping?" or "No slipping back!" or "Don't you be a-slippin on me."

At the end of Wednesday's practice, Kyle approached Coach Brown and said, "Coach, I've been working with Stewart like you asked and things are going good. But I don't think he'll ever run inside. And besides, that kind of grunt work is for Bobby, Billy, and me. I think Stewart should be one of our receivers. He can catch and I guess you know he's the fastest kid on the team. What do you think, Coach?"

"Our quarterbacks have improved a lot," said Coach Brown. "Dale and Kevin think we ought to throw more. What do you think?"

"I think we should and that's where Stewart can help. Nick, Ian, and the Schneider kid from the White team can also catch. I'm not giving up on him. But he can help get teams out of those eight-man lines we're starting to see. We can still spot him for sweeps and the wing-back reverse with George pulling."

"Good idea, Kyle. We'll put a couple of plays in for Sunday. Do you want to discuss it with your student?" said Coach Brown.

Kyle smiled and said, "I already did, Coach, and he likes it. I'll still work with him on how to take a hit."

"Kyle, one more thing ... Let's keep this increased passing idea to ourselves. You know how nervous Coach Cook gets when we throw the ball."

"Right, Coach. If Coach Cook thinks it's my idea, I might get extra laps," said Kyle with a smile.

"So, Kyle, do you want to be a coach someday?" asked Coach Brown with a smile.

"No thanks, Coach. I just want to play. Coaching makes me nervous, if you know what I mean."

After practice, Perry went to the special weigh-in. Although he'd worked hard, he weighed in at 141, one pound above the limit for skill players. Coach Brown tried to plead Perry's case, but to no avail.

Perry was very discouraged. This inflexibility was like so many other frustrating aspects of his life. The coaches explained to Perry he could come back next Wednesday, but would not be able to play on Sunday.

On the way home, Bobby tried to encourage his friend. "Perry, I think you ought to concentrate on nose-tackle. If you make the weight next Wednesday, you'd have to diet for the rest of the season because there's a weigh-in before playoffs. Nose is a good position for you."

Perry did not comment, but when Thursday arrived he approached Coach Brown and said, "Coach, I want to play nose. Bobby thinks it's a good position for me. There's a lot of hitting there, and I like that."

"Sounds good, Perry. I'll notify the league and we'll get you some playing time on Sunday."

Coach Brown looked at Coach Jerman and said, "Now, we're making progress."

* * *

On Sunday, the Redwings traveled to the city for their fifth game of the season against St. Rita. The Mustangs' record was 3–1. They had always been well coached and this year's team was no exception. The Redwings had another good week of practice, and were looking forward to the game.

After the team prayer, Coach Brown addressed the team.

"It's important to build your confidence as we have over the past eight weeks. As your confidence increases, you become a step faster physically and intellectually. You have accomplished this because of repetitions in practice. This may have been boring at times, but you were building muscle memory and internalizing your skills. We have emphasized all season to play free. There should be no fear of failure, because fear serves no useful purpose. It just limits your performance and growth."

Coach Brown had everybody's attention so he continued, "Your skills are there to whatever level achieved in practice. Today, let's just let those skills flow freely to the game we are about to play. Once the play starts, don't think about it. That will only inhibit the flow. Today we are just going to let it happen."

The Redwings took the field enthusiastically in quest of their fourth win of the season. As the game progressed, the Redwings played with increasing confidence, focus, and efficiency. Stewart scored on a fly pattern where he developed 15 yards of separation between himself and the defender. Kyle was quick to voice his opinion. "I told you, Coach. He's a natural wing. He's my man!"

Kyle scored on a draw play, and Mitch from the White team scored on a counter trap with a key block by Drew, one of "George's kids." St. Raphael led 24–0 near the end of the first half, when Perry nervously entered his first game at nose.

On the first and second plays Perry went high at the snap and was buried by a "two-time" block on both plays. After the second play, his opponent leaned on him getting up and gave a little shove. Perry got up frustrated, shoving his opponents, and had to be restrained by his teammates.

On the next play Perry went offside in an obvious attempt at retaliation. With that, Coach Brown sent Bobby into the game to talk to Perry as he didn't want to remove him from the game. It was important for Perry to work out his orientation on the field.

Perry looked to the sideline, expecting to be removed from the game. Coach Taylor called a defense that placed Perry in the gap between the guard and center as opposed to head-up on the center.

Perry got into his stance. Bobby reminded Perry of his technique: low man wins. His nose dropped to not more than six inches off the ground. Bobby leaned on his butt for good measure. The ball was snapped. Perry exploded out of his stance and crashed into the fullback, knocking him into the tailback, and they both went down in a heap.

As he got up, his teammates banged Perry on the helmet. You would have thought Perry made a game-saving stop instead of a tackle on the last play of the half of a 24–0 game. When he finally realized what had happened, he raised his arms as though in a Rocky movie and looked to the sidelines. As the half ended, the players jogged to the sidelines, except Perry.

Perry sprinted to the sidelines and proclaimed, "I'm psyched. I love this stuff."

The eighth graders smiled as Bobby said, "That's great, Perry. I think you just crossed Coach Brown's bridge to where football becomes fun." Bobby knew Perry might not be all the way across the bridge, but he had taken a big step, and he wasn't going to let him return.

As the season progressed, Perry improved as a football player and a person. His attitude toward school, his grades, and his overall social skills improved significantly. His schoolmates became aware he played for St. Raphael as Perry proudly wore his St. Raphael sweatshirt to school almost every day. His classmates thought it was quite an accomplishment for Perry to be a member of the team, given the apparent conflict between his reputation and that of the St. Raphael football program.

As he improved, he received more recognition from his peers. The more recognition he received, the more he grew. The more his confidence improved, the more his performance improved in school, on the football field, and in his life. The same vicious circle of personal experience that had driven him in the wrong direction was now propelling him down a road of unprecedented success.

* * *

When Coach Brown returned home after the game, he had an urgent telephone message to call one of the parents of a second grader in the in-house program. Coach Brown called and the parent explained how his team had been cheated out of a win and it ruined their undefeated season.

In the Mighty Mite in-house division, no ball carrier is allowed to carry the ball twice in a row. That is to prevent a single player's domination of a game, and it allows more players to carry the ball.

The parent explained on the last play of the game, the opposing coach had his best player carry the ball twice in a row, and he scored the winning touchdown. He said he called it to the referee's attention, but the referee hadn't noticed.

He said one of our parents offered to show the referees a video of the last two plays, but our coach refused and said it's only a game between seven-year-olds, and winning the game wasn't that important. It was a good game, the kids had a good time, and he wanted to join his kids before they devoured all of the treats.

The parent said his son was devastated by the loss of his undefeated season. Something had to be done to improve the refereeing in this league. He wanted the game to be declared a no-contest and not count in the standings. He also said the coaches should know the rules and be more aggressive in their enforcement.

Coach Brown listened with a few clarifying questions but without rebuttal. He then asked the parent to wait until about 7:00 PM and ask the child who won the game.

The parent was initially upset with the request, but agreed to run the experiment. He then added, "Do you want me to ask, or would you like to ask so you can hear the answer firsthand?" Coach Brown agreed to take his word for the child's response.

At about 6:30 PM, Coach Brown got a call from a very embarrassed parent who said, "I am so sorry. Johnny's grandfather called a few minutes ago. My son told him about the tackle he almost made, the oranges at halftime, getting a star on his helmet, a big bump on his hand that doesn't hurt anymore, treats after the game, and his cowboy uniform that looked just like the pros. During the conversation, his grandfather asked him who won the game. I guess you already know he had no idea who won. I think you also know who was devastated by the loss and who was not able to put it in perspective.

"Oh, yes, my wife wants you to know both she and Johnny have things in perspective and she wasn't home when I called you. I probably would not have been allowed to call and embarrass myself if she had been home. You won't have any more trouble with me. Thank you for the lesson learned."

The discussion with the parent proved to be an entertaining interlude as Coach Brown approached one of the most trying weeks of the season.

PLAY NUMBER TWENTY

Listening is one of the most powerful motivational tools available to those in leadership positions. Perhaps, even more valuable than effective speaking. Most leaders are effective because they have built positive relationships with those they're leading. There's no better way to do this than to listen empathetically. Empathetic listening means trying to understand both what the person is saying and feeling from the other person's perspective. In order to be an empathetic listener one must do as Stephen Covey suggests in his best-seller, *The Seven Habits of Highly Successful People*. He says, "A person must first seek first to understand, then to be understood."

21
The Suspension

"We've had boys who've served suspensions in the past. The solution to your problem is easy because it's totally within your control. I understand from your parents you're both smart and have done well on your standardized tests. All you have to do to get good grades is do your homework. If you don't know the answers, just ask your parents or refer to your resource books or the Internet. If your homework is 25% of your grade, you control 25% of your grade at A or close to it." Coach Brown winked at the moms, who had "sock-it-to-them" grins on their faces. They were enjoying this more than a spa treatment.

WEEK NINE OF THE SEASON GOT OFF TO A GOOD start with a White team come-from-behind victory over a strong team from Batavia. Matt and Mike played well. Several other players, including Dan, Mikie, Blake, Brady, and Chris, an emerging quarterback, also played well.

However, there was some bad news. Billy showed up to watch the White team on crutches with a broken ankle. Coach Brown was puzzled, as Billy finished the game on Sunday with no apparent injury.

Billy sheepishly approached Coach Brown and said, "Coach, I injured my ankle in gym class. It's just a small crack. I'll be out four to six weeks. I figure I'll be back for the championship game."

Coach Brown inquired, "How'd you do it?"

"Some kid was chasing me. We were just having fun and I stepped in a hole," replied Billy. "It's not as bad as it looks."

After Billy joined the others on the sideline, Kyle approached Coach Brown and said, "Isn't that unreal about Billy? He plays football for seven years without an injury and his girlfriend breaks his ankle."

Coach Brown asked with an inquisitive expression, "What? How'd it happen?"

"Billy broke up with his girlfriend and she chased him, trying to hit him with her backpack, and he turned his ankle. Didn't he just tell you about it?"

"He told me he stepped in a hole on the playground when a kid was chasing him. So, I guess he did," said Coach Brown. "Things are starting to follow form. In the history of St. Raphael Football we've had three times as many players miss games due to off-the-field injuries than on. Parents can't believe it when I tell them their children are safer on the football field than anyplace else."

"Don't tell Billy I gave you the details. He'll be ticked. I thought he told you," said Kyle.

"Okay, I don't need to know the details. Anything else going on I should know about?"

"No, Coach," said Kyle as he ran away as quickly as possible.

* * *

That evening, Coach Brown got a call from George's mom and Greg's dad. Midterm grades were sent home and both boys were performing well below family standards. Both parents had decided to hold the boys out of football in order to get their attention and allow more time for study. Both parents requested Coach Brown to talk to the boys at practice on Tuesday.

On Tuesday, the boys arrived at practice accompanied by their moms. They had been schooled in how to notify their coach of their suspensions. They indicated they were behind in a couple of subjects and their homework had been late and substandard. With coaxing from their moms, they vowed to do their homework and do better on their tests. When they finished, they said they were sorry and started to leave, relieved that this uncomfortable ordeal was over.

Coach Brown asked, "Wait a minute. Do you remember your commitment at our goal-setting session? One of them was to finish your homework before practice so there'd be no suspensions. This week we play St. Monica. They are undefeated and will be one of the teams we must beat to be champions."

The boys nodded their heads in unison.

"We've had boys who've served suspensions in the past. The solution to your problem is easy because it's totally within your control. I understand from your parents you're both smart and have done well on your standardized tests. All you have to do to get good grades is do your homework. If you don't know the answers, just ask your parents or refer to your resource books or the Internet. If your homework is 25% of your grade, you control 25% of your grade at A or close to it."

Coach Brown winked at the moms, who had "sock-it-to-them" grins on their faces. They were enjoying this more than a spa treatment.

"So, follow me here. If you do your homework well, do you think it'll be easier to study for the tests? ... and get a better grade?"

The boys nodded again.

"So, if doing your homework well is totally within your control, then getting good grades is also within your control. So there's no reason not to do your homework. Wouldn't it be great if we had that much control over the outcome of the game on Sunday?"

The boys smiled a little and nodded again.

"I have a story for you," said Coach Brown. "This will help you see the value of good grades and the consequences of bad grades. Let's sit down. This may take a few minutes. Gary was a boy who played for one of our football teams several years ago. He was an outstanding player and a natural leader. All the kids looked up to him, even when he was a seventh grader. His coach stayed in touch by going to his football games and continued as a role model for the boy after he went to high school. All through grade school, Gary's parents and this coach tried to get him to work to his full potential academically. He always said he'd try, but there was always something that got in the way. Even missing football games didn't get his attention. Nothing worked. In high school, Gary was recommended for a leadership camp scholarship. His coach wrote an extensive recommendation. Gary did not win the scholarship and he wrote his coach the following letter."

Coach Brown took a wrinkled piece of paper from his playbook and began to read.

> Dear Coach,
>
> Sounds like things are going well for you. I'm happy to hear that. Thanks for asking about the camp. I apologize about not getting back to you sooner. Well, unfortunately I didn't make it. I knew going in my grades were probably going to hold me back, and well they did just that. So there was definitely something to learn from that. I have been taking it as a positive experience. Since then my grades have improved, because I know that I have all of the potential to go on to greater things in life, but your first priority has to be your grades.
>
> Thanks again for your excellent recommendation. I can't stress enough how much I appreciate the time you put into that. I'll make sure that I keep you up to date on all the news with my grades and football.

"Gary's coach wrote the following letter in hopes of helping him achieve his goal of improving his grades."

Gary,

I'm sorry you didn't win the scholarship to the camp. However, this could be a blessing in disguise. For some time your parents, teachers, and I have tried to convince you achieving the best grades possible was very important. The reason we have all made this effort is because we care about you and your future.

We all see in you exactly what I wrote in my recommendation and in the case of your parents and teachers even more. I hope you will read the recommendation often and utilize it as a source of strength and motivation for achieving the level of determination required to do something much more important and difficult, getting the best grades possible. This isn't going to be easy because you've not worked at it the way you have worked at becoming the person I described in the recommendation. The person I described in the recommendation is also partially the result of natural talent. When you redirect your efforts to getting good grades you may find this isn't going to come as easy as some of your other accomplishments, such as learning to play football or improving your bench. But it's far more important. Although getting good grades is going to be very difficult, you are very fortunate to be the person I described in the recommendation. Because the strengths and values you applied to becoming that person are the same as those required to achieve your academic objectives. You are also very fortunate to have a tremendous support system around you. It will be important to utilize it in your quest for excellent grades. But, in the final analysis, it's up to YOU.

In order to achieve it you'll have to make it your number-one priority and develop a passion and a routine for doing whatever's necessary to achieve your goal. You'll have to endure the same pain as two-a-days, maybe more. At times you'll be as discouraged as when you lose to Central or when we lost to St. Mary's. But if you overcome this adversity you'll not be the same person. You'll be a stronger person. And this strength will help you achieve this goal and many others. So Gary, I'm going to end with a story. You know how I love to tell stories.

Once upon a time in a faraway land, there was a boy who was good looking, a good athlete, had a lot of friends, including girls, and people liked him, even his teachers. This boy sailed into high school with huge expectations. He was still good looking, quarterback on an undefeated football team, had more friends, especially girls, and people liked him, even most of his teachers. So this immensely popular boy decided to run for class president. Much to his surprise he lost badly to a boy who was a good athlete (tailback), of average looks and a nice person, had friends including a steady girlfriend, and excellent grades. The quarterback asked one of his best friends why he'd lost to John. His friend answered, "Even though I'm your best friend, I voted for John because I think he'd make a better president. He's an all-A student." So the quarterback went to work and improved his grades from a few B's and C's to mostly A's and a few B's. He stayed a nice person with lots of friends, including girls, got better looking, and people liked him, even his teachers. At the senior awards ceremony, John won the Walters Award that went to the best student athlete. But, our friend the nice, good-looking quarterback with lots of friends including girls and teachers was a close second. Good luck, Gary.

I know you're serious and I'm looking forward to my next e-mail about your progress. PS When you get a little discouraged, read this e-mail. It might help. I like your handle RedBull78. You were all of those things at St. Raphael.

"A few weeks later, Gary's coach received the following letter from Gary's mom."

Dear Coach,

I'm sorry it has taken me so long to thank you for your wonderful letter. I tried to call you several times, but each time I called I started to cry because I am so moved by what you've done for my son. He has framed the letter and your recommendation and put them on his desk in his room. I'm sure he looks at them every day. Gary has started to study more, and has allowed us to help him more frequently with his studies. It has become a family project and an excellent vehicle for enhancing our relationship with Gary. We used to limit our enjoyable discussions to sports because when we went into other areas, he seemed to become uninterested and would not fully participate. Discussions about studies seemed to have opened up a whole new vista of important topics we were dying to discuss, but were previously off-limits. You have a gift for helping children. I know you have helped several others. I know you get a lot of satisfaction from it. But, no level of satisfaction measures up to the impact you have had on Gary and others. Gary's in the process of writing you an e-mail. I believe he is having difficulty with the words. He wants it to be just right. I hope he lets us see it. When I see you, I hope Gary's not around, because I am going to give you a big hug. Even though Gary has made a lot of progress, I don't think he's ready to see his mom hug his favorite coach. I will call you soon.

Kathy

"Now, get out of here and we'll see you Sunday. Your parents said it'd be okay to dress, but not play or practice until your school performances improve. You guys know you've not fulfilled your commitment to the team. They may want to talk to you about that when you return."

The boys nodded and agreed to work hard at earning reinstatement to the team.

The moms thanked Coach Brown and said, "I think the boys expected a reprieve. Thanks for putting first things first. We'll work with them to get them back as soon as we can."

"I think you're making the right decision," said Coach Brown. "Too many parents are uncomfortable with tough love. They let things pass and stick up for their kids even when they're wrong. This is an opportunity to teach a life lesson. I'm glad you took it. ... And it's also an opportunity to support them in their effort to return to the team."

"Coach, how'd this boy turn out?" asked one of the moms.

"He turned out great. He earned a Division 1 football scholarship and started for his team. He graduated and has a good job," said Coach Brown proudly. "The job's so good, he paid for my lunch the other day and is taking me to a Cubs game this summer. He said he had great seat connections."

The rest of Tuesday night's practice went well. The players were excited about playing St. Monica since they had been their chief rival since 1969. Nobody had kept track of the win/loss record over the 50-game history, but it was close to an even split. The players weren't aware of the details, but folklore about the rivalry had been exaggerated many times as it was passed from one team to the next.

The Redwings beat St. Monica twice last year on their way to the finals. This would be a significant motivator for the 2008 team.

The Redwings would be short-handed, but this would give several White team members a chance to play. This game had play-off implications, especially for the Redwings, since teams with two losses seldom made the playoffs. The Redwings' strength of schedule, however, would be helpful as a tie-breaker.

 PLAY NUMBER TWENTY-ONE
As coaches teach, they often validate by asking their players what they think about what they just learned, how they can improve, what plays are working best, etc. Coaches find that listening will enhance their relationship with their players because it demonstrates respect. If coaches listen, the children listen because coaches are their role models. When coaches listen, they also find out whether their players understand their teachings long before the opening game.

22
Another Suspension

That evening, Coach Brown got a call from Sarah. She opened the conversation quickly. "You can't believe what's been going on since practice. I'm getting calls from several parents including the girl's parents, who are saying I should let Kyle play and find another way to punish him. They're saying why punish the team for what Kyle did. They don't care what I do to him as long as he plays. Kyle's also getting calls with the same suggestion. And of course, he's loving it. My husband's on a business trip and I think he's hinting in support of them. What do you think?"

ON WEDNESDAY, AS THE TEAM HAD COMPLETED ITS warm-up exercises, Coach Kelly asked, "Did anybody get a call from Kyle?" All the coaches shook their heads no.

Coach Kelly flipped open his cell, called Kyle's mother, listened carefully, flipped the phone shut, and said to the other coaches, "We've got a problem. Kyle's mother is on her way to the field to explain. We may not have Kyle on Sunday."

About twenty minutes later Kyle's mom, Sarah, approached the coaching staff. Her eyes were red with emotion, but there was anger and disappointment in her expression.

"Guys, I'll give you the bottom line. Kyle's grounded indefinitely. I came home early from work, and found him and his high school girlfriend drinking in his room. I've checked the liquor supply in our locked cabinet and there's quite a bit missing. Some bottles are watered down. I haven't assessed the extent of the problem, but Dave and I will over the next few days. He will not play on Sunday. Kyle told me you're playing St. Monica and you're a little short, but we can't let this pass. I hope you understand."

Coach Brown said, "We do! It'll be important to define the extent of the problem, and then make sure there are no long-term ramifications. Sarah, please keep us informed to the extent necessary and we'll help any way we can. We had this situation a few years ago and it worked out fine. When you get things sorted out, give me a call."

"I will, Coach," Sarah replied. "Thanks for your understanding. This afternoon, I discussed the situation with a couple of parents who suggested I ground him after the St. Monica game. But I can't do that. I hope you understand."

"We do," said Coach Brown. "Kyle's health is far more important than any game. His football participation must be considered only when it's part of the solution. He's come a long way this season in non-football areas. Maybe his development in these areas will help him deal with his problem."

"Thanks, Coach. I'll stay in touch."

That evening, Coach Brown got a call from Sarah. She opened the conversation quickly. "You can't believe what's been going on since practice. I'm getting calls from several parents including the girl's parents, who are saying I should let Kyle play and find another way to punish him. They're saying why punish the team for what Kyle did. They don't care what I do to him as long as he plays. Kyle's also getting calls with the same suggestion. And of course, he's loving it. My husband's on a business trip and I think he's hinting in support of them. What do you think?"

"Sarah, I sense from the watered-down bottles, this is not the first time," said Coach Brown.

"That's right. I talked turkey with Kyle and he said they've been drinking since school started. He met Megan in his advanced math class at Central. He's even been to a couple of high school parties where there was liquor."

"Do you think withholding football is your best chance of getting his attention?"

"Yes!" responded Sarah. "I don't have much else to work with. You can't beat a kid today. They'll throw you in jail."

"Then, I think we should take this opportunity. I'm working with three past players right now who are suffering the consequences of excessive drinking. The first was expelled from his high school football team and school for multiple DUIs. Another boy almost lost his life in an automobile accident. The third football player, I accompanied to AA. That was an eye-opener. I think you have to play your best cards now in order to try to prevent bigger problems in the future," said Coach Brown.

"Ok, I'll stay with the plan. I'll ground him indefinitely. Maybe you can help me emphasize the seriousness of what he's done. Can you tell him about the kids you're working with? Let's see what kind of progress he makes. Maybe you can have him back if he responds well and the team makes the playoffs."

"Yes, I'd be happy to meet with Kyle. Let's discuss how my meeting with him can be integrated into a total plan for impressing Kyle about the consequences of excessive drinking."

* * *

On Thursday night, Coach Brown discussed Kyle's situation with the team. There was very little reaction. Some of the players acted as though they knew about Kyle before his parents. They understood the grounding and a couple of players expressed their disappointment in Kyle, for letting the team down. They also expressed their enthusiasm for beating St. Monica on Sunday. But the coaches knew they were just going through the motions.

Near the end of practice, Coach Brown called the team together as usual, but tonight was going to be different. He said, "Coach Taylor has a special announcement to make."

Coach Taylor began to announce the starting defense for the St. Monica game. When he got to nose-tackle he said, "As you all know, Perry's worked hard since joining the team. You all have helped him get better. On Sunday, due to his hard work, he'll start at nose."

When he announced Perry's name, Perry stood motionless, not knowing what to do. Brian, one of the captains, began a staccato clap and the rest of the team joined in. The players recognized the importance of the moment. Bobby put his arm around Perry and whispered something in his ear. Then, Bobby and Perry walked to their position for the walk-through. Perry got down on one knee, which was the custom, but had to put his head down in order to hide his emotions. Bobby put his hand on Perry's shoulder to steady this rough, tough boy from the city who was shaking with emotion and said, "Man, I can only guess what this means to you."

Mike and Marie called that evening to express their feelings about this evening and the last six weeks. Mike began by saying, "You will never know the significance of the past six weeks in Perry's life. His football experience broke a death spiral. One bad experience was providing fuel for the next. Perry had no hope. He felt he was a victim. And, he thought he had no personal resources to stem the tide of defeat and discouragement. Originally, our objective was to just slow things down a little, so he could stay out of juvenile and the experts could start the reversal process. We thought football might help. We didn't expect it to be the solution."

Marie, who was on the second line, broke in and said, "But fortunately, Perry was provided with a defining fork in the road of his life. He was given a choice of a football team or a youth home. Fortunately, there were people near Perry who helped define his choices and assume the risk associated with driving him toward the right choice. That has not been easy for Perry. I think he'll have some setbacks. But, I think he's beginning to believe he has some personal resources for solving his own problems."

Mike continued, "Perry is very nervous about Sunday. On the way home, he went from expressing feelings of confidence and high expectations to all that goes with the fear of failure. I believe his salvation this weekend will be your comment about 'not starting him if you didn't think he was ready.' I think we'll be quoting you quite often this weekend. Bobby also told him, the nice thing about playing nose is it's simple, and a nose never won or lost a game. We can't wait until Sunday."

"We can't either," said Coach Brown. But, as he reviewed the scouting report relative to the depleted Redwing resources, he knew it would be a long afternoon.

PLAY NUMBER TWENTY-TWO

St. Raphael coaches explain to their players early and often that they plan to create a learning environment in which they will teach fundamentals until everybody understands; plan to use positive reinforcement only; support those who do not understand right away; expect all players to treat one another with respect; and focus on the continuous improvement of all members of the team. The least experienced players must learn the most for a team to be successful. Let them know there will be adversity and the best players will make dealing with adversity a developmental experience.

23
St. Monica 40, St. Raphael 6

Now, with three minutes left in the game, the referees called a time-out. One referee went to the St. Monica sideline to encourage their coach to play his second string since the St. Raphael first string had been on the sidelines for over seven minutes. The other three members of the crew came to the St. Raphael sideline and told the Redwing coaching staff their team had demonstrated the best sportsmanship they had ever seen in their 30 years of refereeing games at any level. Bobby was singled out as one of the best sportsmen they had ever seen as he continued to say "nice run" and "good hit" as he took his beating and never gave in. The head referee said, "Tell him what we said." Coach Jerman looked at Bobby as he sat dejected on the bench and said, "Why don't you tell him yourself? I think he could use a lift about now."

SUNDAY DAWNED A BEAUTIFUL DAY FOR FOOTBALL as the team traveled to the St. Monica Crusaders field. But as Coach Jerman had said for many years, "There's no such thing as a bad day for football."

The coaches tried to keep the players loose, but they knew they were in for a tough day without six key players. Just before leaving for the game, the coaches were notified Garrett, the left tackle, would also miss the game because of the flu. Bobby was also sick from either the stomach flu or the game flu, knowing he would be the primary ball carrier with Kyle and Billy on the sidelines.

The St. Monica team was imposing. Each lineman stood 5'10 or better and over 150 pounds. Their backs were all over 130 pounds and their best running back, O'Malley, was sporting a week-long growth of facial hair.

As the kickoff approached, the coaches could see Perry was nervous as he paced the sidelines. The offense took the field first and moved the ball successfully, but was forced to punt. Nick punted the ball 50 yards and it was downed by Riley at the St. Monica 3-yard line. The defense enthusiastically took the field.

On the first play, Coach Taylor called a "gap-eight." This defense called for eight players on the line of scrimmage with all of them in a gap. Perry was located between the right guard and center. The St. Monica quarterback called the play on a long, uneven cadence. As he did, Perry, being a little over-anxious, jumped offside.

As the St. Monica players clapped, the referee walked off the penalty to the 8-yard line. Perry got up, banged his hands on his helmet, made apologies to his teammates, and got ready for the next play. He didn't look to the sidelines. He didn't shove an opposing player. He didn't even appear discouraged.

One the next play, he was in the gap again. This time he came across low and hard. He hit the fullback just as he took the handoff, causing a fumble. The fumble was recovered by Todd at the Crusader 6-yard line.

As Perry and his teammates ran confidently off the field, the coaches knew he had taken another step across the bridge to a new and better life both on and off the field. His football experience had served as a vehicle for initiating an environment of self-discovery. What Perry discovered, he liked. For one of the few times in his life, he was proud of himself. He was proud of what he had accomplished. This feeling originated from far more than making a single tackle behind the line of scrimmage. It was the feeling of positive self-esteem that went deep, to his very soul. He could feel his emotional fuel tank being filled with gallons of self-confidence that he could transfer to other parts of his life.

On this day, he didn't know exactly where he was going, but he knew for the first time he enjoyed looking forward to his future. He knew the burden of his past would be with him for some time. But instead of pulling him down, it would be only an ever-diminishing impediment to a bright future. Perry breathed a sigh of relief, signifying not only the end of his first defensive series as a St. Raphael starter, but his first few steps toward a more productive life.

Unfortunately, the rest of the game was not as positive. St. Monica held St. Raphael at the 2-yard line. Then, they moved the ball relentlessly to score four touchdowns before halftime.

In the third quarter, the Crusaders showed no mercy as they scored twice for a 40–0 lead and a running clock. The Redwings played hard, but they were overmatched without six key starters and injuries to three additional starters during the game. The team, however, grew individually and as a team. They played their hardest, never complained, and never gave up.

Stewart took his hits without fumbling, had to be removed from the game, but clamored to return. Jeff played tough on defense. Mark, Blake, Mike, and Matt all fought hard and made significant strides toward becoming eighth graders. Perry continued to battle and improved every play. He served as a role-model of toughness and class as St. Monica pounded him play after play, as they ran the ball inside. Unfortunately, Mike and Danny, the 90-pound corners, had to make 15 tackles between them. Bobby took the worst beating of all as he carried the ball over 20 times for only 42 yards. Brady emerged from the White team as a tough replacement for Kyle on defense.

Coach Brown put in the White team to start the fourth quarter. St. Monica kept six defensive starters on the field. It was obvious they wanted a shutout. On the first play of the fourth quarter,

St. Monica put nine players in the box and gang-tackled 90-pound Mikie, from the White team, for no gain. Mark, the White team tailback, was stuffed for no gain and got up slowly, waving "I'm all right" to the sidelines. Coach Brown sent Brian, Todd, Bobby, and Perry back into the game to give the White team running backs some protection while they ran out the clock.

On third down, Danny, who played quarterback in the fourth grade, entered the game. Harrison went to tailback. Danny called the play "Brown Bomber on two."

The Redwings came out of the huddle, with looks of disbelief, then smiles on their faces. They had practiced this play for weeks. It was intended for a critical game situation. Now they would use it in the most unlikely of circumstances.

It was a St. Raphael tradition for players to bring plays to practice. If the Redwings scored on the play, it was named after them forever. This was Danny's play and he was going to attempt putting his name in the Redwing playbook forever. They had to make it work.

When St. Raphael snapped the ball, the Crusaders had nine players within a few yards of the line of scrimmage. Danny took the snap and pitched the ball to Harrison going right. He was the player with the best arm. After he pitched the ball, Danny circled left end and went straight down the field. St. Monica was so intent on crushing the Redwing back, they didn't see diminutive Danny head up the field.

Once Danny was in the clear, Harrison threw him the ball just as he was buried under a host of Crusaders. Danny caught the ball, bobbled it, then took it to the end zone. As he crossed the goal line he was flattened by a Crusader tackler. Danny came quickly to his feet, handed the ball to his frustrated tackler, and ran off the field as though he had made a game-winning touchdown. The shutout was gone. The St. Monica coach threw his playbook to the ground in disgust. The Redwings celebrated. Matt did his disgusting dance as he possessed no rhythm whatsoever. It was better that way.

After the ensuing kickoff, St. Raphael cleared its bench. Bobby and the others had lived up to all the stickers on their helmets. They played hard, did their best, never gave up, and showed no fear.

Bobby took the beating particularly hard. He was seated alone, towel over his head, probably hiding the impact of mental and physical exhaustion. He had grown tremendously this season and, with Kyle and Billy on the sidelines, felt a self-imposed pressure to carry the team.

Bobby was normally soft spoken, but had grown to lead his team by example on and off the field. He had an unlimited willingness to help and support others. He never said, "Hey look at me" and was embarrassed when others reminded him of his accomplishments. When he walked, his shoulders were always stooped, his gait slow and deliberate as he tried hard to just blend into his environment and ignore the responsibility he knew was his.

The pressure of this responsibility grew and finally boiled over just before the game as he experienced stomach cramps. His condition was compounded by how it had affected the rest of the team's preparation. Coach Jerman had seen this before and terminated the pregame routine early. He called Bobby and the team to the middle of the field and reminded them of what had gotten them to this game.

When the game started, two or three St. Monica players shadowed Bobby everywhere he went. Bobby battled and his team fought but they took a beating that October afternoon.

Now, with three minutes left in the game, the referees called a time-out. One referee went to the St. Monica sideline to encourage their coach to play his second string since the St. Raphael first string had been on the sidelines for over seven minutes. The other three members of the crew came to the St. Raphael sideline and told the Redwing coaching staff their team had demonstrated the best sportsmanship they had ever seen in their 30 years of refereeing games at any level. Bobby was singled out as one of the best sportsmen they had ever seen as he continued to say "nice run" and "good hit" as he took his beating and never gave in. The head referee said, "Tell him what we said."

Coach Jerman looked at Bobby as he sat dejected on the bench and said, "Why don't you tell him yourself? I think he could use a lift about now."

So, the referees held up the game while they walked to the bench where Bobby was sitting, blood running down his arm and an ice pack on his ankle. He had a towel over his head to hide his disappointment and probably his tears. The referees talked to him for more than a minute. Each referee shook his hand. Bobby could not say a word as he was too overcome by the emotional conflict between the agony of defeat and the pride he felt from a possible life-defining moment.

When the referees returned to the game, Bobby stood alone, not knowing what to do or say. He made eye contact with Coach Brown and he could see he was equally moved by the experience. He and Coach Brown walked toward one another and gave each other a hug that lasted a minute or more. As they hugged they could feel one another's emotion. At the end of the hug, Bobby and Coach Brown looked each other in the eye, unashamed of the emotion they displayed.

You see today, the coaching staff reaffirmed that when they coached they grew to love and respect their players. And when that happened, the coaches realized more than ever why they coached and why they and their players have such a profound and lasting impact on one another.

PLAY NUMBER TWENTY-THREE

One of my past players called me the other night to discuss his nine-year-old daughter's performance in a gymnastics meet. She had difficulty with her first two events, falling twice on the bars and vault. She then had a choice. She could pack it in, or deal with the adversity and try to do her best for the rest of the meet. She chose to do her best and did. The next morning, her father complimented her on her comeback and did not focus on her mistakes. He talked about how this experience will make her stronger in the future. She smiled and said, "Daddy, I can't wait for practice next week. I know I can fix my vault and bars." Later that month at a meet, she finished third on the bars and the beam with personal bests.

24
Dealing with Defeat

Coach Brown began. "We're so proud of you! Everybody on this team lived and played by the stickers on their helmets. We lost a game to a better team today, but you all grew so much." Coach Brown paused to allow his opening comments to sink in as he made eye contact with each player, then continued, "You may not realize it, but we're all better off for this experience. Everybody got better today, including your coaches. We found out how good we've got to be to be champions. More importantly, we discovered our hearts and they are huge. You all did your best, so you shouldn't feel bad about losing. Yeah, I know that's easy for me to say. I wasn't the one taking the hits."

THE COACHES BROUGHT A TIRED, BEATEN, BUT unbowed bunch of Redwings to the center of the field for a final word. The team took a knee while Coach Brown stood in the middle of the circle of players, cradling the head of a sobbing player against his leg. He paused to collect himself as he looked into the eyes of his players, who had given all they had but experienced a crushing 40–6 defeat. They wondered if the coaching staff would recognize their effort or be upset with them because of the score.

Coach Brown began. "We're so proud of you! Everybody on this team lived and played by the stickers on their helmets. We lost a game to a better team today, but you all grew so much."

Coach Brown paused to allow his opening comments to sink in as he made eye contact with each player, then continued, "You may not realize it, but we're all better off for this experience. Everybody got better today, including your coaches. We found out how good we've got to be to be champions. More importantly, we discovered our hearts and they are huge. You all did your best, so you shouldn't feel bad about losing. Yeah, I know that's easy for me to say. I wasn't the one taking the hits."

Coach Brown paused as a few members of the team laughed a little, then he continued. "About twenty years ago, we had a season record of 0–7–1. Our team was outscored about 250 to 25. It was our worst record ever, but Coach Jerman and I will never forget that team and the effort they put forth, especially in the final game of the season. Just like we'll never forget the effort you all gave today."

Coach Brown looked at Coach Jerman as he nodded his head in agreement. "That team had only seventeen players, had lost all their games, and had to play an undefeated team their last game of the season. It was raining and about 35 degrees when their coach called and asked for a forfeit. I agreed to cancel the game but would not agree to a forfeit. They wanted the forfeit to enhance their winning streak, which had grown to forty games over the past four seasons."

The players became increasingly attentive as today's game slipped further into the past, so Coach Brown continued. "So, the St. Thomas team of 50 players made the 60-mile trip to our field of mud for the game.

"On the opening kickoff, the St. Thomas runner fumbled. It was caught in mid-air by Kevin and he ran it in for a score. The score stayed that way as neither team could move the ball in the ankle-deep mud and snow. But, the Redwings got tired in the fourth quarter, and St. Thomas scored with two minutes left in the game. They tried to run for the extra point, but failed by inches ... with a little help from the referees."

Brian interrupted, "Is that why you hired Dr. Death ... I mean Coach Cook?" Everybody laughed, even Coach Cook.

Coach Brown smiled at Coach Jerman as he enjoyed the memory of the game. "Their coach was so angry, he wouldn't join his team for the handshake after the game. The league suspended him the following year.

"So, enjoy your effort, your improvement, and come to practice on Tuesday ready to continue our preparation for the championship game. I think we can beat these guys."

As Coach Brown and Coach Jerman left the field for their cars, Blake's father, Rick, stopped them and said, "I would like to thank you guys for coaching our kids the way you do. Thanks for being so calm, cool, and collected through the ups and downs of this season. You set such a good example for these kids, it'll be a life lesson. I thought Blake would be more disappointed with the loss today. I think Sue and I felt worse than he did because we're feeling for ourselves and our child.

"But Blake had enough maturity to help us deal with our disappointment. Can you believe that? Today, he was the teacher and we were the students. I think you guys ought to know you're getting through to these kids. When I talk to Blake, I have no idea if he's heard or cared about a word I've said. Today, Blake told us it was the most fun game he'd ever played, because the game was played with such intensity and at such a high level. He said he did his best and so did everybody else. He said it was his best game of the year. He got more playing time today because of the missing starters. He said he did all he could to win the game."

Rick paused to check on his family, then continued, "I could see the kids coming to the team huddle after the game, not knowing what to expect. They knew the coaches wanted this game badly, because of a 50-year rivalry they knew little about. I could see some of the boys crying. They were all looking to you guys to say something to make them feel better. I thought to myself, I wouldn't trade places with you guys for a million bucks. You took the boys to the middle of the field where they could unwind in relative privacy. However, we could see you were cradling the head of a sobbing player against your thigh and had your other hand on a bowed head of another player. Sometime I would love to hear what you said to them, because in five minutes they went from what they thought was the worst day of their lives to laughter, a cheer, and a proud walk off the field."

Rick paused to wave at his son, who was obviously worried about his father's extended conversation with his coaches. Then, he continued, "That cheer was punctuated by handshakes, helmet bangs, and head slaps all around. It seemed as though these boys didn't even bother to wipe away their tears. They almost wore them as a badge of courage, evidence of a day that almost measured up to their expectations even though they lost 40–6."

Lou stepped forward, thanked Rick, and said, "I can't remember everything we said, but I'll tell you this. When you talk to the kids after an experience like that, you can't try to introduce new concepts. All you can do is remind them of something they already know or feel as the result of their past experience. You can only help them organize their thoughts. They must have internalized the basics of your talk to be effective." Lou paused and looked at Coach Brown to see if he had anything to add, then continued, "We reminded the boys, if you work hard and give everything you've got in practice and games, you'll win every game you're entitled to win and some you aren't. If you do your best and lose, knowing you did your best helps you deal with the loss. The loss, originally thought to be a failure, is put into perspective by knowing you did your best. That's an accomplishment in itself and far more significant than a loss you couldn't control."

Rick shook his head and said, "Lou, those are great points. Thanks again for coaching our kids ... and one final comment. Blake thinks they can beat St. Monica if they meet again in the playoffs. That's amazing. They just got beat 40–6. I guess I better keep the faith."

* * *

On Monday night, the White team played well as they defeated Batavia Red 20–7. Several players excelled even though they were a little tired from their Sunday experience.

For support, the whole Red team attended and worked out before the game. The coaching staff was surprised and pleased as Red team attendance at White team games was optional.

Coach Brown asked Todd, "How'd this practice get organized? Did I call it on Sunday in the heat of the moment?"

"No, Coach. Kyle called us. I think his mom put him up to it. But it was a good idea. We got a lot done, didn't we, Brian?"

"Yeah, Coach," said Brian. "I think we ought to practice every Monday without the coaches. I think we did some good stuff. I can tell you one thing, we'll beat St. Monica next time if we get a chance. A lot of other guys on the team think so too. I figure with two losses we're going to need some help making the playoffs. I went through some scenarios with my dad."

"Did you tell the team about your scenarios?" asked Coach Brown.

"Yeah, Coach. Most of them don't get it," said Brian. "So we're just going to win our last two games and see what happens."

"That sounds good, guys. I think the Monday practice is a good idea too. I'll get a trainer and one of the coaches to be there but not involved. Okay?"

Todd asked, "Will Kyle be able to participate? He really feels bad about letting the team down."

"We're going to talk tonight. But I don't think he'll be back until the playoffs," said Coach Brown.

"George and Greg will be back for the last game, and I see Garrett's here tonight. Billy's also doing well, and his parents think he might return for the playoffs if we get there. But we've got to get there first."

 ### PLAY NUMBER TWENTY-FOUR

St. Raphael coaches also encourage all the coaches and players to do their best during practice and games. Because, if everybody does their best, the team will win every game they should and a few that they shouldn't. They also tell the children, if they do their best they should not feel bad about losing a game. This approach to winning reduces the amount of unnecessary pressure and permits the children to play freely and positively, thus achieving higher levels of performance. If the children know they're playing in a risk-free environment, they'll learn faster and perform better because there's no fear of failure. Failure doesn't exist for anyone who knows they did their best. This even applies to coaches who may not sleep too well as they second-guess themselves about their play calling in the fourth quarter of that big game last Saturday.

25
A Developmental Discussion

All of us approach many forks in the road throughout our lives. You are at one now. You could take one road, which leads to becoming a Joe. You could take the other road, which leads to a Ryan. Your coaches, parents, and friends will not always be able to direct you down the right road. You'll have to make many choices on your own. You'll make some more mistakes, as you did the other day. Your parents and I are trying to teach you to make the right choices by making you aware of the consequences of the wrong choices. There are also rewards when you make the right choice.

AS THE WHITE TEAM GAME CONCLUDED, KYLE and his parents arrived at the shelter near the north end of the park. Coach Brown greeted Kyle and his parents and said, "Kyle, I think your organization of the informal practice was good. That's an example of the type of leadership we discussed earlier in the season." By the look on Sarah and Dave's faces, they knew nothing of the practice.

As previously discussed with Sarah, Coach Brown and Kyle walked to the other side of the shelter for a private discussion. Kyle and Coach Brown sat across from one another.

Kyle nervously opened the discussion, "Coach, I'm sorry for what I did and how I let the team down. Todd said they took a pretty good beating on Sunday, especially the White team guys. He said they played real tough, but St. Monica's good. Guess they ran up the score a little."

"Yes, the team missed you and the others who were suspended and injured. Do you know what the team missed most from you?" asked Coach Brown.

"Well I'm a two-way player. I run the ball a lot and make a lot of tackles," said Kyle.

"That's not it. What they missed most was your leadership," said Coach Brown. "Once you became the leader of the team, the players grow to depend on you for leadership. Once you assume leadership there's no time off. You must be a consistent leader. It's a big part of a team's success. Do you understand, Kyle? You must fulfill that responsibility."

"Yes, I think so, Coach. You mean I can't do things that get me suspended, because the team needs me to be a leader."

"That's right, Kyle. It's especially bad for the leader to do something like that because as a leader you're also a role model. If you drink, your teammates think it's cool. If you do it, they'll have an excuse to do it. You have a lot more responsibility than you think"

"So, organizing the practice tonight was a good example of leadership," said Kyle. "How many kids came?"

"Kyle, they all came. That's what I mean about leaders being influential. If you weren't their leader, they wouldn't have shown up," said Coach Brown.

"Coach, did they all show up, every kid, including Perry?"

"Everybody, even the injured and suspended, showed up. Todd told me they had a good practice and they're going to do it every Monday until the end of our season."

"That's great, Coach. I felt like I had to do something to make up for what I did."

"Kyle, do you understand why your parents and I are so concerned about what you did?"

"Yes, I think so. ... They're concerned that I'm too young to drink and I'll get into trouble."

"That's right. But more importantly, we're concerned about the future. Kyle, let me tell you a couple of stories about how kids damaged their lives because of alcohol."

Coach Brown told Kyle the following story: "There was a boy named Ryan who played football in high school. Ryan worked hard and overcame adversity many times to become a good football player. Ryan had always been a leader. He was captain of his freshman team, his sophomore team, and hoped to be elected captain of his varsity team his senior year.

"Over the winter, two of his teammates were caught drinking at a party and were disciplined. One of the players (we will call him Joe) received a DUI, lost his driver's license, and was suspended for several games.

"At a social gathering, several of the players complained about the severity of the punishment. They believed the DUI blood alcohol standard was too low. They complained they had more to drink than Joe that night and they were able to drive home safely. When asked his opinion, Ryan disagreed.

"This punishment might have been good for Joe because he'll learn a lesson without serious consequences. Joe could have killed somebody while driving drunk. Solving this problem early in life will be in Joe's best interest. Joe let the team down by his suspension and he also set a bad example for the underclassmen.

"Most of the kids thought that Ryan's opinion was "lame," and word spread throughout the school that he did not support his teammates when they were in trouble. Ryan found only his very best friends supported his position."

"A few weeks later the team elected their captains. Although Ryan got significant support, he was not chosen. Ryan was very disappointed and unsure of what to do next. His friends told him his lack of support for Joe was the reason he wasn't elected. The final captain was to be elected after two-a-day practices in the fall.

"Ryan was faced with a dilemma. Should he change his opinion and campaign to be the final captain or should he continue to act from his values and maintain his current position? Ryan talked to his parents, his friends, and an ex-coach. Should he condone Joe's behavior in order to enhance his chances of being elected the fourth captain? Should he trade part of his value system for enhancing his chances of being captain?

"Over the winter, Ryan had many discussions about his dilemma. From these conversations, he discovered God in his infinite wisdom gives a person two choices and two guarantees when dealing with adversity. A person may chose to be proactive and deal with their problem positively or they can feel sorry for themselves and say, 'Why me, Lord?' The guarantees are: People will always have adversity in their lives; and regardless of their decision, they'll not be the same person they were after dealing with adversity.

"Ryan also learned if a person is proactive, they will emerge a stronger person and more capable of dealing with adversity in the future. If they're reactive, they will emerge a weaker person, less capable of dealing with future adversity.

"Ryan finally concluded he could best serve his team and himself by not condoning Joe's behavior. He decided instead to provide leadership by example in order to be elected.

"He provided that leadership during the winter weight-lifting program by achieving his goals, helping others, and setting a record in two lifting categories. He came to practice in the best shape of his life, and provided leadership in sprints, drills, and endurance runs.

"At the end of the two-a-days, he wasn't elected captain. However, to his surprise, he wasn't as disappointed as he was after the first election. He concluded, after a discussion with a past coach, the reason he wasn't more disappointed was he'd become a leader without being elected captain. He decided he'd be the same person he was when he was captain of his previous teams. He decided leaders are not always elected. Sometimes they emerge by their actions from the unelected. He decided to be one of those people.

"Ryan also discovered he'd become a leader by example in an arena much larger than the football team because there were many schoolmates and faculty observing how he handled this difficult situation. By not abandoning his values for short-term recognition, he'd serve as a role model for other students, many of whom he'd never meet.

"Ryan had a very successful season, making the all-area team, was on the homecoming court, and made many new friends. He signed a letter of intent to attend a Division 1 college as a preferred walk-on and earned a full scholarship after his first season.

"Joe was suspended from the team for the season for drinking a second time and entered AA. He had a difficult winter, but relied on Ryan as part of his support group and emerged a better person. At the football banquet, the head coach introduced Ryan as 'an athlete who was the unelected captain of our team.' He received a standing ovation as he walked to the podium to accept his varsity letter with a 'C' in the upper left-hand corner.

"Kyle, which points of the story relate to you and your situation?" asked Coach Brown.

"You and my parents are concerned I'll be like Joe and get kicked off the high school team if I keep drinking," answered Kyle.

"That's right. What else?" asked Coach Brown.

"You want me to be a leader like Ryan when I get to high school."

"That's right, Kyle," said Coach Brown. "All of us approach many forks in the road throughout our lives. You are at one now. You could take one road, which leads to becoming a Joe. You could take the other road, which leads to a Ryan. Your coaches, parents, and friends will not always be able to direct you down the right road. You'll have to make many choices on your own. You'll make some more mistakes, as you did the other day. Your parents and I are trying to teach you to make the right choices by making you aware of the consequences of the wrong choices. There are also rewards when you make the right choice. Do you understand what we're trying to teach you?"

Kyle thought for a minute and said, "Yes! I felt terrible on Sunday. Sunday night the guys told me Bobby took a beating in my place. There was nothing I could do. I know I let a lot of people down. I want to make up for it, but can't undo what I did. Scheduling the practice was the only thing I could think of to make up for what I did. I'm glad it worked out. My mom wanted me to ask if I could work out with the team to stay in shape for the playoffs. She said if I continue to do what's been asked of me, they may lift the grounding in two weeks. She wants to know if they lift the grounding, would you lift the suspension?"

"Yes, I will, Kyle. I think you're learning a valuable lesson. The players will be happy to see you at practice again."

 PLAY NUMBER TWENTY-FIVE

Coaches should realize children and their parents take their cues from the coach, often when they least expect it. If a coach is consistently calm, thoughtful, hardworking, respectful, determined, has a passion for coaching, and never says anything negative to a referee, his players and parents will do the same. The children learn more from what coaches do rather than what they say. So, consistent behavior by coaches has a positive effect on performance. St. Raphael coaches have found the best way to develop the consistency required for coaching success is to act from their values. Coaches who act from their values are usually decisive, very consistent, and seldom have to second-guess themselves.

26
Jeff Returns

"Also, Coach, I really didn't do anything to help with the acceptance thing," said Matt. "The coaches have been honest with us all season. So, whatever the coaches say, the players believe. You told us at the beginning of the season, the coaches and players would make mistakes, and we should just admit them, and learn from them. The coaches made a mistake. They admitted it. So, what's the big deal?"

AT THE BEGINNING OF PRACTICE ON TUESDAY, Coach Brown told the team they needed help from other teams in order to make the playoffs. As the coaches discussed practice plans with the team, the players decided they wanted to play their best game of the season on Sunday even though they might not make the playoffs. By playing their best game, they reasoned, the eighth graders would leave on a high note and the seventh graders would begin their quest for the championship in 2009.

Greg and George returned from the academic suspensions and paid the price at the Coach Cook university of re-admittance by doing some extra conditioning. Garrett also returned from the flu.

Billy was walking with a boot and doing rehab, with an anticipated return for the playoffs.

Consistent with his therapist's recommendation, Jeff took some snaps from center and participated in passing drills. Things went well and Jeff was pleased with his progress, but didn't push it.

At the end of a very good practice, the coaches told the team they had Wednesday off as a reward for practicing on their own on Monday night. The coaches expected the announcement would make the players happy, but, on the contrary, there were several moans of disappointment accompanied by several looks of disbelief. The coaches were puzzled and pleased by this unexpected reaction.

As Coaches Brown and Jerman walked up the hill to their car, three of the players caught up with them and said, "Hey, Coach, you got a minute?"

As expected, one of the players was Matt, accompanied by Brian and Todd. Todd pushed Matt to the front of the group and said, "Matt will do the talking. It was his idea."

Matt began with an innocent question. "Coach, haven't you always told us that practice was good for us?"

Coach Brown replied, "Yes!" and started to enumerate some of the reasons. Matt was obviously not interested in the review, as he interrupted Coach Brown and said, "Well, if that's true, why, as a reward for our play and practice on Monday, did you take away something that's good for us?"

The coaches were stunned. Neither could utter a word before Matt said, "Coach, have you given up on us?"

As those seven words and three faces of hope and expectation carved their place in Coaches Brown and Jerman's minds forever, Coach Brown searched for the words that would correct this misconception.

After an uncomfortable silence, Coach Brown said, "Oh, no, Matt! We never, ever give up! I'm sorry we left you with that impression. We didn't mean to. What can we do to correct it?"

The players looked at each other briefly and again selected Matt as spokesman by their silence.

"On Thursday, just explain things to the team as you just did to us and everything will be okay." Then Matt added, "It wouldn't hurt to practice on Friday to make up for Wednesday either."

"Okay, we'll do it. Thanks, guys," said Coach Jerman.

After the boys left to a waiting group of players, Coach Jerman said, "These kids never cease to amaze me." Coach Brown shook his head in agreement. "We may not win the championship, but we have a championship team."

* * *

On Thursday, Coach Brown explained things as Matt had suggested and planned a walk-through practice for Friday. During the explanation, Matt, Todd, and Brian elected to stand next to Coach Brown as an indication of support. As Matt had predicted, the players accepted the explanation at face value.

Thursday and Friday were two of the best practices of the season. There was one hundred percent attendance at each one. Two of the coaches rescheduled business trips when they were told of the misunderstanding.

It also helped greatly when Coach Martynowicz reworked the various win/loss scenarios, and found if the Redwings won their last two games, and two other teams lost either week, St. Raphael would be the last team into the playoffs. This was a remote possibility, but it provided all the hope that the players needed to reach their highest levels of enthusiasm and focus of the season.

After practice on Friday, Coach Brown asked Matt to stay for a minute to thank him for bringing a potentially serious problem to the coach's attention. He thanked him for his honest feedback and for whatever he did to facilitate the players' acceptance of the coaches' explanation.

Matt responded, "Thank you, Coach, but I was just doing what the coaches have encouraged us to do since the beginning of the season. They have asked us what we think, so I just told you what the players were thinking. I guess I got selected because I got the biggest mouth.

"Also, Coach, I really didn't do anything to help with the acceptance thing. The coaches have been honest with us all season. So, whatever the coaches say, the players believe. You told us at the beginning of the season, the coaches and players would make mistakes and we should just admit them and learn from them. The coaches made a mistake. They admitted it. So, what's the big deal?"

Friday night, Coach Brown got a call from Kathy. She said, "The therapist thought it would be good to put Jeff in a game at quarterback if the game was secure, win or lose. Jeff thinks he's ready, too."

* * *

On Sunday, before the game with St. Michael, Coach Kelly gave Jeff extra snaps at quarterback. At first, there were some drops attributed to nerves. Once Greg slowed the snap down everything went nicely. The real proof would come under game conditions.

The game went well as St. Raphael built a lead over St. Michaels of 27–6 at the end of the third quarter. At the beginning of the fourth quarter, Jeff nervously entered the game at quarterback.

As the season progressed, people connected with the team became aware of Jeff's condition and were very supportive. Because of this, almost everybody at the Benet Academy football stadium that day understood the significance of a third stringer entering a game for what would normally be mop-up duty.

Kathy was in the stands, her hands clasped tightly in her lap, unaware of anything except her 13-year-old son, trotting bravely onto the field for a self-imposed test of his mental condition. She thought, if he fails the test, what then?

Doug was on the sidelines as a member of the chain gang. As Jeff trotted on the field, he gave the down marker to the closest coach and nervously moved to a better vantage point.

With the game in hand at halftime, Coach Brown had informed the head coach of the opposing team, who was a good friend, about Jeff. He told the coach he wanted to keep his first string on the field for three plays in order to give Jeff confidence.

As Jeff entered the huddle, the players came together and put their hands on top of Jeff's as a show of support. Jeff called the play. "I right 46." The team broke the huddle and sprinted to the line of scrimmage. Jeff set the team, called the cadence, but unfortunately the ball was snapped prematurely and Jeff dropped it. He recovered it for a 2-yard loss.

Greg, in his anxiety, had forgotten the snap count. Jeff got up off the ground and looked to the sidelines. Coach Brown thought for just a second he might want to come out. But he just raised his hand to assure the coaching staff he was all right. Greg banged his helmet and pointed to his chest, as a gesture of "my fault."

Jeff called the same play. The team lined up for the second down and 12 play. This time the ball was snapped, handed off successfully to Bobby for a 4-yard gain.

Coach Brown called the third down play to the right again, because Jeff was right handed. However, when the ball was snapped, Jeff handed off to Michael going left on 45 mini-train for a 5-yard gain. This play required a fake right and a handoff left. Jeff wanted to show he could fake and run plays in both directions.

As the punt team entered the game, Jeff trotted off the field as though nothing special had happened, but everybody knew differently as the crowd roared their approval. To the coach's surprise and joy, Jeff headed straight for his father. They erupted into a long tearful embrace. Then, father and son walked arm in arm to the end of the bench for what had to be one of life's great discussions.

After the game Jeff and his father approached Coach Brown, and Doug extended his hand. "I just wanted to take a moment to thank you and your staff for what you did for Jeff ... and for me as well. Our therapist said football was a primary vehicle in Jeff's recovery. Thank you so much. The whole experience has helped me redefine my role in our family and my relationships with others."

Doug paused and smiled sheepishly and asked, "By the way, do you still want to hit me? You had every right to during our first meeting."

"No, Doug. I wasn't too proud of the way I responded either. Jeff showed a lot of courage today," Coach Brown said as he smiled proudly at Jeff.

Doug continued, "Jeff has something he wants to say, Coach."

"Coach, my therapist and I thought of an analogy about my sickness that might be helpful to you when you come across another kid like me. Here it is. My life was like a pendulum that had swung too far in one direction and I got sick. Like all pendulums, when they go in the other direction they go a little too far. That's probably why I didn't want to play quarterback again. But, when the pendulum started to swing back to the center as I was getting well, I grabbed it. And now I'm directing it to where I want it to go.. That's why I don't plan to play football in high school. I plan to concentrate on baseball. What do you think? Pretty good, eh? Will you be able to use that sometime?"

Coach Brown was speechless and before he could respond, Jeff said, "Enough said, Coach. Come on, Dad, let's go. I hope you never have to use it, Coach. But if you do, you don't have to give me credit. ... Oh, one last thing, I'm retired as a quarterback. Defense is a lot more fun."

As Coach Brown started to pick up a few water bottles and his playbook, Mike and Marie approached with another couple, Perry, and Perry's social worker, Sue, and said, "Coach we have a surprise for you. This is Gary and Brenda Stevens. They are Perry's permanent foster parents. Perry was told yesterday. That's probably why he played so well today. He wanted to wait until after the game to thank you so it wouldn't be a distraction."

Perry let the announcement sink in as tears welled up in his eyes. Embarrassed, not knowing what to say, even though he had practiced in his room the night before, he trotted toward Coach Brown. As he arrived he paused, then he lunged at his coach enthusiastically. As he hugged him, he banged his helmet off Coach Brown's temple. Perry had a habit of wearing his helmet from the time he left the car until he returned. Perry held on tight as a welt began to form on Coach Brown's head and said, "Thank you, Coach. Thank you so much."

Then Perry turned, embarrassed at his emotion, and trotted to the car.

Sue said, "Coach, since you and your staff have been so close to this situation, I want you to understand the significance of football in Perry's rehabilitation. He was hours away from entering the juvenile system. We focus on rehabilitation, but we normally can't offer something like St. Raphael Football as a vehicle for a child's rehabilitation. Thank you. I'm sure Perry will never forget St. Raphael."

"You're welcome," said Coach Brown. "We all enjoyed this experience. If you think we can help again, let us know."

"Are you sure of that? You've got a good-sized welt growing on the side of your head. ... and most of our cases don't turn out this well," said Sue.

"I'm sure," said Coach Brown as he smiled and fingered the growing welt on his head.

* * *

Once home, after a satisfying day of football and a refreshing beverage, Coach Brown got a call from Susan, a parent of a Mini

Mite football player in the in-house program. "Do you remember me? I'm the lady you talked into letting her son play football in the first grade. I think I threatened you if he was injured."

"Yes, I certainly do! How could I forget? You threatened to kill me. Of course you were just kidding, but I wasn't so sure at the time. How'd it go?"

"It went great," responded Susan. "So great, that I have to tell you a story."

"Okay. I like stories. Does it have a happy ending?" asked Coach Brown.

"I'll let you be the judge," laughed Susan. "My son Nick could not do a situp or pushup at the beginning of the season. Sometimes, he would just lie down in the middle of the practice field whenever he got tired. The other night, I went to practice and could not believe what I saw. He was out in front leading the exercises. He was exhorting the kids to do extra pushups so they would beat somebody."

"That's great!" said Coach Brown. "I'm glad it was good for him. That's our goal."

"That's not all. The next day he told me he was doing the rings at school. You know, the hand-over-hand, ring-to-ring exercise. He said the kids told him he was the best in the school at the rings."

"That's great," said Coach Brown.

"That's not all. After he finished the rings, he said one of the girls wanted to be his girlfriend. He did not like that. Then, the little girl chased him at recess. She said she wanted to marry him, but he ran away. He said he was fast and she couldn't catch him," concluded Susan.

"Did you tell him to keep on running like a Forrest Gump until he was in a position to choose?" asked Coach Brown.

"No! I did not! Isn't that a great story? I just had to tell you. Thank you for talking me into it," said Susan. "I think I'll let him play next year."

PLAY NUMBER TWENTY-SIX

Coaches have the greatest impact on team success because they are primarily responsible for the creation of the learning environment that enables everybody to achieve their full potential. The extent to which this environment is achieved and maintained determines the ease and speed at which learning takes place. Coaches must realize this is especially true in youth football, because the players are very impressionable. When they're placed in positions to succeed both physically and emotionally, they will learn at an incredible rate. If two teams are even at the beginning of the season, the team with the best coaching staff will be ahead at the end.

27
Run Freddie Run

*The main purpose of the call was to thank you. I can't believe
the positive impact this experience has had on my son. He's
more confident, has more friends, is doing better in school,
and is more sociable. He says a bunch of kids from his school
are playing next year.*

AT THE BEGINNING OF PRACTICE ON TUESDAY,
Coach Brown reminded the players they had to win their last game,
and two teams had to lose, in order for them to get into the playoffs.
Practice went well as the players wanted to play their best. Everybody was there, including Kyle, but he was out of uniform. He was
helping any way he could to get the players ready for what could
be their last game of the season. His parents had not decided yet
whether he would return for the playoffs.

When Coach Brown arrived home that evening, he had a call
from Freddie, a first grader who'd called him at the beginning of the
season to intercede with his mother since she would not allow him
to play Mini Mite football. As soon as he thanked Coach Brown
and told him a few disjointed highlights of his season, he gave the
phone to his mom, who told the following story.

Freddie was a small, quiet six-year-old boy who was picked on at school and did not have a lot of friends. He liked to play football in the backyard with his eight-year-old brother and his friends, but was only invited to play when there weren't enough kids for a game.

Freddie's mom, Judy, began, "One day Freddie brought home a flyer from school about the St. Raphael Football Program that allowed kids his age to play tackle football. He ran into the house, dropped his backpack, and declared, "Mom, I want to join the football league. They play real football just like on TV."

I read the notice and said, "Freddie, this is tackle football. I don't want you to get hurt. You know you always get hurt playing with your brother and his friends.

"After some begging, a discussion with you, his father's intervention, and more begging, I allowed him to play. Do you remember him?"

"Yes, I do," said Coach Brown.

"Well, as the boys prepared for their first Saturday game," continued Judy, "the coach told them to wear their jerseys to school on Friday for good luck and team pride. Freddie could hardly wait to show all his friends his Green Bay Packer jersey. Much to my surprise, things didn't go well at school that day. When I picked Freddie up at the bus stop he started to cry.

"At first, Freddie didn't want to tell me what happened. But after we got home, he told me the kids made fun of him at school. They didn't believe he was on a tackle football team because he was so small. He said he didn't want to wear his jersey to school again.

"I told him, I thought wearing your jersey was important. If you don't wear your jersey and stand up for yourself, the kids will never believe you. Maybe you could invite your best friends to watch on Saturday, and they'll tell the other kids that you play football.

"On Friday, Freddie wore his jersey to school and the kids made fun of him again. This time he told them his friends Tony and Sarah were coming to his game, and they would tell him that he played.

"After the previous Saturday's game, I told his coach about what happened at school. The coach listened and then said he knew what to do.

"Freddie normally played safety because he was small and a little timid. The coach wanted to keep him safe. That was fine with me and Freddie. He was happy just being on the field and making new friends.

"During next week's practice, the coach put in a play where Freddie carried the ball. Freddie's small, but he's fast. On the way home, Freddie told me he scored a touchdown in practice, but I didn't believe him.

"Saturday arrived and I picked up Tony and Sarah. Freddie's friends were impressed with all the players in uniform. They wanted to feel Freddie's shoulder pads and liked his helmet with all the award stickers.

"At the start of the second half, Freddie's team was close to the goal line and he went in at running back. Freddie looked to the sideline and gave me a little wave. I about died. Freddie almost smiled as he saw the horrified look on my face. Unfortunately, the ball was centered while he was waving. The quarterback pitched the ball to Freddie and he dropped it. He then ran off the field toward me. He had tears in his eyes. I felt so bad."

Judy paused to collect herself.

Coach Brown said, "So far, so good. Go on."

"Well, fortunately, the coach caught him before he got to me and they had a talk. Then Freddie went back into the game at running back. Now I'm really a mess."

"I bet you wanted to kill me about then," laughed Coach Brown.

"The thought crossed my mind," said Judy. "Well, the ball was snapped again, but Freddie did not move to get the ball. He just stood there."

"The coach yelled, 'Freddie, take the ball.' The quarterback ran to Freddie and handed him the ball. The team blocked everybody and the quarterback pushed Freddie to get him going in the right direction.

"Once he got going nobody touched him. He ran and ran, scored a touchdown, and ran right out of the end zone. After he scored he kept running to the sideline and tried to give me the ball. I think he saw that on TV.

"The main purpose of the call was to thank you. I can't believe the positive impact this experience has had on my son. He's more confident, has more friends, is doing better in school, and is more sociable. He says a bunch of kids from his school are playing next year."

"Thanks for the call. I enjoy getting calls like this. Did Freddie hear your description of his game?"

"Yes, he did. He has a big smile on his face."

"I bet he does, and well he should. You tell him I hope he plays for me on the travel team someday," said Coach Brown.

Judy responded, "No way, Coach. We're going to take this one year at a time. I saw some of the second graders play on the next field and I swear there were some 100-pounders."

PLAY NUMBER TWENTY-SEVEN

The players are so impressionable that whatever a coach says or does, they are going to learn—right or wrong—because at this age the kids do not have the body of knowledge required for sound judgment. They may not be able to evaluate, but they are able to absorb information at an incredible rate. The inherent danger is, if you teach kids the wrong things, they will learn it almost as fast as if it were the right thing. Often kids believe they don't need a filter because you are the COACH. And coaches are some of the most respected members of a child's society.

28
Dealing with Adversity

Kathy leaned down and put her face inches from Coach Brown's and said through clenched teeth, "Don't be a hero. By now, every player knows their coach is down. Do you think they'll be just a little distracted with you calling plays today? The other coaches can take care of things. You just let us take care of you for a change." Coach Brown smiled, "You got me. You're a very persuasive woman. You can get out of my face now. We don't want people to think we're dating." "Glad you haven't lost your sense of humor. But don't try to get up or I'll get Doug to pin you down. I think he'd like that," said Kathy.

AT GAME TIME OF THE PIVOTAL GAME WITH ST. James, the temperature hovered near freezing. The wind howled out of the north at 30–40 miles per hour, accompanied by a driving rain-sleet storm. The players had worn several layers of clothing but were soaked to the skin by game time, but they never complained. They were intent on doing what was within their control, and then hoping for a miracle. None of their contracts were up for renewal next year. None of them were concerned about endangering their careers by playing in inclement weather. They were just intent on doing their best for the sheer satisfaction of performing at that level.

The St. James Jaguars were a very good team. They had soundly beaten St. Francis early in the season. St. James would be up for this game, as they needed to win to make the playoffs.

Coach Brown was a little late getting to the game. He drove close to a paved area leading to the field and unloaded his playbook and other football materials required for the game. He then drove his car to the parking lot adjacent to the field. Upon his return, he routinely bent over to pick up his playbook and other materials.

As he started to stand up, he got light-headed and fell to the ground. He had just enough time to break his fall with his elbows. However, as he fell, he landed unevenly, twisted, and crashed the back of his head full force onto the concrete.

He laid motionless for about a minute, then he moved a little and started to sit up.

At that moment, Kathy, who was a nurse at Edward hospital, started running across the parking lot screaming, "Stay down! Stay down!"

Coach Brown continued his effort to sit up, but felt light-headed again and laid down cautiously on the cold cement. When Kathy arrived she asked, "What happened? I saw you go down. How are you feeling?"

"I'm a little light-headed, but feel okay. My head hurts a little."

Kathy lifted Coach Brown's head onto his playbook. As she took her hand away, it was covered with blood. She then reached into her purse and retrieved a tissue, and held it firmly against the wound. When she took it away, there was only a small quantity of blood.

She said, "Coach, your head wound is superficial. Not to worry. How are you feeling?"

"I'm feeling better," said Coach Brown. "This same thing happened about a week ago after climbing a flight of stairs. I was okay. Just hurt my knee a little when I fell. I think I can get up."

As Coach Brown started to rise, Kathy placed her hand firmly on his chest and said, "Stay put. There's no need to get up. Let's wait a while. We want to make sure you're okay. Could somebody put an umbrella over Coach Brown?"

As she spoke, she signaled to her husband to call an ambulance. Doug said, "I already did. It's on its way."

Hearing this, Coach Brown started to get up again. "I don't need an ambulance. I don't want to ride in one of those things. I just want to coach my game."

Kathy leaned down and put her face inches from Coach Brown's and said through clenched teeth, "Don't be a hero. By now, every player knows their coach is down. Do you think they'll be just a little distracted with you calling plays today? The other coaches can take care of things. You just let us take care of you for a change."

Coach Brown smiled, "You got me. You're a very persuasive woman. You can get out of my face now. We don't want people to think we're dating."

"Glad you haven't lost your sense of humor. But don't try to get up or I'll get Doug to pin you down. I think he'd like that," said Kathy.

As Kathy rose to one knee, the siren of the emergency vehicle was heard for the first time.

"Coach, do you want somebody to call your wife?" asked Kathy.

Coach Jerman, who had just arrived from the field, said, "I'll take care of that. Is she at home, Jim?"

"No, she's at Susan's," said Coach Brown. "Here, take my cell. She's under Marcia."

As the emergency vehicle arrived, Coach Brown asked Kathy, "If the medics say I'm okay, would you drive me to the hospital? I don't want to ride in that thing."

"If they say you're okay, and release you, I'll take you to Edward. But we can't take any chances," said Kathy, as she turned and started to give the paramedics an update on what had happened.

The paramedics examined Coach Brown and cleared him to ride with Kathy to the hospital. Coach Jerman and Kathy helped him to his feet. He stood unsteadily for a minute or so, then walked slowly to the car, which had been brought close to the accident area. He looked at Coach Jerman and said, "I feel fine, Lou. Please make sure you convince the kids. They've got enough pressure today, especially with this weather."

Just as Coach Brown was about to enter the car, Kyle, Todd, and Brian arrived with Coach Grosso.

Kyle, wearing his jersey and jeans, stepped forward and asked, "You okay, Coach? The team sent us to find out how you're doing."

"I'm okay. I just got light-headed and they want to run a few tests at the emergency room. See, I'm not even riding in the wagon. So don't worry about me. Just kick some butt today."

As Coach Brown turned to get in the car, Kyle reached out and affectionately patted Coach Brown on the shoulder. Coach Brown turned and gave Kyle a brief hug as the other players wished their coach good luck. As Coach Brown seated himself in the car, Brian said, "Don't worry about the game, Coach. This is our kind of weather."

After he locked his seat belt, Coach Brown looked at Kathy. She shook her head side to side and said, "Now I know why I'm taking you to the hospital instead of the emergency vehicle. You didn't want the kids to worry. Do you ever stop coaching? This ride better go smoothly or you won't be coaching for a while."

The ride to the hospital went smoothly. As Kathy pulled into the carport outside the emergency entrance, an alerted medical staff was present with a wheelchair. Coach Brown was wheeled to an examining room for further tests, which led to his admission.

* * *

Kyle, Todd, and Brian entered the pregame huddle and assured the team Coach Brown was okay. The players looked confused and didn't know whether to believe their captains. Kyle and the coaches gave additional assurances, but the team was distracted.

Then Kyle stepped into the huddle and said, "Look, I talked to Coach myself. He's okay. He got into a car by himself. He didn't even need the meat wagon. Do you think the doctors would let him go to the hospital in a car if he wasn't okay? There ain't nothing we can do to help him except win the damn game. So let's do it. These guys are good, but we are so much better than we were at the beginning of the season, with or without me. I'm sorry I did what I did. I let you guys down."

The team accepted Kyle's assessment and his apology enthusiastically. The fact that St. James had also improved with time never entered their minds. They knew what they had accomplished and they were ready to play. Such is the innocence of youth.

The Redwings won the toss and elected to take the wind in the first quarter. Santos boomed the kickoff to the St. James 5-yard line, where the fired-up Redwings held the Jaguars for no gain. They were forced to punt into the wind.

The punt was blocked by Danny, and Perry recovered it in the end zone for a touchdown. Santos kicked the extra point with ten players on the field as Perry forgot he replaced Kyle on the kick team. The score was 8–0. This meant St. James had to score twice, since they didn't have a kicker.

St. Raphael scored two more touchdowns in the first quarter. Stewart caught a 30-yard pass from Harrison, and Nick scored on a wing-back reverse behind George and Todd. Santos kicked both extra points for a 24–0 lead at the end of the first quarter. St. James had only 18 players, and had been held to negative yardage in the first quarter. St. Raphael played 22 players, which allowed them to keep relatively warm.

However, St. James got the 40-mile-per-hour wind for the second quarter. Coach Taylor told the team, "If you can hold them one more time, we'll win this game because all of their players have had to go both ways."

St. James made two first downs, but were worn down by the worsening conditions, which now included a driving sleet storm. The Redwing defense, led by George, Brian, Garrett, Perry, and Todd, took over on downs.

The Redwings held the ball for the rest of the quarter, as Bobby and Michael, combined with Jimmy, Brian, and Mark from the White team, pounded the ball inside. The Redwings used a fresh ball carrier each down, and were careful not to fumble. They drove 70 yards for a score. Santos kicked the extra point into a strong wind and St. Raphael led 32–0 at halftime as the sleet storm worsened.

At the end of the half, the coaches decided to call the game because of the weather. The Redwings had won. They had done everything they could in spite of horrible conditions. They had done what they controlled. Now they must wait for the outcome of events they didn't control. The victory celebration was non-existent because of the weather, the possibility their season was over, and of course, their concern for Coach Brown.

As the kids knelt in the team huddle, the talk was not about disappointment, it was about pride in their accomplishment. They had come within an eyelash of making the playoffs. There were no "what-if's," only pride in their effort and accomplishments under difficult conditions.

There was an abundance of respect in each congratulatory look, handshake, and private in-the-ear discussion of topics the boys didn't want to share with anyone except the intended recipient. The parents gathered at a respectful distance. Several boys waved to their parents to join the team in the middle of the field. The parents advanced, tentatively, some in tears, unable to predict the mood of their child. They were no longer aware of the terrible weather. They were just in touch with their own feelings, and in most instances, hoping their boys were not experiencing the same level of disappointment. Their disappointment had little to do with not making the playoffs, but the disappointment a parent feels for a child in pain. However, the coaches could see an emerging sense of pride, as one parent after another hugged, kissed, or shook hands with their child. There was a developing sense of relief, then amazement, and then learning, as the parents began to experience the mood of their children.

These kids had played so hard all season under such adverse conditions, and had developed a different perspective. They had come so close to their objective, yet apparently failed. Many of the parents came prepared to help the child deal with anticipated disappointment. But the children they hugged seemed over it. They were on a different page. Instead, they were so proud of what they had accomplished. Because of the intensity of the moment, many parents were overcome by emotion as they learned that their children had truly internalized a bigger objective over the season. That objective was to do their best, improve as much as they could, and they would always be winners. As the players and some parents "took a knee" for one last time, Coach Jerman addressed a group that was unaware of the horrible weather conditions.

"First of all, I've talked with Coach Brown and he is okay. They're running a series of tests and he'll stay overnight for observation. He said he thinks you guys finally got to him with all your shenanigans." Nobody laughed until Coach Jerman said, "Come on, guys, that's a joke. I'm just kidding." Since this was out of character, only a few players laughed politely. Coach Grosso interrupted and said, "I talked to him as well and he's in good spirits. He told me he'd coached too many games and the pressure finally got to him." There was still no laughter. The players respected their coaches, but sensed they were being protected from the truth. There was a pause and Coach Jerman continued, "Coach Brown ask me to tell you guys, this is simply the most improved team he's ever coached, and I agree. You accomplished more than any of us thought possible as the season progressed. All of us should learn from you today about how much can be accomplished when you take control of your effort and performance. You did that today, and all season, under the worst of conditions." Coach Jerman paused, looked into the eyes of each player, and continued, addressing the parents. "We had trouble coaching the game today because we were distracted by the pain our players endured paying the price to achieve a goal. That pain included their concern for Coach Brown. Your children learned this season that it's difficult to control outcomes. But more importantly they learned how to control their effort. Our players demonstrated for all of us this season what can be accomplished when we focus on controlling your effort. They may not have achieved everything they hoped for, but I bet they achieved more than any of us expected. That's why focusing on what one can control is so important."

Coach Jerman verified he had the group's undivided attention, removed his sleet-soaked glasses, and continued. "This concept will become even more important next year when your boys play high school football. The environment gets tougher and our players will have to reestablish their identity. I hope you all will take time to enjoy your victory today. The coaches will. In addition, I also hope you all will support your children when they experience adversity next year. They will need all the support you can give them."

Coach Jerman paused, making approving eye contact with each of his players, then walked to the sideline to pick up the game ball that had been returned by St. James. As he walked away, he could only think about how fortunate he was to be associated with these players. His thoughts were interrupted by two "Redwings!" cheers; one by the players and one by the parents. Then there was the loudest cheer of all when Coach Cook yelled, "Gino's at five? I'll buy."

* * *

The coaches were well into their celebration at Gino's when Coach Jerman got a call on his cell phone. It was the league president congratulating St. Raphael on making the playoffs. Because of the weather conditions there were two upsets that permitted the Redwings to back into the playoffs. It was a good news—bad news story. The good news was, they were in; the bad news ... the Redwings played St. Monica in the first round. The coaches rolled their eyes as they recalled the 40–6 beating earlier in the season. Then, they erupted in cheers of "We can beat those guys," and a little good-natured sarcasm directed at the defense: "If we can hold them under 30 points, the offense will take care of the rest." There were calls for another round of pizzas and the planning began.

The coaches' enthusiastic planning was interrupted by the voice of reason from Coach Aimonette. "Don't you think we ought to start calling the players? Let's not do it by e-mail."

The coaches began calling the kids with the good news, which they thought would be wildly received. However, many of the players were less excited than anticipated. Each child asked about Coach Brown, and they were told, "He's doing fine, although nobody really knows."

A puzzled Coach Jerman asked Brian, the next relatively subdued player he called, "I understand you're concerned about Coach Brown, but why aren't you and the other players more excited about making the playoffs? Is it because we're playing St. Monica? We've just achieved one of our team goals."

Brian replied without much hesitation, "Coach, we're concerned about Coach Brown, but winning the playoffs is our real goal. Most of the guys think we can beat St. Monica with our full team. You know St. Raphael teams always make and do well in the playoffs. I think the guys expected to win the championship. So, making the playoffs just doesn't seem that special." Coach Jerman said to the coaches, "Isn't it interesting? The players have already adjusted the goal. I think they did it right after the St. Monica game. Practices have been focused and all business since that game.

"Isn't it interesting that the players had adjusted their goal before we did? And, they understood something as subtle as tradition. I think they were able to do this because they were capable of assessing their own performance level better than we were. They've always been capable of a lot more than we thought. I believe our players are able to excel because they're kids without the encumbrances of maturity. I've coached for 40 years and the kids never cease to amaze me. "

After the last player was called, Coach Jerman got a call from Marcia, who reported, "The doctors don't know what caused Jim to pass out. They're going to keep him overnight and perform tests in the morning. Jim's been treated for an irregular heartbeat for quite a few years. His condition may have gotten worse with time. He's in no danger and will be monitored overnight."

Coach Jerman was not comfortable with so little information about his friend of 40 years. He was going to the hospital on Monday to find out for himself.

 PLAY NUMBER TWENTY-EIGHT
Sometimes coaches volunteer because they want their son to play quarterback or some other high-profile position. One of the most important responsibilities a coach has is to put his players in the right positions. If quarterback's the right position for the coach's son, then a child should not be denied this position because he's the coach's son. But if this is not his best position, placing him there will have a negative impact on the team and more importantly the child. He will feel the pressure of failure and judgmental pressure from his teammates and parents.

29
Playoff Preparations

Kyle tossed the ball to Coach Brown and said, "The guys thought you deserved the game ball. Actually, they said I should use it as a bribe so I could play in the St. Monica game. My parents have cleared me to play." Kyle's mom nodded her head, smiled, and said, "We think he's learned his lesson, so it's up to you, Coach. Besides, I can't take any more inane chatter on this subject. You'd think if this knucklehead plays, St. Raphael can't lose. Father Ted even mentioned him in his sermon on Sunday ... I'm just kidding." "Kyle, you can play," said Coach Brown. "But the team was right. No game ball, no St. Monica game. The bribe was all it took. And make sure you tell the team I snatched the ball out of the air when you tossed it to me. That's a condition of your probation."

ON MONDAY MORNING COACH JERMAN DROVE from Chicago to visit Coach Brown. Although he had called him Sunday night to discuss the game and the playoffs, he knew little about his condition.

He arrived at the hospital about 10:30. Coach Brown was asleep after his breakfast of pancakes and eggs. After some small talk about the playoffs and the players' reaction, Coach Jerman got to the purpose of his visit, "So, what's wrong? What caused you to pass out?"

"The doctors don't know. They gave me some preliminary tests last night and everything looked good. The emergency room doctor said seventy-five percent of people who pass out leave the hospital unaware of the reason. There are many reasons why people pass out. Some are serious, most are not."

"If that's true, why are you still here?" asked a skeptical Coach Jerman.

"I've been taking medication for a small heart problem, an irregular heartbeat. The drug I take is for high blood pressure, but is used for an irregular heartbeat as well. One of the nurses said most people would not have been kept overnight, but my heart doctor wants to run some more tests today. He's in Houston, and wants to see me in the hospital when he returns on Tuesday night. I think they're being extra thorough because several people here had children in the program. The admitting nurse said I have influence here."

Satisfied that Coach Brown was in good hands, Coach Jerman changed the topic of conversation to Sunday's game with St. Monica. After they discussed the game plan, Coach Jerman said he'd return on Tuesday night with the game video of the first game. "This'll give you something to do if you're still here. You don't look very sick to me. I'll let everybody know."

After reviewing the scouting report, having an echocardiogram, and taking a few telephone calls, Coach Brown slept most of the afternoon, At four o'clock, he received a call from George and Greg on the speaker phone from Greg's home.

"Coach, this is Greg and George and our moms calling," said George. "They said we should call and let you know we've been cleared to play. Our grades are better, so can we come back? If you say okay, we'll talk to Coach Cook about our extra conditioning and stuff."

"Have you guys been doing your homework before practice?" asked Coach Brown.

"Yeah, Coach. We can't go anywhere after school until we get it done and checked," said Greg.

"Who's checking it ... your girlfriends?" asked Coach Brown playfully.

"Coach, we don't have girlfriends. Our moms are checking it," said Greg.

"Returning sounds good. The team can use you guys for the St. Monica game. Don't forget to see Coach Cook."

"Thanks, Coach ... What, Mom? ... Oh yeah, Coach ... How are you feeling?"

"Good, George. Thanks for asking."

As the boys hung up, Coach Aimonette and Coach Martynowicz entered the room carrying George Patton's book on leadership and a fifth of "cough syrup." Coach Aimonette handed both to Coach Brown and said, "One is for now and one is for later. I hope you can figure out which is which. I'm sure if you are unable to decide, the nurses will give you some help."

After the coaches discussed some ideas on how to beat St. Monica, Kyle and his mom entered the room, with a muddy football with 32–0 scrolled across it. Kyle tossed the ball to Coach Brown and said, "The guys thought you deserved the game ball. Actually, they said I should use it as a bribe so I could play in the St. Monica game. My parents have cleared me to play."

Kyle's mom nodded her head, smiled, and said, "We think he's learned his lesson, so it's up to you, Coach. Besides, I can't take any more inane chatter on this subject. You'd think if this knucklehead plays, St. Raphael can't lose. Father Ted even mentioned him in his sermon on Sunday ... I'm just kidding."

"Kyle, you can play. But the team was right. No game ball, no St. Monica game. The bribe was all it took. And make sure you tell the team I snatched the ball out of the air when you tossed it to me. That's a condition of your probation."

"I will, Coach ... snatched ... got it ... and thanks, Coach. I won't disappoint you again," said Kyle as he shook Coach Brown's hand with both hands.

The ensuing conversations were interrupted by a nurse entering the room to draw blood. "I hate to break up the party, but Coach owes me some blood. I'll wait until you all leave so as to not damage his macho-man image."

Coach Brown continued to have tests throughout the week. Eventually the doctors discovered an enlarged ventricle. This condition caused an irregular heartbeat that if not treated could have been fatal. To correct this condition, the doctors decided to install a pacemaker and a defibrillator. The pacemaker would pace the heart to maintain appropriate beat and timing. The defibrillator was there in case something went wrong.

The coaches later referred to this device as the "little engine that could," "energizer bunny," or "coach's happy button" that they tried to push if Coach Brown got overly excited. They also wanted to know if they could use the implantable defibrillator in case something happened to them.

A coaching contingent visited every night. The planning for this game was unparalleled in the history of St. Raphael Football. The coaches brought gifts, some of which showed incredible imagination. The best gift of all was delivered on Thursday night before the scheduled surgery on Friday morning. The delivery consisted of over 50 cards of various sizes signed by over 1,000 players from the in-house program. That evening after all the visitors were gone, Coach Brown stayed up well beyond his recommended bedtime to read every card.

Early Friday morning, Coach Brown was prepared for surgery. The operation went well with no complications. He awoke, underwent some final tests, and went home Friday afternoon. He had to keep his left arm relatively immobile so a scar tissue pocket could develop to stabilize the device location.

* * *

The quarter-final game with St. Monica was scheduled for 2 PM at St. Ignatius Prep School located in the heart of the Chicago Loop. The school was over 100 years old, and had served the children of Chicago superbly for its entire history. As the players took the field for warm-ups, they looked up at the imposing Sears Tower, hovering over the synthetic turf field. The team was at full strength. Even Billy was dressed, ready to give all he had in spite of a heavily taped ankle.

Because the land was worth millions an acre, there was only room for stands on one side of the field. The St. Monica supporters were enthusiastically supporting their team. They were confident of victory. The St. Raphael parents were more subdued. They were happy their children had reached the playoffs, considering the adversity they faced throughout the season. They were impressed by all the statements of confidence uttered by their children throughout the week. They encouraged their children, but knew in their hearts there was little chance the Redwings could beat St. Monica. They hoped they would be safe and were preparing to help them deal with the agony of certain defeat.

The Crusaders arrived late as their players straggled in, delaying team warm-ups for fifteen minutes. They warmed up casually, stretching, catching a few passes, and talking to each other.

Coach Jerman looked across the field at the St. Monica coaching staff trying to get the attention of their obviously overconfident players. He had experienced this himself this season as he prepared the Redwings for their loss against St. Ann.

By contrast, the Redwings were focused. The stretching drills were crisp, done correctly without any urging from the coaching staff. Each coach walked from player to player shaking hands, and giving a few last words of encouragement. This was not orchestrated. It just happened. Everybody had done their best to prepare.

Now, it was time to just let it all hang out. The Redwings were as good as they could be. They had paid the price. Soon, they'd find out if they were good enough to overcome a talent level discrepancy evident in the 40–6 loss just a few weeks ago.

As warm-ups neared completion, Coach Brown emerged from his car parked at the far end of the field. He was driven to the game by his son, Dan, and they had gotten lost. They had planned to get there for warm-ups. The rest of the coaching staff had attended the first game so they could scout next week's opponent, which would be St. Nicholas.

Coach Brown walked slowly, his arm in a sling, and showed the effects of being hospitalized for six days. He had a smile on his face and tried to walk as crisply as possible, but he didn't fool anybody.

Matt was first to see him and spread the word. Coach Brown left his escort and walked cautiously to where the players were on one knee preparing for their pregame prayer. He hesitated at the outskirts of the team huddle as Coach Jerman was about to address the team. Coach Jerman waved him into the middle of the players as he stepped back with a hand gesture and said, "This is your job, not mine. Remember our agreement. You do all the talking."

Then, he paused and said, "What took you so long? I knew I should've picked you up. Where have you been? You missed some good practices last week."

Everybody laughed as any previous discomfort evaporated. The players displayed the innocence of youth as they looked to Coach Brown as if nothing had happened. They were awaiting his pregame message ... just like always.

Coach Brown began, "I'm a lucky man. The doctors figured out what was wrong and installed a pacemaker/defibrillator. It's like I have an implant that runs my heart. I'm like the energizer bunny, so I'll have more energy than ever before. The defibrillator is there just in case I get too excited coaching you guys. So it will be important for you to win this game quickly so I don't have any unnecessary stress."

There was only minimal laughter. The players were ready.

"The coaches told me you've had a great week of practice and are ready to play. You have paid the price. You are the most improved team we've ever had. You're ready to beat these guys. I noticed, as I walked to the huddle, their warm-ups are not going well. They may be thinking they just have to show up to beat you guys. They are ripe for the picking. Let's just do what's on your helmets and we'll play our best game of the year. If we do, we'll beat these guys. What do you think?"

The team responded with a firm, focused, "Yes!" It was not a raucous "yes." It was consistent with the mood and personality of the team.

As the team finished their response and prepared for their prayer, Matt stood up and walked to the middle of the circle. "Coach, we have a surprise for you and the other coaches. The team wants to do Bull in the Ring as our final warm-up drill."

With that said, the team formed two circles, backs and linemen, and began to hit with an enthusiasm not seen at any practice. The coaches called it off after about five minutes and said, "Let's save it for the Crusaders. You sure got their attention, though."

The team, breathing heavily, took a knee in preparation for their prayer. Coach Grosso began.

> Men, take a moment and put yourselves in the presence of the Lord. In the name of the Father, the Son, and the Holy Spirit.
>
> Lord, your message from the gospel of Luke hits us right between the eyes. No one can serve two masters. You can't be all things to everyone and you can't please everyone all the time. It certainly is something all of us try to do and surely something our politicians try to do all the time. There's the master of gaining and accumulating material things and there's the work to follow your son Jesus. These are two very different paths for sure.
>
> Men of St. Raphael Football, there's only one Master and that is our God. He's the boss, he's the coach of our lives, and the one to follow.

In your own heart you can't serve two masters. You must follow the path of hard work, honor, and character.

You can't line up next to a teammate and then make fun of him behind his back. You can't high-five a teammate, then wish he'd fail so you can play in his place. You can't run down the field and not make a block just to make a teammate look bad. You can't say yes to a coach, then not deliver with your best effort.

Men, you can't waste your God-given talents. You can't serve the master of laziness and shortcuts and then two plays later look like the best player on the field.

Serve the Master and you will be able to handle all the ups and downs of this game and life. It's a very simple formula and flat out the biggest challenge you'll ever be faced with as a man. Do what our warrior Jesus would do. You don't give up and you stay true to your Father, just like Jesus did.

There's nothing your opponent can do to you today if you serve the Master and display your talent on every play. There's nothing this opponent can do to you today if you serve your brothers on this team.

This team and this bond will live forever. Follow the Master Jesus and what you do in life will change the world.

Lord, be with us on this field. You are the Master and thus we will follow.

AMEN!

PLAY NUMBER TWENTY-NINE

The most successful coaches make the investment required to teach their players about the right balance between internally and externally generated discipline. This is important because once the game starts the players determine team and individual discipline. When external discipline is required, it should always be constructive and never be intended to embarrass or ridicule a child. If players feel positive about a disciplinary experience, they will respect the coach, and apply more self-discipline in the future.

30
St. Monica Game

The players got their water and headed to the end zone for rest and words of advice. Coach Brown walked to the center of the group. Nobody talked or fooled around. The team was focused and involved. Coach Brown began in a slow, somber voice. "There will be no adjustments. Just keep doing what you're doing. Each play, each matchup, has to be approached all out. This game will be decided by who wants it the most. You're playing great ... best of the year." Coach Brown looked at the team, his excitement rising. He raised his arm, sling and all, and exclaimed uncharacteristically, "We're ahead. They're getting tired. This is why Doctor Death trained you so hard. This is what will determine our margin of victory. Just relax. Rest! Then, let's go after it. We're not holding anything back."

AS GAME TIME APPROACHED, THE WINDS IN-CREASED to 40 miles per hour from the north, a huge advantage to the team defending the north goal. St. Monica won the toss and confidently elected to receive. The Redwings took the wind in the first quarter. It would play a significant role in the outcome of the game.

Santos tried to kick it deep and away from O'Malley, their strong 140-pound running back, but it went directly to him. He started up the left sideline, but was knocked out of bounds at the 30-yard line. The Redwings held the Crusaders for no gain on their first three plays as Perry and Todd made three successive tackles with help from Nick, Brian, Kyle, and Ira from the White team. The St. Monica punter dropped the snap from center, picked it up, ran to his left, and punted only 13 yards to the 43-yard line.

On the first play, Coach Brown decided to play aggressive, calling "48 with the works." Joe pitched the ball to Kyle, who ran outside a vicious crack-back block by Nick, made a cut inside his pulling linemen George and Todd, broke several tackles, and went 43 yards against the grain for the score. Santos kicked the extra point and the jubilant Redwings led 8–0.

The Redwings held the Crusaders to one first down. On third and 12, Brian, starting his first Red team game, intercepted a pass that hung up in the wind, and ran it back to the 27-yard line. The Redwing fans were elated as their team drove the ball to the 7-yard line. There, an off-side penalty and a key Crusader tackle ended the drive.

But the resilient Redwings held the frustrated Crusaders without a first down, forcing another punt into the wind that went only 9 yards to the 21. From there, Bobby ran for the score. Santos's kick made it 16–0 at the end of the first quarter. The teams changed ends and so did the Redwing fortunes.

The Redwings kicked off into the wind and held the Crusaders on downs, forcing a punt to the 49-yard line. However, on the first play, St. Monica intercepted a pass and ran it back to the Redwing 31-yard line. They pounded the ball to the 20, where the drive stalled.

But, on fourth and 13, the Crusaders quarterback fooled the entire Redwing team as he executed a perfect boot leg for a 20-yard touchdown. The two-point conversion was good to cut the lead to 16–8.

Disappointment and frustration showed on the faces of Redwing players. It was fourth and 13 and they allowed the Crusaders to score. As the Redwings huddled for the kickoff, Keith stepped into the huddle and said, "Come on, guys, that is just one score. We are still ahead. Let's deal with it."

The St. Monica kickoff was blown to the 10-yard line. Stewart returned it to the 30-yard line. The momentum shifts continued as the Redwings lost yardage, and were penalized to the 8-yard line.

From there Coach Brown decided to quick kick in hopes of backing the Crusaders up to at least the 30-yard line. It was blocked and rolled out of the end zone for a safety to make the score 16–10.

After the safety, the Redwings punted just 25 yards into the 40-mile-per-hour wind to their own 45. From there, St. Monica needed only two plays to tie the score at 16. Perry blocked the extra point with four minutes left in the half.

Kyle called the players together before the kickoff, pointed to his "don't give up" sticker, and said, "Times are tough, but so are we. Look at them jumping around over there. They think they've won the game. Let's show them what we've got. Nobody quits! Nobody quits!" as he banged several helmets.

The Redwings charged onto the field. Kyle carried for three, nine, and seven tough yards. He got up slowly after the third carry and turned his head as O'Malley said something to him. Billy ran for five yards and a second first down. But, time was running out. There were only 90 seconds until halftime.

Coach Brown called, "Flankers left and right. They'll be looking for Stewart. Throw it to Nick on a fly pattern."

Harrison made a deep drop and heaved the ball into the 40-mile-per-hour wind. Nick out-battled two defenders for the 30-yard catch and a first down. The Redwings huddled quickly. "Flankers left and right, post and fly." Both receivers were double-covered. The pass was incomplete. It was fourth down.

"Flankers left and right, look-in to the left end." Both receivers were double-covered again. Garrett, the tight end, fought his way off the line of scrimmage. The look-in pass was complete for a first down. ... Time out!

"Flankers left and right, post and fly ... pick your target, Harrison," yelled Coach Brown over the roar of the crowd.

The Crusaders best defender chose Nick. The safety drifted to Nick's side. Harrison tapped his helmet, indicating the ball was going to Stewart on a post. But the safety committed to Stewart. The ball was away and Stewart went high and snatched the ball away from two defenders ... Touchdown!

But wait ... there was a flag. Coach Brown forgot to take Kyle out of the game. The referee marched off five yards to the 18. It was fourth down with 40 seconds left in the half.

"Flankers left and right; if there's double coverage, go tight end seam." Harrison checked. Both receivers were doubled, so he zipped a seam pass to Garrett for a first down with 20 seconds left.

Harrison was hit just as he released the ball and got up slowly. Joe replaced him at quarterback and had to throw the ball away in order to avoid a sack. There was also a flag ... holding. The Redwings were penalized to the 17-yard line with 10 seconds left. Ian, from the White team, entered the game as a sub for Stewart, who limped off the field with a cramp.

"Flankers left and right ... Ian, run a post and get to the end zone ... I'll throw it high," said Joe. "Just go get it like it's a rebound."

Joe rolled right from the shotgun ... lofted the ball ... Ian was double-covered but he jumped ... caught the ball, and crashed to the turf with the ball held tightly to his chest. Touchdown!

The players rushed to congratulate Ian, but he did not move. He had banged his head hard on the unforgiving turf. The trainer raced to his aid. As Kate, the varsity trainer, arrived, Ian opened his eyes and asked, "What's going on?"

Kate asked, "Where are you?"

Ian looked around and said, "I got a headache."

Kate asked again, "Where are you?"

Ian didn't answer as he tried to get up. Kate looked at Coach Brown and mouthed the words, "He's got a concussion."

After Ian was helped to the sidelines, Santos kicked the extra point hard against the wind, but it banged off the upright and the score remained 22–16 at halftime.

The players got their water and headed to the end zone for rest and words of advice. Coach Brown walked to the center of the group. Nobody talked or fooled around. The team was focused and involved.

Coach Brown began in a slow, somber voice. "There will be no adjustments. Just keep doing what you're doing. Each play, each matchup, has to be approached all out. This game will be decided by who wants it the most. You're playing great ... best of the year."

Coach Brown looked at the team, his excitement rising. He raised his arm, sling and all, and exclaimed uncharacteristically, "We're ahead. They're getting tired. This is why Doctor Death trained you so hard. This is what will determine our margin of victory. Just relax. Rest! Then, let's go after it. We're not holding anything back."

Coach Grosso rose, placed his hand on Coach Brown's pacemaker, and said, "I hope this happy button's working. Let's not have an incident." The kids laughed. This was a good sign and exactly what Coach Grosso intended.

St. Monica kicked off with the wind to start the second half. The Redwings made a first down but were forced to punt into the wind. The snap was low and Nick's knee hit the ground as he tried to catch the ball. The Crusaders were elated as they got the ball at the Redwing 29-yard line.

On the first play, O'Malley went 29 yards for a score. Ira blocked the extra point. The score was tied at 22 with four minutes left in the third quarter. The coaches looked at the players before the kickoff. They weren't shocked or disappointed. They were focused and determined. Mentally, they were in championship form.

After the kickoff neither team could move the ball. The hitting was ferocious as one player after another demonstrated how badly they wanted this game. Players shuttled in and out of the game because of exhaustion or minor injuries.

St. Raphael punted to St. Monica at the 39. After two losses, the Crusaders completed a pass to the Redwing 20-yard line, but the receiver was called for offensive interference. Instead of having the ball first down on the 15-yard line, the Crusaders turned the ball over near midfield. This was a huge break for the Redwings.

From there, Nick caught a 30-yard pass from Joe. The Redwings were at the 20-yard line ready to score. However, St. Monica stiffened and took over on downs at their own 15-yard line.

On the next series of plays, St. Monica demonstrated why they were undefeated as they moved the ball easily to the 50-yard line. The momentum had shifted again. But on the next play, St. Monica fumbled, and Keith recovered the ball at the 40-yard line.

The Redwing fans were elated, as they pounded their feet on the metal bleachers. After one first down, the Redwings were forced to punt. The Crusaders took over at the 15-yard line.

From there St. Monica relentlessly moved the ball 81 yards to the 4-yard line against the wind and a fatigued Redwing squad. It was first down and four to go for what could be the winning score.

With each momentum shift, the other team reached down and tapped their reserve tank of adrenalin. One more play ... two more plays ... each play could provide the desired margin of victory and this was no exception.

On first down Brian stuffed the St. Monica runner for no gain. After a fumbled snap and a short gain, it was fourth and goal at the 2-yard line. Both crowds, sitting side by side, were screaming their support for their respective teams.

St. Monica's huge line came to the line of scrimmage, confident they would dominate the smaller Redwings as they had done during the current drive. Everybody knew O'Malley would get the ball, but where was he going to go?

The Crusaders went on a long count. Nobody jumped offside. The ball was snapped. Perry and Todd were gapped and went on ball movement. Kyle went with O'Malley to the hole. But there was no hole. Perry had penetrated and hit the lead blocker in the backfield. Then, Kyle and Brian tackled O'Malley, but he twisted away. Then he was driven awkwardly to the ground by Ira, one of Matt's nine White team starters.

O'Malley went down and didn't get up. The Redwings took over on downs as O'Malley limped off the field.

On the first play, Kyle was nearly caught for a safety by the blitzing Crusaders. After two plays moved the ball to the 2-yard line, Coach Brown called a time-out with five minutes left in the game. If the Redwing punt was blocked, it could be recovered by St. Monica for a touchdown and a sure win. Or, if the Redwings got the punt off, the Blue Streaks would get the ball at about the 30-yard line with plenty of time to score.

After he conferred with Coach Aimonette, the Redwings' chief strategist, and Coach Jerman, Coach Brown decided to take a safety. This would give St. Monica a 24–22 lead, but the Redwings would get a free kick from the 20 with a 40–50-mile-per-hour wind. He instructed Nick to catch the ball and step out of the end zone.

As Nick stepped out of the end zone, the crowd murmured as they tried to comprehend the unexpected. Then, the Crusader faithful cheered, and the Redwing fans were left in shock.

There were expressions of disbelief and more. Had Coach Brown lost his mind? Or worse yet, had his pacemaker failed? The coaching staff looked at Coach Brown in disbelief.

Then, as Coach Aimonette smiled, the rest of the staff slowly understood what just transpired. The Crusader coach stared across the field in disbelief. Then, when he realized he was without O'Malley, he smiled, pointed a finger at the Redwing sideline as if to say, "Nice move, but you've got to stop us."

With adrenaline pumping and a 50-mile-per-hour wind blowing, Santos kicked the ball over the Crusader returner's head. It rolled and was blown to the 10-yard line. Nick, Danny and Mike buried the ball carrier at the 15-yard line.

On the first play, the Redwings stopped St. Monica for a 3-yard loss, then, for no gain on successive plays as Perry, Todd, Keith, Garrett, and George smothered the Crusader runners as soon as they took a handoff.

On the final play, Perry tackled the Crusader runner near the St. Monica sideline. The Crusader runner kicked Perry out of frustration. Perry got up quickly, looked at the St. Monica player, pointed his finger, and just walked away. On another day and another time, Perry's reaction might have been considerably different.

St. Monica punted to the 50-yard line with the benefit of a fortunate bounce. There was 2:39 left in the game and maybe the St. Raphael season.

"48 with the works," Joe said calmly. The ball was pitched, but it hit Bobby in the back. After a scramble, the ball was recovered by Jason, who had replaced Billy, for a 2-yard loss. In his excitement Joe had pitched the ball to the wrong player. Nobody said a word as the team rushed to the huddle. "Flankers left and right ... slant," said Joe.

Joe looked to his left ... then right and saw soft coverage left and pointed to his right. The defensive back crept up into press coverage. Joe took the snap from center and threw a perfect pass to Nick on his left for 15 yards and a first down at the 30.

"Flankers left and right ... 7-yard hook right. ... Complete to Nick! ... Second and 3 at the 23 with 1:15 left. Time out."

Coach Brown called two plays. "Draw and boiler set, 10-yard inside hook." On the draw, Kyle gained 3 yards. The referees called a time-out to measure for the first down. It was third down and a yard for a first down. There were 52 seconds left in the game.

"Hammer right, tight end drag," called Coach Brown. "They won't expect it, and we have to get going."

The Crusaders went into a gap eight expecting a run. Joe faked the ball to Kyle, who was stopped for a loss, then threw a perfect pass to Mathew for a first down at the eleven.

"Boiler set right ... fake 7-yard hook ... Drag."

Both receivers sprinted to the end zone and drew double coverage. Joe looked at them, then dropped the ball off to the tight end, Mike Schneider from the White team. Mike bobbled it for a second, and was knocked out of bounds at the 1-yard line.

"Time-out," screamed Coach Brown as the clock ticked down to 18 seconds.

The Redwings needed one foot for a first down and one yard for a touchdown. There were no more time-outs.

Coach Brown looked around the huddle. All eyes were on him as the players pleaded for the right play. It was quiet in the huddle, as the cheers and advice from the stands and coaching staff could not penetrate the invisible shield that surrounded the huddle. One play for the win ... or one play for the loss. Which would it be?

Mike, the seventh-grade center who replaced Greg because of an injury, mustered all his courage, pushed the older kids aside, and said excitedly, "Coach, I can get us into the end zone. I can put that Smith kid on his back. I will roach him," as he pointed to the sticker "Never give up" on his helmet. A couple of the older players smiled in admiration and disbelief.

Coach Brown had many plays available and a lot of advice from assistant coaches. But his instincts dictated, "Have faith in those who think they can." The kids nodded their heads in agreement and touched their stickers. They all knew where they were.

"Okay. Hammer right, QB sneak."

Brian said, "One play! ... All the backs push Joe into the end zone. Hands in ... REDWINGS."

Coach Brown held Joe back for a second and said, "If you don't make it, line up quickly and spike the ball. Make sure you spike it forward."

Just before the ball was snapped, the Crusaders' best lineman moved from tackle to guard, right where Joe was going to run. The Redwings broke the huddle and came to the line of scrimmage for their season-defining play. All the linemen went into four-point stances for extra traction and thrust. All those butts that had been so high all season were now as low as they could be. The energy and anticipation continued to build as the fans from both teams went totally silent.

The ball was snapped. Todd, George, and Mike all got out low and under the St. Monica linemen. There was a push, as the energy of the moment was released. There was a stalemate as both teams wanted this moment and the game. Then, there was another push as Billy, Bobby, and Kyle crashed into the pile of linemen. The pile moved forward into the end zone, and Joe moved with it to victory. The players erupted. They had won 28–24 over the team that had beaten them 40–6 just a few weeks ago.

The celebration was short, but intense as the players quickly assembled at the 50-yard line for a sincere exchange of congratulations for a game well played. The procession took longer than normal as players took extra time to congratulate specific opponents for their effort.

The team assembled at the center of the field for postgame remarks by the coaches. They were still excited when Coach Brown arrived after a lengthy discussion with the St. Monica coach.

"Needless to say, you played your best game of the season today. I want you to enjoy this win today and Monday, but that's it. You can enjoy it again when your season's over. Many teams celebrate way too long after a big win. They're still celebrating as they try to play the following week and they lose ... and they can't figure out why they lost. We will not make that mistake. It will take another effort just like today's to beat St. Nicholas. They have only one loss and have outscored their opponents 240–30 over nine games. Do you understand what I'm saying?"

Kyle stood up and said, "Coach, even I understand. We won't celebrate until we win the championship in two more games. But when that happens, I hope that thing of yours is Gatorade-proof." The players laughed.

Coach Martynowicz then said, "Let's have the whole team lead the Redwing today ... ONE, TWO, THREE ... REDWINGS."

Coach Brown lingered a little while to take in the aura of the now quiet stadium. He looked up at the Sears Tower. It almost seemed to nod its head in recognition of an unexpected accomplishment. He had been through an emotional week, but it was awash now in the joy of the moment.

Coach Jerman stood behind his friend of 40 years. "Are you okay?" he asked, concerned the pacemaker had been overtaxed by the excitement of the final minutes.

"Yes, Lou, I'm more than okay. Aren't you?" Coach Brown looked around one more time as the parents walked to their cars with their exhausted children. "It had to be one of our greatest games ever ... and yes, it was a good test run for this $50,000 unit. It's worth every penny, don't you think?"

"I'd say priceless, my friend," as Coaches Brown and Jerman embraced for the second time that day. The game was worth more than the traditional handshake.

As they walked off the field, John, a 25-year referee in the league, approached and said, "Just wanted you guys to know your teams are known for their unique style of play around here. People call them a bunch of choir boys. They compliment the other team. They don't trash talk. They don't swear. But they sure know how to play football once the ball is snapped. It's important to exhibit good sportsmanship when nobody's looking. Your players do that. I just thought you ought to know."

"Thanks, John," said the coaches simultaneously as John hurried away.

"I got to go. I can't be seen with you guys. The league will think something's up. Good thing they don't know my son referees in your in-house league," said John over his shoulder.

Coach Brown looked at Lou. "Honest, Lou, I didn't know. You know Coach Kanis is always looking for referees."

Coach Jerman smiled, shook his head, and said, "You got to keep me out of trouble. I'm on the board."

 PLAY NUMBER THIRTY

Discipline should never be applied from anger. It should never be intended to embarrass or ridicule a child. When this occurs, the child will not hear much of what you say, he will lose respect for you, and require more discipline in the future because he sees very little value in self-discipline. Furthermore, this type of coaching will cause the child to work at pleasing the coach as opposed to taking the risks required for growth. Since it is difficult to predict what pleases others, the child will make additional errors and experience additional misunderstood discipline. When this happens, there is no useful learning taking place.

31
St. Nicholas Game

After doing a little dance and raising his arms to the cheers of the crowd, Matt trotted toward Coach Brown. As he approached he yelled, "The will to win is important, but the will to prepare is vital. Do you know who said that, Coach? ... Joe Paterno. He's my favorite coach." Matt had dedicated himself to preparing for this opportunity, not knowing if it would ever come. He must have believed preparing for an unknown opportunity, in itself, was a worthwhile experience.

THE PRACTICES WERE COLD AND RAINY ALL WEEK, but the players were more focused than expected given the conditions. They worked hard preparing a special defense to stop the famous St. Nicholas power off tackle play. St. Nicholas would run this play indefinitely if a team was unable to stop it. The players became increasingly confident, and by the end of the week believed their special defense would stop a bigger, stronger St. Nicholas team.

The practices were also sparked by the return of a former quarterback. Joe had an exceptional year in high school. He earned the starting varsity quarterback position as a sophomore. Unfortunately, his team was upset in the first round of the playoffs on a last-minute score. Although he was very disappointed, he called

Sunday night to see how the Redwings did and offered to fulfill his commitment to help coach.

This was beneficial from both a motivational and functional standpoint. The players respected Joe and listened to him all week as he spoke about the physical and mental aspects of the high school game. He told them how much they'd improved since the beginning of the season, and how abruptly it could all end with a single loss. As the coaches listened they saw small pieces of themselves in this 15-year-old boy. They were also reminded once again of the tremendous growth potential of a child and the debt of gratitude they owed these children as they constantly reminded them of the simplicity in what was really important.

At the end of the week Coach Brown thanked Joe for coming. Coach Kelly complimented him on fulfilling his commitment to help even though he must have been very disappointed about his team's loss.

Joe responded, "I'm disappointed, but mostly I feel sorry for the seniors who had hopes of winning the state title. It was their last game, and it happened so suddenly. You have to enjoy what you have. You never know when things are going to be taken from you. It wasn't until I got to high school that I realized how much we had learned at St Raphael. Giving a little back was fun, and it helped take my mind off the seniors. Heck, I'm still in the playoffs. I'll see you Sunday and be back next week, if you need me."

* * *

Sunday dawned a beautiful day for football. Coach Jerman reminded everyone once again, "I could remember only a handful of Sundays in 40 years that were not beautiful days for football even in November."

Everything got off to a good start. The coaches knew the players and the parents were psyched because they all showed up at the practice field on time, they had all their equipment including mouth guards, nobody asked about who they were playing, and everybody drove to the game without getting lost. Warm-ups went well. The form tackling drills were so intense Coach Brown had to tone them down a little for fear of an injury.

Coach Brown called the team together and asked them to take a knee. "In order to succeed, a team must start early at a difficult pace and maintain that pace as long as they can. If a team does that they'll achieve something exceptional. You have done that. We haven't said much about it, but all of you met most of the individual conditioning goals established at the beginning of the year. That's great! Your coaches have monitored and varied the pace of your development so there was no burnout. So you are ready to play today."

Coach Brown looked around and every eye was focused on the task at hand. "We have maintained a difficult pace, and everybody kept up at their definition of that pace. The definition of the right pace varied by player, but you all kept up. We focused on the mental and physical skills. The mental skills were the most difficult to develop. Natural ability helped, but mental skill development required the most effort and discipline. Mental skills have the biggest impact on the game because they're the key to physical skill development. It's hard to develop and maintain the mental state required for continuous improvement. You guys have done that and it's your edge today. Now you just have to let it happen. Just play free and let the slogans on your helmets come to life. You are ready for St Nicholas."

"Now Coach Grosso will lead us in prayer."

My brothers, take a moment and put yourselves in the presence of the Lord in the name of the Father, the Son, and the Holy Spirit. In today's gospel there was a father and two sons in a vineyard. The father needed work done and the one son didn't want to do it but did it anyway. Son number two said he would and didn't. Which son are you? There's toughness with the first son, for he didn't want to do it but did it anyway. He did it because he loved his father. As you take this field today against this opponent, you will be faced with the same question each and every play as you were during each practice. Each of you said you'd give your best in practice and you did. That's why we're here. How will it be after this game today? What decision will you make? Lord, we ask you today to give us the same courage you gave son one in the vineyard. Today's vineyard is this football field. We need your help so we can fulfill our commitment to each other because we love this team as son one loved his father. It will be hard, but we want the strength to dig deep to fulfill this commitment to each other. Lord, help us deliver this commitment. AMEN.

The game proceeded as expected. The St. Nicholas Raiders took the opening kickoff and relentlessly ran their off-tackle play, moving the ball for a first down at the Redwing 25-yard line. The customized defense wasn't working like it did in practice. The players were losing faith in it.

But on the next play St. Nicholas fumbled and Alex, a seventh-grade linebacker added to the starting lineup for the St. Nicholas defense, recovered the ball. St. Raphael was energized but were unable to move the ball and were forced to punt.

Nick, the normal punter, was injured on the kickoff, and would not be able to play for the rest of the game. Mark, the second-string punter, was pressed into service. This was Mark's first game back after dislocating his finger. He had practiced punting all week, successfully catching the snap from center with his bandaged finger, but on this day it was not to be. The ball was centered, hit Mark on the finger, then the ground, and was recovered by St. Nicholas on the Redwing 15-yard line. From there, St. Nicholas scored for a 6–0 lead. Mark, an incredibly well-motivated first-year football player, came to the sidelines, emotionally distraught, claiming, "I just cost us the game and I don't want to punt anymore."

Coach Kanis, the special teams coach, assured him they'd have many opportunities to win this game, but he wasn't buying it. Coach Brown watched as Coach Kanis comforted Mark before delivering a message of encouragement designed to rebuild his confidence. He told Mark about a time in high school when he made a big mistake in a playoff game and never got a chance to redeem himself.

"You are fortunate," said Coach Kanis, "because you'll get another chance a lot sooner than you think. The way St. Nicholas is playing, we're probably going to punt again very soon and you're our punter. Anybody who volunteers to punt with a bad hand has to have courage. Players with that kind of courage are going to make a few mistakes. Remember, you also volunteered to run a fake punt as long as you could run out of bounds after you made the first down so your mother wouldn't get angry." Mark smiled for the first time.

Coach Kanis continued, "Some people, including myself, who've tried a lot of difficult things are going to make mistakes. Unfortunately, there are many players who never volunteer or take a risk. These players make few mistakes, but experience little growth. Now you have a great opportunity to grow. The difference between the really great athletes and the other athletes lies in their ability to come back from adversity. Great athletes have short memories. You just made a mistake, but you punted well all week. Now you have an opportunity to deal with that mistake. Nobody on the team is mad at you. I'm sure they all think you'll do just fine the next time. Also, the coaches would never consciously put you in a position to fail."

Coach Kanis paused to see if Mark had heard anything.

"Now, tell me, Mark, what's the difference between great and ordinary athletes?"

Mark reluctantly repeated, "The great athletes try again after they make a mistake. Should I take some snaps from Greg? It looks like the guys are worried about my punting. They're playing a lot better now."

While Mark was reconnecting with the world around him, Joe executed the perfect option play, going 70 yards through the entire St. Nicholas team to tie the score at 6–6. The extra point was blocked. The Raiders came right back, requiring only six plays to take the lead 13–6 and the momentum.

St. Raphael fought back and reclaimed the lead by driving 70 yards in eight plays with Bobby going the final 22 yards on a perfectly blocked counter trap as George flattened two Raiders. Santos kicked the extra point for a 14–13 lead.

The Raiders continued their relentless attack, moving the ball to the St. Raphael 20-yard line. There, Mike intercepted a pass, and ran it to the St. Nicholas 30-yard line. From there, Kyle scored behind Garrett's "pancake block" and St. Raphael went to halftime with a 20–13 lead.

The Raiders began the second half by moving the ball with ease 65 yards in 12 plays to score. Brendan, Perry, and Todd stuffed the extra point and the Redwings retained a 20–19 lead. The hitting was taking its toll, as several players from both teams went to the bench with minor injuries.

After the kickoff, a fired-up Raider team pinned the Redwings at their 15-yard line. Mark's time for atonement had arrived as the Redwings prepared to punt into a stiff wind.

Mark was prepared as he trotted onto the field before anybody had chance to say anything to him. The coaches had no idea about his state of mind. They only knew it was someplace between "let's get it over with" and an intense resolve. Mark did not enter the huddle, but went straight to his spot on the goal line. He stretched his leg and shook his bandaged hand a little, as though he was checking for circulation.

Harrison set the team for the most important play of the game. The stadium went silent. When he was ready, Greg, who could center at the high school level, sent the ball back hard on a line directly at Mark's outstretched hands. The interior line, sensing the importance of the hour, held. Mark CAUGHT THE BALL! He then carefully positioned the ball, laces up. He started his stride, extended his arms, dropped the ball directly onto his instep, extended his leg, and kicked the ball low into the wind.

Fortunately, the St. Nicholas coach had emphatically waved his punt returner up to the 35-yard line. The ball sailed over the player's head and began to roll end over end as only a football can. The Raider player finally retrieved the ball on his own 35-yard line, then gave ground to avoid the St. Raphael pursuit. He was tackled by Bobby and Kyle on his own 30-yard line.

Mark bounded off the field and was mobbed by coaches and teammates. He had passed a test, learned a lesson, and benefited significantly from a mistake. After things quieted down a little, Mark found Coach Kanis and said, "Thank you, Coach. Now I have a story to tell a player someday when I'm a coach at St. Raphael."

Mark's punt provided a much needed injection of enthusiasm, but soon it waned as the Raiders drove the ball to the St. Raphael 20-yard line. The team had sustained some minor injuries that kept Greg, Todd, and Garrett, all two-way starters, on the sidelines.

The team reached down and found enough resolve to hold St. Nicholas and force a fourth down and one at the 11-yard line. However, on the third down play, Perry got the wind knocked out of him making a tackle. Over his objections, he had to leave the game for one play.

As Coach Brown looked toward a depleted bench, he saw Matt standing next to him snapping his chinstrap. He looked up at Coach Brown with a matter-of-fact look in his eyes and said, "Look no further, Coach, I am all you got. This has been a tough day for linemen."

While Coach Brown took one last look at the bench, Matt began telling Coach Brown what he thought he'd say as though he had lived it a thousand times in his dreams.

"Coach, I know what you are going to say. Stay low because low man wins. Keep your eye on the ball and go on ball movement. They are coming at me because I'm a replacement. And I can do it because they aren't as good as Garrett and George .... right?"

All Coach Brown could do was nod his head and say with a smile, "Matt, you take all the fun out of coaching when you do my job too. Go get 'em."

As Matt trotted slowly onto the field, Coach Brown could see the Raider coach looking to see where the replacement was going to line up before he called his play. Matt was greeted so enthusiastically by the team, he had to put his arms up to ward off the helmet slaps. Matt wandered around a little before getting into his position, hoping to confuse the opposing coach, but to no avail.

When St. Nicholas broke the huddle, everybody in the stadium knew where they were going as their 180-pound tackle moved to guard directly in front of Matt. Matt saw this, pointed at him as he got into his four-point stance. This caused Billy and Bobby, the two middle backers, to creep up directly behind Matt.

When the ball was snapped, Matt came off the ball quicker than ever before with his nose only inches off the ground. He was two-timed by the guard and center, driving his face into the mud. But the blocks were too late. Matt had achieved penetration and could not be pushed off the line of scrimmage.

The St. Nicholas fullback banged into the pile Matt had created. Matt was now "king of the ring." The ball carrier, having no place to go, tried to run to his left, but ran directly into Mike, who was now playing defensive end. The ball carrier was stopped for a 2-yard loss and St. Raphael took over on downs.

As the players unpiled, the Raider tackle pushed Matt a little. This was the greatest form of recognition Matt could have received. Matt and Mike danced off the field with Matt proudly displaying the mud caked to his facemask as a badge of honor. Matt had pushed himself for an entire season, dreaming of such an opportunity. When the opportunity came, Matt was prepared.

After doing a little dance and raising his arms to the cheers of the crowd, Matt trotted toward Coach Brown. As he approached he yelled, "The will to win is important, but the will to prepare is vital. Do you know who said that, Coach? ... Joe Paterno. He's my favorite coach."

Matt had dedicated himself to preparing for this opportunity, not knowing if it would ever come. He must have believed preparing for an unknown opportunity, in itself, was a worthwhile experience.

Matt's effort sparked the team as they drove 87 yards in six plays for a touchdown, with Stewart going the final 40 yards on a screen pass play. This touchdown made the score 26–19. While the kids were celebrating in the end zone, the coaches were struggling with one of those dreaded decisions that have inflated youth coaching salaries over the years. If the Redwings kicked the two-point conversion, they would put the game out of reach. If the Redwings went for one point, and made it, St. Nicholas had plenty of time to score against a depleted Redwing squad and tie the game with a kick. The special team's Coach Kanis asked Santos how he felt about kicking the point.

Santos, who was normally a quiet kid, said firmly, "Coach, I can do it. My grandfather flew here this week to help me with my kicking. He used to be a kicker in college."

Coach Kanis asked, "Is your grandfather in the stands?"

Santos replied, "Yeah, Coach."

Coach Kanis looked at Santos for a second to see if the answer was in his eyes. Apparently it was, and he said, "Coach Brown, we're always talking about being proactive. Let's kick it and get these guys off our back for good."

The Redwings raced back out onto the field and set up for the kick. The St. Nicholas coach called a time-out. He'd decided it was going to be a fake.

After the time-out, Greg made a perfect snap from center, St. Nicholas did not rush the kicker, and Santos boomed an extra point that would have been good from 30 yards. Coach Kanis looked at Coach Brown, and said as he looked to the stands, "Sorry to push you on that one. There are some things that are more important than the game. Besides, we would have held them, don't you think?"

As the coaches looked to the stands, which were very close, Santos's grandfather could be seen boasting emphatically, "That kid's my grandson. I taught him to kick like that." He was also winning what looked like a death struggle with Mrs. Santos, who was trying to pull him back into his seat.

The score and a nine-point lead gave the Redwings much-needed breathing room, but Coach Brown knew the game was far from over. St. Raphael was tired, without five starters, and there were eight minutes left in the game.

After a 50-yard kickoff, St. Nicholas drove the ball to the Redwing 30-yard line. If they could score and execute an on-side kick they could still win the game. St Nicholas moved to the 20-yard line with four minutes left. They had to hurry. On third down and one at the 10-yard line, the Raiders surprised the Redwings with a pass into the end zone. The pass was intercepted by Danny and St. Raphael ran out the clock. The game was over and St. Raphael moved on to become an unlikely opponent for St. Genevieve in the finals of the Chicago Catholic League Championships.

PLAY NUMBER THIRTY-ONE

Many unsuccessful coaches believe children must adjust to their coaching style because, after all, they are the boss. Successful youth coaches learn to become a bit of a child, so they can adjust to the learning style of the children. More than once, I've heard parents compliment their coaches by saying to each other, our coaches are great because I don't think they want to grow up. Try to have as much fun as your kids do.

32
Parental Appreciation

*As I watched today, I could see them building huge chunks of
character that emanated from their consistency. They knew
what to do when we all thought they wouldn't or couldn't!
They performed as if there were no consequences, only
opportunities. They acted from a platform of values they had
developed over the course of the season through instruction,
discussion, testing, reinforcement, support, role-modeling,
caring, and so on.*

AS THE GUN SOUNDED, THE CELEBRATIONS AND
disappointments were superseded by mutual respect, as the players
shook hands immediately in the middle of the field, not waiting for
the traditional receiving lines to be formed at the 50-yard line. After
the handshakes, some helmet slaps, and some brief discussions, the
Redwings made a brief, halfhearted attempt at celebration, but they
were just too tired, mentally and physically. Even Matt's celebration
was subdued, as he could only dance a few steps as he raised his
mud-caked helmet skyward, and said, "I'm not cleaning this helmet
until Monday. I'm so psyched."

The team jogged or walked to the sidelines, got their cans of pop, emotional hugs from their parents and coaches, and started for their cars. Their full appreciation of what they had accomplished in beating a heavily favored St. Nicholas team would just have to wait until they finished their parental discussions and traditional naps on the way home in the car.

There was no team meeting required after the game. The players knew they had done their best and it was darn good. They knew practice was on Tuesday. The team they would face in the finals was undefeated St. Genevieve, who had reached the finals by winning their two games by a combined score of 75–12. Their physical and psychological tanks had to be refilled before they could even think about their final game.

As the coaching staff collected their stuff, Don, a father and one of the most supportive parents, called them together to express his appreciation he had accumulated over the past five years of his children's participation in St. Raphael football.

He began by saying, "Today, I was inspired by these kids, win or lose. I thoroughly enjoyed their effort because of its innocence and purity of purpose. They were oblivious to a past that would have suggested they couldn't succeed. They played without fear. They performed under the most demanding of physical and mental conditions. Yet, they were unaware of their environment. Their execution was relentless and exciting. Each time there was adversity or a breakdown, they were able to ignite the fire required for breakthrough. These kids supported one another in ways that would not allow failure."

Here Don stopped to collect his thoughts and his composure.

He continued, "As I watched today, I could see them building huge chunks of character that emanated from their consistency. They knew what to do when we all thought they wouldn't or couldn't! They performed as if there were no consequences, only opportunities. They acted from a platform of values they had developed over the course of the season through instruction, discussion, testing, reinforcement, support, role-modeling, caring, and so on."

Don paused again, then said, "Bear with me, guys. This has been building for five years."

The coaches all nodded their heads and Don continued, "I've heard my sons talk about hard work, respect, never giving up, good attitudes, working for improvement, helping your teammates, and making friends. I believe your players have internalized these values, and built their own platforms on which to perform. They don't think about it, they just let their performance flow from their values. They have built confidence in their football skills, and confidence in each other. I have heard my kids say if they do their best, they'll achieve everything that's possible and perhaps a little more. In the past, I'm not so sure I listened to all of that stuff.

"Well, they convinced me today. I saw them achieve much more than I thought possible when driving to the field today. Their actions today reminded me of all those discussions with one another riding to and from practice."

Don paused for a second to see if the coaches were still listening. They were. In fact, they looked awestruck by the passion of his commentary, so he continued.

"Believe it or not, many of the parents saw their children as role models today. That may sound like the exaggerations of an emotional parent, but that's the way a lot of parents are feeling right now. Some of them even admitted it to each other during the game. And, isn't it beautiful, the players don't even realize the impact they've had on us today. It even transcends winning this game. Listen to my kids over there. They're yelling at me to get going so we can get a pizza on the way home. They have no idea what I'm feeling about them right now, but I'm going to tell them a little at a time. Do you think they'll understand?"

Coach Jerman answered what could have been a rhetorical question by saying, "Over the years, I have greatly underestimated the capability of our players to understand."

After Coach Jerman's remark, the coaches thanked Don and started to leave, but he was not finished. "I was reading a book the other day you guys ought to read called *The Winner Within* by Pat Riley. He told a story about his dad. At the end of the story Pat said his father told him, "Every now and then there comes a day where someplace, sometime, you simply have to plant your feet, stand firm, and make a point about who you are and what you believe in." Don paused. "Today, I think our kids did that. And I mean our kids."

Don stopped for a second to gain his composure and then continued very firmly, "You may not realize it, but you guys create the environment that makes all this possible. You don't seem to be fully aware of the contribution you're making. I can see by your expressions, you almost act like my kid, more interested in the pizza than talking about your accomplishments. I want you to take some time to do that."

Don stopped again to gain his composure and then said very slowly, "I want to thank all of you for helping me raise my children!"

Then, Don hugged each coach, shook their hands, and walked away, glad it was a half a mile to his car, where his kids were hanging out the windows, yelling for their pizzas.

All the coaches could do was look at one another. They all knew Don had just experienced what the coaches have an opportunity to experience every year. Coach Cook said it all when he yelled, "GOD, I LOVE COACHING! HOW ABOUT A CELEBRATION IN THE FOOTBALL ROOM?"

All the coaches declined. They felt as tired as their players. The video review could wait until next week. All the coaches knew, even though they had trouble remembering their wives' birthdays, they could all do a play by play of today's game without the video.

PLAY NUMBER THIRTY-TWO

The coach should ask the parents not to criticize the coach to their child. This causes the child to lose confidence in the coach and impacts the coach's ability to teach their child. If the child doesn't pay attention because he thinks poorly of the coach, it impacts his learning and his play. The coach should make himself available and encourage the parents to make their suggestions directly. Most criticisms are due to resolvable misunderstands that take on a life of their own with time.

33
Championship Game Preparation

The players grew quiet much quicker than usual, as they refocused on the game, only minutes away. The fact they were in a locker room and a high school stadium for the first time added to the atmosphere of excitement surrounding the game. They were underdogs, and they knew it. League coaches said this was one of the best teams they had seen in the 35-year history of the league. When Coach Brown called St. Nicholas to get a scouting report, their coach said, "Just have your kids enjoy the experience of being there, and have fun."

CHAMPIONSHIP WEEK PRACTICE HAD A UNIQUE atmosphere. The practices took place under the lights in 15–20 degree temperatures. The players didn't mind; only the coaches shivered and complained.

The players were quiet, attentive, focused, and easily frustrated as they tried to cram for their final exam against St. Genevieve. They knew they were facing an undefeated team who had outscored their opponents this season 325–18, because they had found the league website scoreboard on the Internet. They also read the assorted postings on the website from confident Saints players and asked, "What does it mean to be taken to the shed?"

At the end of practice on Tuesday, Coach Brown called the team together and handed them a letter written to one of St. Raphael's most memorable teams. It was not one of the nine championship teams, but the 1970 team that went 0–7–1.

"Do you remember the team I told you about after the St. Monica game?" began Coach Brown. "That team symbolized all of the stickers on your helmets and so do you. We sent this letter to them and only one other team. The second team upset an undefeated team to win the Catholic League Championship in 2003. The coaches decided to give you this letter before your last game because we're so pleased with your accomplishments this season. Sunday will be frosting on the cake, and we are very confident about our chances. We are peaking at the right time, and I have a feeling St. Genevieve is a little overconfident by the looks of their postings on the league website."

Coach Brown paused as the coaches distributed the letter and advised several players not to stuff it into their sweaty helmets and pants. Then he said, "Read the letter carefully tonight. I believe it contains your keys to victory on Sunday."

As Coach Brown solicited comments from other coaches, only one person stepped forward, and it wasn't a coach. It was Matt. "I think my oldest brother got this letter. He showed it to me at the beginning of the season. He says he's read it many times, especially when he's had problems. Each time he reads it, he's a little older and says he understands a little more. The only guys on this team that have half a chance of getting it are Brian, Keith, and Todd ... and of course me. So, if you guys don't get it, show it to your parents."

Then, Coach Jerman called the team together. "Hands in ... one, two, three, ... Redwings." Just then the automatically timed lights went off as if for emphasis. Everybody looked at one another as Coach Martynowicz exclaimed, "Even Coach Jerman's getting into this game. Yeah!"

* * *

On Sunday morning, the team met at Market Meadows as usual for the trip to Chicago. Margi carefully took roll. Nobody was late. The players and parents stayed in their cars because the temperature was 9 degrees. There had been a six-inch snowfall during the night. It was going to be a tough drive to the city, so everybody was anxious to leave for the game.

At exactly 11:45, a huge tour bus pulled into the parking lot. Coach Martynowicz said, "Why don't we ever take a bus to our games? Every other team in town does."

Coach Grosso laughed and said, "Gotcha! Didn't you and Taylor get the memo? That's our ride. It was arranged by the offensive coaches. It's only going to cost each coach 50 dollars. Just give your money to Coach Kelly."

Margi greeted the bus driver, then went car to car informing the parents. The players were excited as they fought for seats in the rear of the bus. The parents were relieved that they didn't have to make the one-hour drive to the city. They were also conscious of the hush that developed in the back of the bus as they approached their destination.

* * *

The team mood was somber and focused as the players trudged into the high school locker room at Jack Cronin Stadium before their game with undefeated St. Genevieve.

It had snowed six inches in the city too, and there were only enough interested volunteers to clear the yard stripes and field boundaries before the game. The temperature had risen to 15 degrees at game time, but a north wind had driven the windchill to several degrees below zero.

The players acted unaware of these horrible conditions as they took their seats in the locker room after warm-ups. Several were sweating profusely, and most refused hot chocolate offered by Margi and Terri. Several players laughed at the sight of steam rising from the heads of those who'd removed their helmets.

The coaches, on the other hand, were nervously blowing on their hands after removing their mittens. They were also kicking snow from their boots and pulling their stocking hats down over their ears in preparation for a long, miserable afternoon.

Unlike the Notre Dame locker room, the cheerleaders were allowed to stand near the door warming their hands and giggling about their presence in the boys' locker room. Coaches Cook and Bus stood in front of the girls as if to shield the players from any unnecessary distractions prior to the game.

St. Genevieve was from a tough Chicago neighborhood. They'd beaten St. Nicholas 26–0 earlier in the season. They had a line that averaged over 150 pounds and a quarterback who was being recruited by several Chicago Catholic high schools. And, rumor had it, their tailback had a mustache and drove his own car to the game.

The players grew quiet much quicker than usual, as they refocused on the game only minutes away. The fact they were in a locker room and a high school stadium for the first time added to the atmosphere of excitement surrounding the game. They were underdogs, and they knew it. League coaches said this was one of the best teams they had seen in the 35-year history of the league. When Coach Brown called St. Nicholas to get a scouting report, their coach said, "Just have your kids enjoy the experience of being there and have fun."

So, with these comments in mind, Coach Brown rose to address the team. He began with a question, "What do you think got us here today?"

After the question was repeated, several players raised their hands. Garrett said, "We played our two best games of the year the past two weeks."

"I felt our hard work was worth it because we got a lot better during the season," added Billy, who had been cleared to play again on a heavily taped ankle.

"For the first time," said Kyle, "I felt like we depended on each other."

Jeff stood, looked at the floor and said, "You guys supported me when I had problems. I wanted to do more for the team, but couldn't. You all learned we're in this together. You helped Perry. You helped me. You all stepped up when we lost players for a whole bunch of reasons, and this made us all stronger. As Coach told me, dealing with our problems made us stronger."

Matt stood looked at Mike, Brendan, Matt, Brady, and other White team members and said, "I count nine of my White team members who are starting ... not including me. My work is done unless you need a big stop late in the game."

Everybody laughed. They needed the relief of a good laugh.

At this point, with other hands in the air, Coach Brown decided to summarize what the team had said. "So, what I heard was that this team grew to support each other, learned how to deal with adversity; to depend on each other to do your best, and be honest about your effort."

The team, as expected, answered this question with a resounding, "Yeah!"

With this answer resounding in the locker room for St. Genevieve to hear next door, Coach Brown asked what he thought was a concluding rhetorical question, "Does anybody else have anything to add?"

There was a pause, as the team's emotional level rose sufficiently to propel them through the locker room door onto the field and maybe beyond. As the players started to stand for the sprint to the field, Brian, a quiet team leader all season, decided to speak.

"Coach, all year you've told us not to focus on winning, but to do what it took to get better. You don't have to convince us we belong here. We believe we belong here because we're here."

Coach Brown and the other coaches thought for a minute, realizing they had been a little shortsighted. They had focused on convincing the kids they belonged here. Brian and others knew they belonged here simply because they were here. Coach Jerman, realizing nothing else needed to be said, said, "Let's go live up to the stickers on the helmets and have some fun."

At this point Kyle stood, called the team together with a "hands in," and the team yelled, "Redwings." Then he led them, walking with a determined gait, each player with their own thoughts, to the field of battle. As they approached the field, Perry could no longer control his emotions, and broke ranks and started to run. The whole team followed, unable to control their excitement for another second. They were ready for some football.

As the coaches followed, Coach Jerman said, "Aren't these kids amazing? I guess they heard more than we thought."

After the team prayer, the captains walked hand-in-hand to the center of the field for the coin toss. They had not joined hands all season, but this was a special moment.

The result of the coin toss was a good news–bad news story. The good news was the Redwings won the toss, deferred, and were kicking off with a 30-mile-per-hour wind. The bad news was that the captains got a close look at four of the reasons why the St. Genevieve Saints were 10 and 0. Upon their return to the sidelines, they reported the St. Genevieve running back did have a mustache, their right tackle had a lot of dark hair on his legs, and they were all tall and had firm handshakes.

With that, Bobby said, "I could grow a beard if I wanted to, and I have dark hair on my legs. So what's the big deal? And I'm only in the seventh grade!"

PLAY NUMBER THIRTY-THREE

Once team values are understood the team becomes more grounded and this grounding creates the platform from which excellence is achieved. This works the same way for individual children. When a coach teaches positive values it's like filling the values tank so there is no room for undesirable ideas and characteristics. If the right values enter the tank early, they serve as an intellectual immune system. When kids are young they are sick all the time because they have no immune system. Each time they get sick they improve their future immunity to disease. Experiences in life that are characterized by success and failure serve the same purpose as disease in the development of the intellectual/values immune system.

34
Championship Game

*At halftime, Coach Taylor asked Kyle how he knew what to
call on the interception. "They took extra time in the huddle
so it had to be something they hadn't run before," said Kyle.
"You know how long it takes us to call new plays. When their
tailback flanked, I knew he was going to get the ball. I had
deep coverage if Mike or Jeff missed the interception. We
needed a spark on a cold day. So, we had everything covered."
Brian pushed Kyle. "That's the worst joke I've ever heard.
Spark on a cold day, but I like it."*

SANTO'S KICKOFF RODE THE 30-MILE-PER-HOUR
wind over the safety's head. The ball skidded in the snow and
refused to stop rolling until it reached the 10-yard line. There, the
St. Genevieve safety was pummeled by Perry, Kyle, and a host of
Redwings. St. Raphael was fired up, and ready to play.

From there, however, St. Genevieve easily drove the ball 90 yards
in just eight plays for their first score as the Saints dominated the
line of scrimmage. The extra point was good and they led 7–0 after
four minutes of the first quarter.

After the kickoff, St. Raphael ran three plays, lost four yards, and were forced to punt from their own 25-yard line. The punt was blocked by the Saints' 180-pound tackle. On the first play, the St. Genevieve mustachioed tailback ran 20 yards for a touchdown, and made the score 14–0 halfway through the first quarter.

Perry called the team together before the kickoff. He looked each player in the eye and said firmly, "We're playing like we're afraid of these guys. They're from my neighborhood. If they think you're afraid, they'll bury you. Let's hit these guys like we did last week. It's not enough to just be here. I want this game."

The second quarter went better for the Redwings as they made two first downs on pass plays while St. Genevieve scored only once to take a 20–0 lead just before halftime. The field and weather conditions worsened and several players were forced to the sidelines with numbing extremities and minor injuries.

The Redwings were overmatched, but were not giving up. They were getting stronger as the quarter wore on. Some of the Saints were getting up a little slower, and the swagger was gone as they realized they'd have to play the full forty minutes in horrible conditions to be champions. By comparison, the Redwings were surprisingly oblivious to the temperatures that dropped constantly as the afternoon progressed.

On the ensuing kickoff, Jim Kanis, the special team's coach, inserted Michael and several other White team players into the game. He then called the special kickoff play used at the White team level only.

The ball was kicked end over end to Michael. The return wall formed on the left side of the field. Michael started toward the wall and so did the overly aggressive St. Genevieve players bent on inflicting as much pain as possible.

All of a sudden, he and three other players veered to the right. One block ... then two ... Michael broke a tackle and went 85 yards for a touchdown. The Saints players, in their desire "to lay some serious hurt" on the Redwing ball carrier, had overrun the play. Santos kicked the extra point to make the score 20–8.

The coaches hoped the Redwings could hold on until halftime. But, St. Genevieve moved the ball steadily to the 10-yard line, looking for the score that might ice the game. The wind and cold continued to take its toll on both teams as frequent substitutions were necessary. Even though St. Raphael had played a lot of players, they looked tired and cold, but nobody had given up. Substitutes still clamored to get in the game. Two Redwing players were taken to the locker room during the second quarter by the trainer due to possible frostbite.

The St. Raphael pregame locker room enthusiasm had changed to a more subdued, quiet resolve. They encouraged one another to give it all for one more play ... then one more play ... then another, hoping they could hold on until halftime. Then, they could regroup and maybe come back.

On third down at the 8-yard line, St. Genevieve took extra time in the huddle. In youth football, that usually meant a team was going to try a play they hadn't practiced much. St. Genevieve broke the huddle. Their tailback flanked to the wide side of the field. The defensive coordinator, Ed Taylor, started to yell, but Mike raised his hand as if to say "everything's under control."

Kyle had moved the two inside linebackers into a blitz position on either side of the center. He then moved to safety and called rotate coverage, which meant he would zone-cover the tailback, and Jeff and Mike would "man up." He then said to Mike, "Go for the ball."

Mike nodded his head without taking his eyes off the St. Genevieve tailback.

On the snap from center, the blitzers went after the quarterback, who hurried his throw. Mike backpedaled a few steps, kept one eye on the quarterback and one on the ball. The ball was thrown accurately, but at the last second Mike, knowing Kyle had deep coverage, stepped in front of the receiver, and tipped the ball. Jeff then out-battled the St. Genevieve tailback for the ball at the 5-yard line.

He paused to get his bearings, and then began a 95-yard trudge through the ice and snow to the St. Genevieve goal line. However, his quest was interrupted at the 10-yard line by none other than the St. Genevieve 180-pound tackle, who angrily buried Jeff's face beneath the snow line. Jeff stayed on the ground, and eventually had to be helped off the field. But, with 20 seconds left, St. Raphael had another chance to score.

On the first play, St. Raphael went into a spread formation. Before St. Genevieve could adjust, Joe took the snap, went back to pass, then ran to his right and threw a 10-yard pass to a wide-open Stewart for a touchdown. Santos kicked the extra point. The Redwings had been dominated. They had been outgained 250 yards to 35, but were only behind 20–16. They raced to the locker room as several players yelled, "We're still in this game."

At halftime, Coach Taylor asked Kyle how he knew what to call on the interception.

"They took extra time in the huddle so it had to be something they hadn't run before," said Kyle. "You know how long it takes us to call new plays. When their tailback flanked, I knew he was going to get the ball. I had deep coverage if Mike or Jeff missed the interception. We needed a spark on a cold day. So, we had everything covered."

Brian pushed Kyle. "That's the worst joke I've ever heard. Spark on a cold day, but I like it."

Kyle was right. He had trained himself for that moment as he learned to fulfill a leadership role throughout the season. He knew if he did what he thought was right for the good of the team, everybody would be supportive regardless of the outcome. This had been proven many times when things went poorly early in the season. This supportive environment, under adverse conditions, facilitated his growth into a leadership role.

As the players relaxed and drank their hot chocolate, Brian mentioned to Joe he thought St. Genevieve looked a little discouraged leaving the field at halftime.

Coach Schroeder, the offensive-line coach, overheard the comment and asked the players, "Why do you think they're discouraged? They're ahead."

"Maybe they expected to score before halftime and we'd give up," speculated Sean, a 90-pound nose tackle from the White team. "Then their second string could finish the game and they could get warm. Coach, nobody's complaining but it's cold out there. I admit that I was thinking that before Jeff's interception."

The players laughed, beating on Sean's helmet. Drew, another White team member starting at tackle on defense, interrupted the frivolity and said, "I think they're worried because we scored. They know we're not giving up."

"I think you're right, Drew," said Coach Schroeder. "I think they expected an easy game after the first quarter. When they couldn't put us away, they realized they're going to have to work for it. They're playing about thirteen players and we played over twenty in the first half. It's going to get colder. It will be a war of attrition of wills in the second half. We're in shape physically. We have more players. Let's see how tough we are mentally. If you're tired or cold, take a break. There's no shame in that. Hands in! ... Redwings!" With renewed enthusiasm, the Redwings returned to the field for the second half.

The weather conditions worsened as temperatures dropped and it began to snow. St. Genevieve took the ball to start the second half. This made Coach Brown happy, as he hoped to pin St. Genevieve deep and shorten the distance they'd have to go for another score. The Redwings got their wish as St. Genevieve started their first series at their 15-yard line. After a holding penalty, they were forced to punt.

St. Raphael sent ten players to try to block the punt. The St. Genevieve coaching staff tried to call a time-out but the ball was centered over the punter's head. After a scramble, Perry recovered the ball in the end zone for a touchdown. The extra point was good. St. Raphael led for the first time 24–20. They still had only two first downs and 35 yards of total offense, but for the first time felt like they just might win this game.

But St. Genevieve had other ideas. They were undefeated and wanted this game, too. They took the ensuing kickoff and pounded the ball inside the tackles for 14 plays and a touchdown. They missed the extra point to make the score 26–24.

For the remainder of the third quarter and most of the fourth, the game became a defensive struggle as field conditions deteriorated. There was blowing snow as temperatures dropped to bone-chilling levels. With four minutes left in the game, the Saints moved the ball to the Redwing 30-yard line. St. Raphael went into an eight-man line to stop the St. Genevieve offense, which was relentlessly pounding the ball inside the tackles to apparent victory. Sean, the White team nose tackle, and Perry positioned themselves in the guard-center gaps. The ball was snapped for a routine handoff. On ball movement, Sean shot through the gap, hit the fullback who fumbled, and Todd recovered. The Redwings had one final opportunity to win the game from their own 30-yard line.

St. Genevieve went into a prevent defense. Runs by Kyle, Bobby, and Michael behind George, Todd, Keith, Brian, and Greg moved the ball to the 50-yard line. A screen pass to Riley behind Brian, Billy, and Garrett moved the ball to the 30-yard line. Riley took a big hit from several Saints players and got up holding his hand.

A time-out was called. Kate, the trainer, examined the wrist. It was broken. There were two minutes left in the game as she applied a temporary cast and tried to take him to the locker room. He refused. He wanted to be with his team until the final gun.

On the next play Harrison completed a pass in the flat to Stewart, who went out of bounds at the 20-yard line. Coach Brown was alternating quarterbacks to maintain warm hands and to speed the play calling.

On the next play Joe ran a quarterback draw to the 5-yard line but the play was called back because of an off-side penalty. The team was not discouraged as Harrison and Joe completed hook passes to Nick, Mike, Mathew, and Ian to the 11-yard line. It was fourth down and one with one minute left in the game. Coach Brown called a time-out.

After consulting with the quarterbacks and Coaches Grosso and Kelly, the play was called. The team lined up in their short yardage set called the hammer. The tight end and fullback were in the backfield for blocking. Kyle was to get the ball, Billy and Bobby were to lead blocker as they ran over George and Todd.

St. Genevieve brought nine players close to the line of scrimmage. The ball was snapped. Harrison faked the ball to Kyle, rolled to his right and threw the ball to Stewart, who had lined up at end in this set. The ball was high, but he caught it and was knocked out of bounds at the 3-yard line with 45 seconds left in the game.

The Redwing fans were pounding their feet on the metal stands. The noise was deafening, but as Coach Brown confirmed later, he didn't hear a thing.

Kyle ran to the two. Time-out! Bobby dove to the one. There were 20 seconds left in the game. Coach Brown called the play and Joe started on the field but Harrison held up his hand and said, "I got the play, Coach." What a relief, Coach Brown confessed later.

The ball was snapped. Harrison faked the handoff right to Kyle, booted the ball left, and threw a short pass to Garrett the tight end for a touchdown. Harrison never saw the completion as his face was buried in the snow. But, he heard it. 31–27. He'd called the "widget pass." It was a JV play that hadn't been used all year. Coach Brown didn't even have it on his play card.

The Redwings erupted, then settled down for the extra point, which was no good. There was one play between the Redwings and a championship. The Saints anticipated an onside kick to prevent a runback with only ten seconds left in the game. They had their running backs positioned at the 40-and 50-yard lines with a single safety.

Coach Kanis called the kickoff team together and tried to impress on them the importance of this single play. When the team trotted to their positions, he held Billy, Kyle, and Santos back for a final word.

All the players were poised as Santos approached the ball. Instead of kicking it on the ground, he boomed it deep and left. The wind carried the ball past the safety to the 15-yard line, where it was picked up by Nick. Instead of taking it to the end zone, he took a knee to end the game. The Redwings had won a game they would remember for the rest of their lives.

Before joining the celebration, Coach Kanis just pointed and smiled at a stunned coaching staff. He started to explain his logic of kicking deep, but nobody cared. There would be time for explanations later, if necessary.

After the customary handshakes at the 50-yard line, the parents and the team stood silent as St. Genevieve was presented with their second-place trophy. The Redwings cheered a discouraged opponent. The Saints captains walked to the Redwing huddle to congratulate them one more time.

After the Redwing captains accepted the championship trophy to raucous cheers, hugs, and brief discussions, Coach Brown addressed the team. "This season has to be one of the greatest experiences of our coaching lives." Coach Jerman nodded his head. "Make sure you take all the time necessary to relive it, and cherish it for what you've learned and what you've accomplished under difficult conditions. The coaches want to thank you all for this experience. We won't forget it either. And I especially want to thank Harrison for the last call. I don't remember what I told Joe to call. I think my pacemaker froze up due to the cold and overuse." Coach Brown paused while everybody laughed, then said, "I'm speechless and that's probably a good thing. It's getting cold out here. Let's go celebrate!"

As the players put hands in for one final Redwings, Margi the team mom interrupted. "In recognition of a great season, win or lose today, we've arranged a party at Bruno's tonight at six. There will be game films and Father Ted will be there to conduct modified religious education classes for those of you scheduled at six. See you there."

After the loudest "REDWINGS!" of the season, the lights went out, and a very tired, but happy group of children slowly walked to the bus for the ride home. The players were quiet on the way home, as many of them slept. They were unaware of the true significance of their season's accomplishments, which would only grow with time and maturity.

 PLAY NUMBER THIRTY-FOUR

A primary reason for this team's success was its emotional intelligence. According to Goldman, emotional intelligence is defined as a combination of intellect, values, and getting along with others. If you can improve any aspect of this formula, you become more emotionally intelligent. This is the power of emotional intelligence. Reaching high levels of EI is possible because improvement of any aspect of it is totally within a person's control. That's why improvement is likely. As they grow their EI, team members can easily contribute to one another's growth. When teammates help each other improve, they feel good and personally improve their EI by teaching and improving relationships. Internalization occurs and the cycle continues. That is why emotional intelligence is so important to a team performance. EI can be taught to children without their understanding of the concept. This Redwing team's emotional intelligence was out of sight by the end of the season.

35
Brady's Banquet

*Diane concluded her discussion with the coaches by
indicating, "Brady's performance on the field of life improved
more significantly than his performance on the football
field. His grades have improved a whole point. He enjoys
the recognition from his teachers, his parents, and even his
friends. The quality of his social interactions with his friends
and family has improved. He's become more confident and
even proactive about things. He has even become interested
in having civil conversations with his younger sister, and has
given her advice in a constructive way. After which his sister
wanted to know, what's wrong with Brady?"*

EVERY YEAR, AT THE END OF THE SEASON, ALL THE
players, parents, and coaches assemble for one last time. They have
dinner, introduce the coaches and players by saying something positive about each child, and recount a grossly exaggerated play by play
of the season.

Over the season, positive relationships were developed between
the players and parents and coaches. The banquet served as a way
to enjoy those relationships one more time. There was lots of conversation before the dinner. Almost everybody lingered long after

the dinner and program to express their appreciation. The banquet also served as a means for parents and children to thank the coaches for their time and effort. The players and parents lingered because as one parent explained, "We know when we leave, one of life's significant experiences is over."

The parents' and coaches' conversations lasted longer than normal this year as the players watched the highlight video for the second time. One of the parents named Mike had done a fantastic job of videotaping each game for the coaches' weekly review. He also created a customized highlight video and still shots for each player.

As the evening progressed, Diane, an English teacher at a junior high, approached a group of coaches, including Coach Jerman. She introduced herself as Brady's mom, said she knew little about football, was more into book clubs, and thanked the coaches for a terrific experience.

She continued by describing her son Brady as a boy with a very short attention span, relatively low self-esteem, not interested in his schoolwork, and unable to interact with other kids and the rest of the family in a positive way. He also had a very negative experience this past summer as a part of a very successful baseball team from a win/loss standpoint.

Because of this, she was reluctant to allow her son to participate in the football program. She said she allowed him to play only because he begged to be with his friends and other parents indicated they had a positive experience.

As the season progressed, she routinely questioned her son about practice, the coaches, the other kids. She indicated she was only modestly interested in her son's answers to these questions until they became increasingly positive and often involved more than "yes," "no," or a grunt. She became more interested when Brady initiated short conversations with her about his practice and games. These conversations began to include explanations about the game itself, because, she concluded, her son wanted her to understand the game so she could participate in these conversations.

Brady's attitude and actions relative to other activities in school and the family became increasingly positive. So positive, she questioned other parents about their sons' experiences with the team. She eventually decided to satisfy her curiosity by going to practice. She wanted to determine for herself what had affected her son in such a positive way.

Before doing so, Diane decided to first get her son's permission, since she didn't want the trip to be misinterpreted as an unexplained invasion of his turf. She thought this could be potentially embarrassing for her son, and might disrupt what had been a very positive experience. Her son was surprisingly prepared for this discussion, almost as though he had hoped she would visit.

The resulting ground rules were simple. She was to stand by the bleachers with most of the fathers, should not come closer even if other fathers did, should not talk to the coaches, and should come on Wednesday because that's when they did the most hitting.

So when Wednesday arrived she went to practice after being reminded for the third or fourth time of the ground rules. Then, just before her son left the house, he said, "Mom, thanks for coming, but I probably won't look at you very much."

When Diane arrived at practice she observed nothing out of the ordinary. Her observations were inconsistent with her expectations in that there was no obviously charismatic leader, no yelling or loud instruction, no players running laps or sitting off to the side being uninvolved or disciplined for unacceptable behavior.

The practice had a quiet efficiency about it. Players worked in small groups. They were all active. Nobody just stood around watching others practice. The players listened to their coaches, but the coaches weren't talking a lot. They spent more time demonstrating, sometimes enthusiastically, and rewarded players in various ways with a bang on the helmet, a pat on the back.

The players supported each other enthusiastically with a disgusting gesture where they banged helmets seemingly without regard for injuring one another. The players laughed a lot more than she expected. And, oh yes! The players did hit each other a lot, but were never angry with each other.

About halfway through the practice, one of the older coaches, who was standing dangerously close to those doing the tackling, got knocked down. All the players, and especially the other coaches, were quite concerned. Then, as the coach rejected all offers of assistance in getting to his feet, everybody thought the incident was quite funny. But the coach learned little from his experience as he reassumed this obviously dangerous position and continued to demonstrate various things to the players.

As seven o'clock approached, the practice ended abruptly as the kids ran from wherever they were to a line in the middle of the field. From there, they started running in unison as fast as they could for varying distances until they reached a state of near exhaustion. Then, they all ran together in the middle of the field, and one of the boys led everybody in some sort of cheer. Diane thought they cheered because this demanding ordeal was finally over.

When Brady arrived home, he asked his mom what she thought of practice. She told him he'd played well, especially when he tackled that real big boy. She told him she thought the practice was very efficient and some of the coaches must be teachers, because they had a good lesson plan. And finally, she told him your team must have practiced well because none of the coaches yelled at you.

Brady smiled. He was satisfied with his mom's observations. But his smile became a little tentative when she asked him to sit down for a minute because she had a few questions. He said okay, but remained standing. She assumed this was so he could escape if he didn't like the questions.

Diane began by stating everybody including the coaches had a good time. Then she asked, "Why were you and the other players having such a good time?'

Brady smiled, signifying the first question was okay.

He answered, "The coaches are real nice and they know a lot about football. They don't get mad if you don't get it right away. The coaches want all of us to be friends and encourage each other. I like more of the players now than I did at the beginning of the season. The coaches say the team's more important than any one of us, even the good players. And, they get after us if we get mad at each other."

Brady paused, thought carefully, then said, "And Mom, it really feels good when a coach or even one of the eighth graders says you did good. I think everybody on the team's getting better and it's fun to get better. Sometimes when we do something real good the coaches let us show the other kids how to do it. They do this in front of the team. The coaches haven't chosen me yet, but I want them to by the end of the season."

Brady seemed interested in talking so Diane thought she would push the conversation a little and ask a second question. "Why do you think you and the other kids have improved so much? That's all the fathers could talk about."

Brady smiled and asked rather proudly, "Did the dads say that today?"

After she nodded her head to Brady's satisfaction he began by saying, "The coaches show us a lot of stuff that's used in high school and college. If we don't get it, they show us again. When we get it they get excited and are real nice. They never get mad when we don't get it."

Brady paused again, then continued, "They also said they couldn't make us try our hardest. Only we could do that. When a player's not doing his best, the coaches ask him if he's doing his best. I don't ever want them to ask me THAT question."

Diane concluded her discussion with the coaches by indicating, "Brady's performance on the field of life improved more significantly than his performance on the football field. His grades have improved a whole point. He enjoys the recognition from his teachers, his parents, and even his friends. The quality of his social interactions with his friends and family has improved. He's become more confident and even proactive about things. He has even become interested in having civil conversations with his younger sister, and has given her advice in a constructive way. After which his sister wanted to know, what's wrong with Brady?"

Diane went on to say that she was a teacher and a parent and she thought she knew what happened. She said she had trouble believing that participation on a football team could have such a substantial impact on Brady's development.

She concluded by saying, "You coaches are in a position to have such a fantastic relationship with our children. When they are with you they're doing something they enjoy. They're having fun and they have such a passion for the game. Their eyes, their minds, and their hearts are as open as the sky on a sunny day. You have a marvelous opportunity to influence their lives in such powerful and meaningful ways.

"I'll never be able to describe the impact you're having as role models for our children. They are incredibly influenced by what you say and more importantly what you do. You would not believe what they see, hear, feel, and bring home from practice each night. My husband and I have determined we have some of the same opportunities."

Diane looked around to locate Brady before she continued.

"I just want you and the other coaches to know how profoundly grateful the parents are that you understand the importance of your role in their lives. I could tell you more, but I'm sure you get the point. I do want you and the other coaches to know, however, that you did more than affect Brady's growth in a positive way. More importantly, you have begun to teach Brady how to take the responsibility for his own development."

Diane located Brady again as he watched the video with his friends. She closed the conversation by giving Coach Jerman a prolonged hug that was designed to express her feelings and control her emotions. She felt almost desperate to get herself under control, because she knew her son would die of embarrassment if he realized she'd been emotional with his coaches. This would probably end his football career prematurely.

Then she thought for just a wistful second ... maybe not? Maybe I can tell Brady some of this stuff on the way home. Sometimes he's so mature.

Then, realism prevailed. Tonight was not the night to get carried away with Brady's growth. She decided to save the story for later ... much later.

 PLAY NUMBER THIRTY-FIVE
Coaches need to create an environment with the optimal amount of discipline because discipline is the framework for creative performance. Within this environment, children have to be on their own with implied support in order to maximize growth. Once the game starts, the players have to be comfortable with an independence of action that optimizes performance. The focus required for optimal performance comes from confidence in oneself, devoid of any fear of failure. Too much intensity changes to tension, if there is too much emphasis on winning. Playing for the thrill of the game enhances performance.

36
Recognition and Appreciation

"We realize we didn't do a perfect job of coaching, but not once did I hear a complaint about our imperfections ... er, except once or twice," Coach Brown said with a smile. "Being positive about your coaches impacted the rate at which your children learned. If you had been critical of your coaches the kids would've been less likely to listen and less likely to learn. Because you were positive, they came to practice anxious to learn and they did."

THE 2008 FORMAL BANQUET PROGRAM BEGAN LIKE so many others with coaches, parents, and players seated at their respective tables loudly discussing the events of the season and the prospects for next year.

Traditionally, the dinner was called to order with a prayer. Since Lou Rotta, a parent who has had four boys in the program, wrote an original prayer for each game, it was only fitting that he deliver the prayer before the meal. Everybody expected one of his famous original prayers, but were disappointed as Lou's prayer was very traditional. After delivering the prayer and an announcement that the adults would have first access to the buffet for obvious reasons, Lou winked at his wife Kathy, as if to confirm a future surprise.

After dinner, Coach Brown called the banquet to order for the introduction of the players. The sixth and seventh graders were introduced first by Coach Grosso, as he indicated their position, any significant statistic that conveyed their prowess as a football player, or a story about how the boy benefited from the season. These introductions were short by comparison to the eighth graders who were to follow. The comments made by the coaches were always positive. There is often humor, but never sarcasm because there is always a little truth in sarcasm, which the players often misunderstand.

At the conclusion of the sixth- and seventh-grade introductions, Coach Brown took the microphone and said with a serious look on his face, "Before we continue with this banquet, I have a debt that must be paid. Until I get this uncomfortable task out of the way, I'll be unable to focus on the most important aspects of the banquet … the recognition of our coaches and eighth-grade players."

The audience was quiet and serious, fearing something unfortunate had happened. The only movement was that of Kyle and Stewart as they positioned a TV screen and CD player behind Coach Brown. The audience was relieved by the mischievous smiles on the boys' faces. Coach Brown continued, "At our goal-setting session, I made a huge mistake. It was the first one since the second grade, but it was a big one. You'd think I'd learn from a previous experience but apparently I didn't."

The players started to laugh because they knew what was coming. Several parents gave their children stern looks, as they thought they were disrespecting a still serious Coach Brown.

"In a weak moment, I agreed to write and perform a rap song if we won the championship, as I did in 2003. This is my final performance. I will never do this again, even if we win a national championship. So here goes nothing."

Kyle turned on the TV of a rap video that was music only. Coach Brown took a deep breath and launched into what had to be the worst rap performance ever attempted:

An Ode to a Championship
By Rapper-around

1

It was the night before practice
The team gathered around
Scott and George were missing
But enthusiasm did abound

2

The introductions were made
Season's goals and the how
If a championship was wanted
We must pay the price now

3

The price was defined
So loudly and clear
Commitments were made
And confirmed with root beer

4

With a price so high
We must smooth the way
We must listen to each other
Before having our say

American Idol's worst singer was better than Coach Brown, but he got an A for effort. Only four verses were completed before Coach Brown was taken out of his misery by Kyle and Stewart for humanitarian and safety concerns. Barb, Sean's mother, laughed so hard she fell out of her chair onto the floor, much to the embarrassment of her son.

After Coach Brown and the audience recovered, Coach Kelly said, "You obviously thought we wouldn't win the championship. Now repeat after me. I ... am ... retired ... as ... a ... rap ... singer."

Coach Brown responded as he raised his arms, hoping to induce applause, "I'm not so sure you all noticed, but I was just getting warmed up when I was forced to stop. The other 20 verses will be passed out by my handlers after the banquet" (and they were and the whole song is in playbook one at the end of the book).

As the crowd quieted down, Coach Brown said, "Before I introduce the eighth-grade players tonight, I want to tell you a story about a boy who was sitting in the eighth-grade section several years ago. His name was Andrew. Andrew overcame severe asthma to start as a sixth grader on the 1996 championship team. He was never able to complete the long lap, but each time pushed himself a little farther, always walking the final yards with his inhaler in hand. He went on to start for Benet both his junior and senior year. He wrote me a letter recently and I brought it with me tonight. In it, he reminded me of a T-shirt that Rob Koller, our greatest motivational speaker ever, handed out at the banquet that year. Andrew wrote:

> Today I'm not writing you about football, but how much of a positive influence football had on my life. Football at St. Raphael taught me the most important qualities I possess today. "St. Raphael Hitter—See it, believe it, achieve it, desire, dedication, do it." Do you remember the T-shirt Coach Koller gave us at the banquet? I sure do! Little did I know at that banquet that I would be applying it to my life anywhere outside of Football or more importantly living my life by those standards. St. Raphael Football taught me that nothing worthwhile comes easy, and hard work has to be put in, in order to get what you want. And things are never easy if you choose to do them right, but doing things right helps when you have tough problems to solve.
>
> At the time, even though Coach Koller told us what it meant, it didn't mean much to me. It was just a nice T-shirt. But over the years, especially through playing varsity ball and recovering from my shoulder injury, I have come to realize that it was most important to my success not only

as an athlete, but as a student and a friend. You see, Coach, I wore that T-shirt under my jersey for every game I ever played and if I could I would probably wear it for the games of life that lie ahead.

I don't think I will ever be able to repay St. Raphael Football for what it did for me. But maybe you could read part of my letter at the banquet and help the kids coming out today to realize what they learned a little sooner than I did.

"As most of you know I had a pacemaker/defibrillator installed a few weeks ago. I called Andrew last Thursday to thank him for the letter. During the conversation, I told him about the operation."

"He said, 'I know, Coach. That's why I sent the letter.'"

"Andrew then told me about his shoulder operation and how discouraged he was at first about missing part of the season. He told me it would be real important to make rehab the most important activity in my life. He told me I should never allow the pain to discourage me. He concluded by saying, 'Coach, it's time for you to take some of the advice you've given us over the years and apply it to yourself.'"

"Andrew saw an opportunity for payback and he took it. So I hope you guys, especially the eighth graders, will benefit from what Andrew had to say. Many of the things Andrew talked about, you have already learned but don't realize it yet. We have seen many qualities applied on the field. You may not realize the resources you've internalized until you need them later in life. But believe me, they'll be there when you need them. We're having too much fun tonight to talk about it, so I won't turn this event into a classroom. But sometime in the very near future, you might think about what you've learned this season just in case your parents ask you one of those dreaded parental questions on the way home.

"Over the years, our coaching staffs have been fortunate to have many great groups of parents support our teams. However, this group of parents has been exceptional, and I want you to know how important it was, and how much we appreciated your support.

"Being supportive of your kids had a significant effect on how they played and how they grew. They may not tell you that tonight, but someday they will. One of the primary reasons they played was to gain your approval and recognition. In other words, they like to have fun, but they played for you.

"I had a conversation recently with a baseball player whose team wasn't playing well. They were losing a lot of close games. I asked this player why he thought they were losing. He said, first it's the parents, then the coaches, then the players. If a boy strikes out, his parent yells at him, then he throws his helmet and cries, then the coaches get on the players and everything goes downhill from there. That's a very astute assessment for a nine-year-old child.

"There were several characteristics of this group that were exceptional. I particularly liked the way you came early to pick up your children, so you could watch them practice. I liked the way you complimented your kids after the games, specifically calling good plays to their attention. I like the way you helped with the administrative aspects of the team whenever asked.

"We realize we didn't do a perfect job of coaching, but not once did I hear a complaint about our imperfections ... er, except once or twice," Coach Brown said with a smile. "Being positive about your coaches impacted the rate at which your children learned. If you had been critical of your coaches the kids would've been less likely to listen and less likely to learn. Because you were positive, they came to practice anxious to learn and they did.

"Bob Walters, the coach at St. Joan, commented this year, 'You can tell St. Raphael has had a parish team for a while. Their parents are very professional about supporting their team. It must be passed from generation to generation.'

"I have one final thought before we introduce the eighth graders. One of the lessons this team taught us is to never underestimate your children. If we had, they might have underperformed and met all of our underachieving expectations.

"In the movie *Mr. Holland's Opus*, Mr. Holland had difficulty communicating with his deaf son because he continually underestimated what he could do. Fortunately, the child would not accept his father's view of his potential. He worked hard to prove to his father he had potential beyond anything his father could perceive.

"Once the child opened his father's mind and his heart, Mr. Holland was able to see the potential he'd overlooked. His child taught him to appreciate the relationship with him for what it could be. More importantly, Mr. Holland was able to appreciate the significance of his own life as captured in the comments of the governor, a former student, when she said at the surprise playing of his Opus that he took years to compose, 'We are your Opus. We are the symphony of your life.'

"And finally, I want you to appreciate an exceptional group of coaches. Only two of them have sons on this team. But they coach your children as if they were their sons. They do this for many reasons, the most significant of which is the total contribution your children make to the Opus of our lives. We know we'll always get more out of coaching than we give because we know the more you give children the more you receive. They asked not to be introduced individually, I think because I mess it up each year. But you all know who they are.

"One of our coaches asked the rhetorical question today, 'How much is it worth to have a 30-year-old still call you Coach regardless of where you meet?' Coaches and parents have the power to make children feel really good about themselves and thereby make themselves feel good about their contribution to a child's development. You get to do this with your child and a few others, while we have the same opportunity with a team of 30 every year.

"During the ages of eight through thirteen, children say their parents are their most important source of information. This is when parents must build the platform for future conversations that impact a child when he has lots of influences, some them not so good.

"Now I would like to introduce the eighth graders. Since this was a special group the coaches decided to introduce them in a special way. I can tell by the looks on their faces, they are worried." Everybody in the room laughed except the eighth graders.

Coach Brown continued. "In 1996 we won the Catholic league championship. That year Coach Koller, the most inspirational speaker we've ever had, decided to give each child a Successories plaque to commemorate his season. This plaque represented something significant about the boy's experience that year. This year, we decided to do something similar. The only difference being, the plaque will represent what we've learned from each player. Our coaching staff believes we're teachers. The greatest benefit of being a teacher lies in what you learn by teaching others."

Coach Brown asked that all the eighth graders come to the front of the room to receive their recognition. Once they were all in place, wearing their jerseys for the last time, Coach Brown introduced each player by reading the inscription on the plaque, and what the staff learned from each child. Coach Jerman handed the plaque to each player, along with the team statistic sheet and a booklet containing the names of all this year's 2,600 children in the St. Raphael Football Program and their team affiliation.

George: Attitude, "The greatest discovery of any generation is that a human being can alter his life by altering his attitude." —William James

At the beginning of the season George was saying, "Hey, look at me." By the end of the season he was saying, "Hey, look at you."

Brian: Dare to Soar, Your attitude almost always determines your altitude in life.

Brian soared to such heights playing football and leading others, he made you forget he was an unsighted person.

Stewart: Achievement, Unless you try to do something beyond what you have already mastered, you will never grow.

Stewart is an accomplished dancer. I want to announce, he won the lead in the Nutcracker Suite. His dance coach credits football with helping Stewart differentiate himself from other dancers competing for the lead. Stewart chose football as his vehicle for growth.

Todd/Keith: Excellence, Excellence is never an accident; it is the result of high intention, sincere effort, intelligent direction, skillful execution, and the vision to see obstacles as opportunities.

Todd and Keith were the glue that kept the team together by how they played, and at times by what they said. Their impact is like being stabbed with a stiletto; you don't see their impact until after the contributions are made.

Billy: Teamwork, Teamwork is the ability to work together toward a common vision.

Billy was the consummate team player. He did the dirty work required to make a team function without being asked or noticed. He just knew what to do to create and maintain a team.

Jeff: Be the Bridge, Problems become opportunities when the right people join together.

Jeff had significant problems, which he overcame with the help of others. By overcoming the problems, he became a role model for those who helped him. His achievement was a source of development for all involved.

Mike: Success, Some people dream of success ... while others wake up and work hard at it.

Most of you watching a game seldom noticed Mike, except in the championship game. But he was always there experiencing great success at what he was supposed to do as a defensive back. No team completed a touchdown pass on his watch and he never missed a tackle.

Danny: Never give up, Go over, go under, go around, or go through. But never give up.

Danny weighs 80 pounds on his good days. Teams thought they could pick on him because he was small, but found out to the contrary as he always found a way to do his job. He had to tackle so low, the kids called him the ankle biter.

Perry: Perseverance, In the confrontation between the river and the rock, the river always wins ... not through strength but by perseverance.

Perry had huge problems to overcome when he joined the team. One of the assets he brought with him was his perseverance. Once directed, it served him well this year as it will in the future.

Greg: Character, Adversity does not build character ... it reveals it.

Greg was the rock of stability. He never missed a snap from center. He had a tough, thankless job. He had things to overcome throughout the season. As he overcame, it revealed his character.

Kyle: Leadership, A true leader has the confidence to stand alone, the courage to make tough decisions, and the compassion to listen to the needs of others. He does not set out to be a leader, but becomes one by the quality of his actions and the integrity of his intent. In the end, leaders are much like eagles ... they don't flock, you find them one at a time.

Kyle reluctantly learned he was a natural leader ... But once he learned how to lead, he did it very well.

Mark: Confidence, Those who possess the courage to stand apart gain a rare perspective.

Mark learned that a short memory is required to excel. He failed. He was required to excel a short time later, and he did.

Santos: Focus, Obstacles are those frightful things you see when you take your eyes off your goals.

Santos was born to be a kicker. He could focus better than anybody I can remember.

Coach Brown closed this portion of the program, "This is an exceptional group of eighth graders whom I believe will be as successful in life as they were on the football field."

After all the eighth graders were recognized, Coach Brown had a few more awards to make. The first was the Sparkplug Award. This award went to the player who did the most to motivate the team from the inside out. It was a small wooden trophy with a used sparkplug glued to a wooden background. It was a simple but greatly cherished award. This year's award was unanimous.

Coach Brown said, "This year's award goes to Matt." As Matt came to receive his award, the team, led by Kyle, gave him a standing ovation. As a somewhat subdued Matt received his award, Brian said, "Coach, make him do one more dance before you give him the trophy."

As expected, Matt needed no encouragement. He handed the trophy back to Coach Brown with a "Hold this." Then Matt did his most disgusting dance of the season to the roar of the crowd.

Then, he walked slowly to his seat, doing one final move as he was mobbed by the seventh graders.

Once the crowd quieted down, Coach Brown began his presentation of an award that he always found difficult to present. He had been very close to the Cooney family for 40 years. He coached Mark, who played on the 1969 championship team. He was friends with Jim and Dot. They often had a few glasses of wine after Mass on Sunday afternoons. Mark grew up to be a coach in the program, and a close personal friend of Coach Brown. Coach Brown began his presentation.

"Each year since 1983, the coaches have selected eighth graders to receive the Cooney Award. This award is named after Jim and Mark Cooney. Jim was one of the founders of St. Raphael Football. Jim, along with Ron Baumgartner and Lou Jerman, developed and installed the program's value system which has guided the program for 40 years.

"The award was instituted by Jim's wife, Dot. Mark Cooney was Jim's son, who played on the team in 1969. Mark went on to play at Benet and Benedictine University. He then helped coach the parish team for several years until his untimely death at the age of 38. During Mark's coaching career he passionately installed four characteristics in each of his players. He did this, because he knew how important they were to him in defining how he lived his life. If there had been an award in 1969, Mark would have won it. The four characteristics Jim and Mark held in the highest regard for a football player in our program were leadership, attitude, effort, and improvement.

"Therefore, this award goes to the player or players who most exemplify those characteristics. The past recipients, listed in your program, have not always been the best players on the team. But, in Mark and Jim's mind, they were certainly the most valuable because of these characteristics. The recipients of this year's award are Brian, Billy, Keith, and Todd. "

The four boys walked slowly to the podium and received their awards to a standing ovation.

Once the boys received their awards and walked proudly back to their seats, Coach Brown announced his final awards.

"Since 1985, the league has conducted an All-Star Game between teams from the north and south sides of Chicago. As winners of the championship, we were allowed four players chosen by the coaches. We have more than four all-stars, but were allowed only four so all teams could be represented. This year's all-stars are Kyle, Brian, George, and Billy. Our coaching staff was chosen to coach the north team, which will include St. Monica. We will practice three nights at Nike Park from six to eight. Let us know if any of you have conflicts with basketball."

Before closing the banquet, Coach Brown asked if any of the other coaches had anything to say. No amount of urging could get Coach Jerman to speak at a banquet in the history of St. Raphael Football. But tonight was different as Coach Jerman rose and walked to the podium. "Before the final game of the season, we distributed a letter to each player. I don't know how many of you read the letter, but I did and I wanted to make sure all of you are aware of its content so I'm going to read it tonight."

With that several parents looked at their children with inquisitive looks. Obviously, many players had not read it or shown it to their parents.

Coach Jerman smiled and continued, "I can see many of you don't know what I'm talking about. Let your sons explain the letter to you on the way home." Coach Jerman laughed a little then continued, "We have distributed a similar letter twice; once to our 0–7–1 team in 1978 and to the 1996 championship team. One of the players from the 1978 team reminded me recently of how important the letter had been to him, especially during some difficult times in his life. He was surprised we hadn't given it to another team since 1996. I told him it was because I'd lost my copy. He produced a wrinkled copy from his wallet and gave it to me and suggested we distribute it this year. Our designated reader, Coach Grosso, will read it to everybody tonight. Then, Lou Rotta will lead us in prayer and we can all go home."

Coach Grosso read the following letter:

> We hope you enjoyed your experience this season. Each of you contributed significantly to the team, to yourselves, and to others associated with the team.
>
> We hope you had fun. We also hope you will remember your experience for what you were able to contribute to others. Most importantly, we hope you'll remember the St. Raphael definition of winning which we think you exemplified all year.
>
> Always remember that winners do their best at all times. If you do your best you'll improve as much as your physical, mental, and natural ability will allow. If you improve as much as you can, you will realize all you can be whether it's in sports, your school work, your relationship with God and others, including your family, or your job later in life.
>
> In most competitive experiences, there are always winners and losers. For this reason some people do not get fully involved because they don't want to experience the agony of defeat. However, if people do not get involved and deal with the uncertainties of involvement, they may go through life and never realize their full potential.
>
> If winning is defined as doing your best at all times, you'll seldom be a loser and have to experience the disappointment of losing. If you are always doing your best you'll be inclined to take more risks, thus enhancing your growth and improvement in whatever you do. More importantly you'll be in control. You'll be your own judge so you'll know when you've won because you'll know when you did your best.
>
> Being a winner by this definition will make you more confident, and will make it less necessary, but easier to accept what you cannot control with the same class with which you accept the rewards you've earned. Winners don't make excuses or blame others. They're honest and intelligent in their effort, aren't self-centered, and give credit to others when they've earned it.

We've emphasized throughout the year that football should be fun for all of us. Hard work in practice is required in order to have fun on game day. This will be true in everything you do.

For the eighth graders, this will be particularly important next year when things get tougher as you establish your new identity. Nobody will know what you did this year even if your new coaches read the letters of intro- duction we plan to send. They will want to find out for themselves.

However, what you've learned this year about the importance of leader- ship, attitude, effort, and improvement will help you establish your new identity. We hope the seventh graders will apply this learning as they assume their leadership role next year.

We believe this team, regardless of what happens on Sunday, will have achieved everything it possibly could and a little more. We also believe because of your attitude, free spirit, and willingness to try new things, you'll achieve everything possible on Sunday.

We also believe all the positive characteristics displayed this year will permit you to fully understand this letter, presented from the heart, if not now, then certainly in the future.

And finally, all the coaches wish you the very best and will be looking in on you from time to time. We hope you'll do the same. We wish you the St. Raphael definition of good luck, "when opportunity meets prepared- ness."

We believe you're prepared for victory on Sunday. Your coaches when- ever you need us.

When Coach Grosso finished, many parents looked at their chil- dren in disbelief. Very few had shown the letter to their parents. Coach Grosso added, "If any of you guys have trouble finding your letters, we have a few extra copies at the podium."

Lou Rotta then walked to the podium to deliver the final prayer. As Lou walked to the front of the room, people gathered their things in anticipation of a brief prayer, thanking the coaches and a ride home. What they got was completely unexpected.

PLAY NUMBER THIRTY-SIX

The coaching staff's most significant contribution is player placement. We had a player who was the faster player at the JV level. But he did not grow from the sixth to the eighth grade and fell behind his teammates in size, strength, and speed. He weighed only 90 pounds at the beginning of his eighth-grade year. He was tried at backup quarterback, but his heart wasn't in it and he became a distraction at practice.

Then one night, Coach Taylor asked him to fill in at nose tackle for a few plays for an injured player. The player started slow, but by mid-practice he was so quick off the ball, the first team had trouble completing a play. Thus, a nose tackle was discovered. He relished the contact, the disruption, and the mayhem of the position. He also became an effective backup quarterback, requiring very few repetitions.

37
Coaching Impacts Generations

Football, like no other sport, is a reflection of our Christian journey. There's the preparation, then the games. Each player brings his gifts to the community or team and has to commit to doing his part. There are letdowns and celebrations, times of joy and success, and times when nothing goes right. No one person makes or breaks the team and no one play makes or breaks the game. Just like in life, you have to work hard each and every day and each and every play.

LOU LOOKED TO THE AUDIENCE AND WAITED FOR them to settle down. Then, he looked briefly at his wife, Kathy, and without fanfare began the journey of a lifetime.

"In *My Daily Visitor*, a Catholic booklet which gives highlights of the reading for the Mass and identifies the saint whose feast day it is, today it discussed the life of St. Margaret of Scotland, whose feast it is today.

"She was an 11th-century Queen of Scotland and a model of charity. She knew what was involved in raising children and being a supportive spouse. She encouraged her husband and his keen sense of justice and concern for his royal subjects. She was also able to help her six sons and two daughters become virtuous leaders. Through her influence she was able to impact generations."

Sensing something extraordinary, the audience settled back into their seats.

"The part that caught my eye was the positive impact she had on her family and how her influence carried on and influenced generations through her children and their children. The things we believe in and toil for change people for generations. When I saw the tear in Coach Brown's eye at the end of the first St. Monica game, it confirmed he is a man who will forever change the lives of these young men whom we honor tonight.

"For over 40 years, Coach Brown and Coach Jerman, along with many passionate assistant coaches, have had a hand in the lives of well over 1,000 young athletes. Each young man learned a lot about football, but little did they know they were learning a lot about life.

"Football, like no other sport, is a reflection of our Christian journey. There's the preparation, then the games. Each player brings his gifts to the community or team and has to commit to doing his part. There are letdowns and celebrations, times of joy and success, and times when nothing goes right. No one person makes or breaks the team and no one play makes or breaks the game. Just like in life, you have to work each and every day and each and every play.

"Coach Brown and his staff love the game of football, but more importantly they love life, and they love your children. They use the game to shape these young men so as to better prepare them to deal with success and adversity.

"There was a player from the program who suffered an injury in a car accident several years ago. Many people stepped forward to support this young man. I don't think this kid realized how many people were in his corner pulling for him. He had received many letters, but one really touched his heart. I would like to read it to you."

At this point, Lou began to lose his composure as his voice cracked and he had difficulty continuing. He paused looked at Coach Brown, then at his wife, Kathy, who was seated at the table directly in front of him for support. She was ringing her hands, but had a firm loving look on her face that said, "Take your time, honey. It will be difficult, but I am so proud of you for what you are about to do." Lou took a deep breath and continued down the difficult road he had chosen.

"The letter came in a card entitled Perseverance—The difference between a successful person and others is not a lack of strength. Not a lack of knowledge, but rather a lack of will. I will read the letter tonight, but I assure you, I almost know it by heart."

Dear Matt,

I talked to your mom at football sign-up and she told me you had been in an automobile accident. I'm sure you're very grateful that you survived, but are very disappointed you'll be unable to play football this fall (Matt had made all-conference as a junior and gained over 1,200 yards). Once you recover, this fall will be very rough for you.

Once I was very disappointed about something, and my son Dan, who was 17, said, "Dad, the really successful golfers know how to play out of the rough."

We discussed what he meant and concluded, among other things, that when times are tough, it's important to be proactive and focus on doing everything possible to contribute to your future. This will be difficult because you're tempted to say, "why me?" But God in his infinite wisdom gave us a choice and put the choice totally within our control.

I chose this card because I believe it defines a thought that will be important to you as you focus on building your future. Sometimes this can best be done by learning from what you can contribute to others. For instance, see what you can do to train your replacement or help younger brothers become better football players.

Because of your success last year and who you are, there will be a lot of people observing how you handle this difficult situation. By doing well, you'll serve as a role model for other students and adults. Some of them will benefit without your knowledge.

I will see you this fall at St Francis or at your brother's games in St. Raphael Football. Hang tough!

—Coach Brown

Lou paused, collected himself, and almost shouted, "That kid was my son Matt and he played for Coach Brown."

Here Lou faltered again, but forced himself to finish the message he was so intent on delivering.

"Jim's influence gave Matt not only the tools to be a successful player, but more importantly he gave Matt tools for life."

Again, Lou stopped for several seconds as he looked around the room and took strength from the compassionate expressions of his friends.

"I called Coach Brown to thank him for the letter and let him know how much it meant to Matt. But more importantly, I called to tell him that his letter was doing more for me than it was for Matt as I dealt with the disappointment I felt for myself and my child. I felt deprived of the enjoyment I would have experienced watching Matt play this year. I also wanted Coach Brown to know that Matt was doing well as a role model for me and others as he dealt with his disappointment. For you see, sometimes parents can learn a lot from their children if they take the time to listen and observe."

Lou paused again to gain his composure, but this time continued quickly with a newfound conviction as he turned to the table where his son Mitch and other team members were seated.

"I want you players to take a hard look at these coaches and know that their work is more than just a game of football. They're giving back to life what life has given to them. You may not see it now, but as you grow up you'll become more aware of the lessons of the game and how they apply to life. These men are true role models and their giving back is a lesson for you. Because soon, it will be your time to give back."

As Lou paused, he looked at Kathy as the audience stood as one. They clapped and cheered for several minutes. They were expressing their appreciation for the coaches, but more importantly were expressing a greater appreciation for the courage of a man who wanted to give back what he'd received to everybody in the room, especially the children. Lou, not fully understanding the purpose of the ovation, turned to the coaches' table and joined in the ovation. Lou raised his hand to signal the audience to be seated so he could complete his mission. After the audience reluctantly took their seats, Lou continued.

"Coach Brown, you and all the other coaches have been a great blessing to our community. For Kathy and me and my four sons, it's been a great ride. We are very sad to see it end."

Lou paused again, took a deep breath, and continued, forcing the final sentence from his lips regardless of its clarity. "You all have impacted our lives. We'll take that and I assure you we'll impact the lives of others. Truly, you men have shaped generations."

At the completion of Lou's talk, people stood and cheered him again as he and Kathy hugged near the podium. Lou then walked to the coaches' table and either hugged or shook hands with each coach. Coach Brown looked at Kathy as she clapped and wiped away her tears. Her expression was one of pride, joy, and sorrow. Her husband had just delivered a talk that had great meaning to everybody in the room. They might forget specifically what he said, but they would never forget the impact on their lives. As Lou sat down next to Kathy she whispered, "Each person here tonight will positively impact somebody because of you. I am so proud of you."

The talk was emotionally difficult to deliver. It was from the heart. It was Lou's way of "giving something back" for his entire family. By his actions he said to everybody that evening, "If you don't understand what I'm saying, then I will show you what I'm feeling and that will help you understand." It took courage, but Lou did it for the benefit of all of his friends.

After talking with each of the coaches Lou handed the microphone to Coach Brown to close the banquet. Coach Brown, probably for his emotional well-being, tried to lighten the mood with a little humor as he quoted Paul Harvey, "Now let me tell you the rest of the story.

"As you might imagine, Matt worked hard at his rehabilitation. He became an assistant coach, and helped train his replacement. He worked with his brothers, and even came to our practice to help out a few times. And yes, because St. Francis made the playoffs, and because of Matt's determination, he made a miraculous recovery. He started and played tailback throughout the playoffs.

"Lou learned a lot from Matt, and cared enough to share his lessons with us tonight. Thank you, Lou. And you can be assured, we'll give something back every chance we get because we want to help you shape generations.

"I will close with one final thought. Each year, for 40 years, we've had a season-ending banquet. As you can see, the coaches have had a lot of fun, but there's also a little sadness because we've developed relationships with each child. And as Coach Jerman said at our table earlier this evening, this banquet signifies our players have graduated and are leaving home. You see, that is because the football field has been our home with your children for the past 15 weeks. We have enjoyed our home and we always will. Thank you and good night."

PLAY NUMBER THIRTY-SEVEN

In order to coach your children, we must initiate and develop the relationship required for effective teaching. Going to them demonstrates unconditional love and respect, which they are all too anxious to return. Once this exchange takes place and is nourished, mistakes made by the participants in this relationship are easily resolved. Coaches, parents, and children enjoy the feeling of love, given and received. Children can teach us to love if we let them. Love has its true value in sharing, because you can love as many people as you want. We all have an infinite capacity to love. So the more you love your children, the more they love you in return. Love in a parent/child relationship enhances the potential for coaching and development. Always remember that love withheld is love wasted.

Epilogue

AFTER THE BANQUET, COACHES BROWN, JERMAN, and Kanis transported all the varsity equipment to Coach Brown's house for storage. Since they were still excited about the evening, and the season, they decided to have their 5,000th iced tea together and some celebratory conversation in the "football room," where the storied season began, just twenty short weeks ago.

Coach Brown began, "I received a letter from Matt just before the banquet with two attachments. Matt was involved in a school assignment that is described in the first letter from his teacher. He asked me not to say anything about this project at the banquet, but gave me permission to share it with the coaches."

Dear V.I.P. (Very Important Person),

For a writing assignment centered around giving thanks this holiday season, I have assigned an inspirational essay about a very positive and influential person in each student's life. The students were NOT informed that these papers would be sent to the person they wrote about, either before or during the assignment. Once the composition was in the final draft form, the students were asked to bring in your address. The essay is the result of your influence in some positive way on a young person's life and character. The paper has not been changed in any way. The composition you are about to read is the actual paper written as a class assignment. I hope this message brings some holiday cheer to you whenever you receive it. It is a small gift in exchange for the gift you have given this student. If you care to respond to the student involved or me, please feel free. Have a happy holiday season.

Matt wrote the following report as part of this school assignment.

BY Matt

VIP REPORT

Sometimes people influence you and they don't even know it. One kid I know, Garrett Bova, doesn't even know he influenced me. In fact, I didn't realize he did until late one night. He is on my football team and in the seventh grade. I'll talk more about him later in the paper. Again, he is in the seventh grade. He stands at about 5'3" and weighs about 180 pounds.

We always call Garrett by his last name, Bova. Bova was the starting left tackle on my football team. Anybody who went against him didn't want to ever again. The only time he let my team down was when he got sick for the St. Monica game.

I remember what he did very clearly. He hit me very hard on a football play and knocked me down. He got me very mad. The next play, I hit him hard and made the tackle. After the play he was in a small daze. He challenged me to hit harder.

Now, whenever I hit a person in football, I hit him as hard as I can. If I get myself mad, my adrenalin pumps through my body and I hit harder. Staying low is what gives me the leverage to knock him down. Because of Bova, I do this every time I play football. Sometimes I even get a quarterback sack.

Let's review now, shall we? Garrett Bova influenced me. I know him from my football team and he is a seventh grader. He hit me very hard in practice. I hit people as hard as I can now. This has helped me to become a better football player.

Coach Brown continued, "Matt's teacher and parents tried to convince him to send this composition to Garrett, but he would not. Since Matt is a person who acts consistently from his values, he was unable to send this letter to Garrett. Matt had to make a choice between two values that were put in conflict because of this situation. He wanted to thank Garrett, because he was grateful. However, he respected Garrett a lot and wanted to earn his respect for what he did on the field, not because he wrote something nice about him. Matt struggled with this dilemma and then resolved it in a way that is indicative of wisdom beyond his years. Matt wrote the following letter and sent it to me."

> Dear Coach Brown,
>
> This paper was an assignment in school. After the class wrote the V.I.P. paper, our teacher told us that we had to mail it out to the person we wrote about. I don't want Bova or anyone else to see this because they will think I am kissing up and I will be really embarrassed. I had a hard time trying to figure out what to do. Then I thought that you might enjoy this letter. Good coaching has made some team members look to other teammates for inspiration. That comes from you and the other coaches.
>
> Thanks for a good season!
>
> From Matt

"Lou, I was so inspired by the this assignment and Matt's performance throughout the season, I had to call him, and tell him what I thought and felt about his performance. I also wanted to get his permission to show his letter to the other coaches. He listened to what I had to say. Thanked me, and said it wasn't that big a deal. He said it was intended for all the coaches, so they could see it, but not Bova. After reading the letter, I decided to write Matt the following letter from the coaching staff."

> Dear Matt,
>
> We liked getting your letter and will always keep it. We think it is great that you learned so much from Bova. We also learned some things from

you. First we learned the true meaning and power of commitment. You promised Coach Brown that you would help the team by playing on the varsity and you kept your promise under some very difficult conditions (Playing defense against the first string ... The Bova hits ... The broken and dislocated finger ... The George bull in the ring thing ... Your game-saving hit against Rene ... Your role-modeling of leadership for Kyle ... Your support of Perry, Mike, and Jeff ... Being an assistant coach and leader of the White team ... And the maintenance of a positive attitude throughout the season).

Second, we learned about the importance of learning from others as you described in your letter about Bova. One of the main reasons some people do better than others is that they are able to take advantage of all of the learning opportunities around them. For example, you learned more by playing on the varsity just like your dad is learning by going to night school while working a full-time job.

Third, you reminded us of the importance of creating an environment where we all can be inspired by our teammates. We try to do this. We are happy that you think we are being successful.

Because of the first point, you have become a very famous person (VFP) at DePaul University. Coach Brown gave a talk there as part of a class and used your performance on the team as an example of what you can learn from children about commitment, dealing with adversity, and breakthrough performance. He didn't use your name.

We promise that we will not show your letter to anybody. However, we think that Bova would really enjoy hearing about how he helped you and he wouldn't think you were kissing up. We are really looking forward to next year. We are counting on you to do your running and other exercises and to be one of our leaders next year.

Merry Christmas,

Your coaches

PS Please don't work on the dance. It's perfect!

"Wow! That is quite a series of letters," said Coach Jerman. "Matt was truly exceptional and so were the rest of these kids. I can't wait to coach him and all the other returning seventh graders next year. Before the St. Genevieve game, Matt said we had nine seventh graders starting. It seemed like more than that."

"Lou, I think if we combine our returning seventh graders with the 8–2 JV team, we may have another championship team next year."

"Jim, it seems like I have to caution you every year. Don't you remember what I said at the beginning of this season about winning championships? I think I was sitting on this exact bar stool."

"I do, Lou. You said, 'Championships aren't won in the football planning room while we party. They're won on the practice and game fields, one game and one practice at a time.' So, let's have another tea and start our planning for next year."

Appendix
Rap Song
by Rapper-Around

1

The night of the first practice
The team gathered around
Scott and George were missing
But enthusiasm did abound

2

The introductions were made
Season's goals and the how
If a championship's wanted
We must pay the price now

3

The price was defined
So loudly and clear
Commitments were made
And confirmed with root beer

4

With a price so darn high
We must smooth the way
We must listen to each other
Before having our say

5

A new player introduced
Stewart's lord of the dance
The players disrespected
Brian took a firm stance

6

What else do we need?
Asked the coaches quite loudly
It's nice to have George
Says Todd quite proudly

7

Teamwork must be based
On respect for each other
Coach Jerman announced
We must act like we're brothers

8

Coach Brown says we'll run
Coach Cook wants to train
Coach Grosso says we'll pass
Coach Taylor wants no gains

9

With the meeting nearly over
Lou must have his say
We may do all this new stuff
But with courage we'll play

10

The first scrimmage went well
A good start to the season
Except Jeff became ill
His Dad was the reason

11

The first practice game's over
There's a sigh of relief
George is coming to practice
But his stay is brief

12

Coach Cook works the players
The team gathers around
If we practice like champions
"Redwings" is our sound

13

First game with St. Mark
They were so big it's a sin
Harrison to Stewart
Results in a win

14

The week of the weigh-in
The coaches showed fear
When the team made weight
There's a championship cheer

15

Now on to St. John's
They made some first downs
Kyle and Billy made sure
There were champion sounds

16

The Redwing beat St. Thomas
Todd's defense was abound
Harrison passing to Stewart
Santos's kicking was sound

17

The Redwings got careless
St. Ann's played their best
All the players learned
Any team is a test

18

A plan was designed
Perry made sure it's in place
This made Lou happy
There was a smile on his face

19

Rita got our best
Stewart played to the sky
George led the defense
Coaches thought they could fly

20

The team played St. Monica
Without some of their best
Bobby took a beating
They passed a big test

21

The team was beaten
Forty to six
Nobody gave up
Next time they will fix

22

The team practiced harder
The playoffs the goal
Two games must be won
Pressure takes its toll

23

The wins come quickly
Coach Brown has an attack
The team is quite worried
As to when he'll be back

24

Redwings make playoffs
St. Monica they must play
The team plays their best
The Crusaders did pay

25

St. Nicholas's a tough team
They are one play away
Matt enters the game
He saves the day

26

Mike and Danny intercept
Perry and Kyle hit
Todd and Brian do block
The victory lamp is lit

27

With victory in hand
The boys earned all the cheers
They all paid the price
We can't wait until next year